KU-436-190

HERITAGE VALUES
IN CONTEMPORARY SOCIETY

Edited by

George S. Smith, Phyllis Mauch Messenger, and
Hilary A. Soderland

Left
Coast
Press
inc.

Walnut Creek, California

UNIVERSITY OF WINCHESTER
LIBRARY

UNIVERSITY OF WINCHESTER

363.69

LEFT COAST PRESS, INC.
1630 North Main Street, #400
Walnut Creek, California 94596
http://www.LCoastPress.com

Copyright © 2010 by Left Coast Press, Inc.

All rights reserved. No part of this publication may be reproduced, stored in a retrieval system, or transmitted in any form or by any means, electronic, mechanical, photocopying, recording, or otherwise, without the prior permission of the publisher.

Hardback ISBN 978-1-59874-445-3
Paperback ISBN 978-1-59874-446-0

Library of Congress Cataloging-in-Publication Data

Heritage values in contemporary society / edited by George S. Smith, Phyllis Mauch Messenger, and Hilary A. Soderland.
    p. cm.
Includes bibliographical references and index.
ISBN 978-1-59874-445-3 (hardcover : alk. paper)—ISBN 978-1-59874-446-0 (pbk.: alk. paper)
1. Cultural property. 2. World Heritage areas. I. Smith, George S. II. Messenger, Phyllis Mauch, 1950- III. Soderland, Hilary A.
CC135.H4634 2009
363.6'9—dc22
2009028837

Printed in the United States of America

∞™ The paper used in this publication meets the minimum requirements of American National Standard for Information Sciences—Permanence of Paper for Printed Library Materials, ANSI/NISO Z39.48—1992.

10 11 12 5 4 3 2 1

Cover design by Piper Wallis

Royalties from this book will be contributed to the Society for American Archaeology Public Education Endowment and the Native American Scholarship Fund.

Cover: Each day thousands of people, including Buddhist monks and international tourists, visit the Phnom Bakheng Temple Complex at Angkor, Cambodia, each bringing unique values and conceptions of "heritage" to their shared experience. Photograph by Alex Messenger.

WITHDRAWN FROM
THE LIBRARY

UNIVERSITY OF
WINCHESTER

HERITAGE VALUES
IN CONTEMPORARY SOCIETY

KA 0363859 6

CONTENTS

FOREWORD

I had an epiphany about heritage values a few years ago when I was teaching at Columbia University in New York. The students were required to submit a journal as part of their assessment, and one of them mused on the responsibility involved in looking after the family home. As I read the assignment, it became apparent that this particular family home was a little out of the ordinary—this student is a member of one of the royal families of Europe, and the "family home" is actually a castle. My epiphany was less to do with the surprise that this unassuming and conscientious student was a practicing royal than with the empathy I felt with the emotions expressed. My own background is much more modest—a working class family in Newcastle, Australia, full of people who undertook hard physical labor to support their families (and the occasional convict ancestor)—and yet the feelings I had for the home of my parents were quite similar to those my student had for the castle. Both of us were thinking about our long-term responsibility to care for the particular heritage we had inherited, a line of thought that emerged from the values we attributed to that heritage. Both of us had been taught these heritage values by our parents—people divided by continent, culture, and class.

There are differences, of course. While my student had wide endorsement for concern in caring for a national icon, few people would care if my parents' house survives. However, as an archaeologist, I know that we need to protect the heritage of working-class people as much as that of people who are well-off, particularly since working-class values often elude historical records. History is mostly about the powerful, the rich, the big players. But most people are smaller players: their impact is within a local sphere, and their actions, and views are poorly recorded. One of the great values of archaeology is that it can fill gaps in historical records and provide unique insights into the values, motivations, and behaviors of ordinary people.

I am delighted to see George Smith, Phyllis Messenger, and Hilary Soderland tackle the complex issues surrounding heritage values in the contemporary world. While I have long been aware of each of their work individually, I was fortunate to meet these three as a team when I participated in a Heritage Values workshop on Cumberland Island, off the coast of Georgia, United States, in November 2007. I already knew George Smith well, as we had collaborated on several projects, and I was very familiar with Phyllis Messenger's seminal volume, *The Ethics of Collecting Cultural Property* (University of New Mexico Press 1999). I was aware that they were working with Hilary Soderland, an award-winning graduate from the University of Cambridge. So I expected great things of the workshop. My expectations were more than fulfilled, not only in this particular instance but also over the last few years, as these three scholars have continued to make a sustained effort to convene diverse groups of scholars and practitioners for extended discussions in order to develop a broad international understanding of heritage values.

This is the first book to take a global approach to the question: what is the heritage that people value and want preserved? Through systematically exploring the heritage values of cultures in different geographic regions, this volume breaks new ground in an area that is of increasing importance globally. Throughout the world, heritage is under threat. Sometimes, these threats are overt, such as with mining or urban development, and sometimes they are covert, occurring through oversight, neglect, or a lack of understanding.

Heritage values are contested values. The issues of dispute vary according to region and the history of a particular country, though the contest is rarely between "good guys" and "bad guys." The role of heritage values in conflict and post-conflict reconciliation is one that affects countries and peoples the world over. In Argentina, for example, there is a heart-breaking dispute over the preservation of certain places used for detainment during the military dictatorship. While some survivors want these places to be preserved as the torture chambers they were, the mothers of the "disappeared" want them preserved as memorials to their murdered children. Whose values should prevail? Those of the people tortured? Or those of the mothers who are still in mourning? This is not a question to which I can give an answer.

Can, or should, heritage values be considered a universalist or a particularist norm? Even the axiom "thou shalt not loot archaeological sites" has complex dimensions. During the initial invasion of Iraq, archaeological sites that had been guarded were left abandoned and during the extended period of chaos before "normal" employment was reinstated, some of these sites were looted and the artifacts sold to support families that were in dire straits. On occasion, the looters were the previous guards of the sites. Looting is a problem in Nigeria as well, where antiquity dealers encourage clandestine excavations by local people so they can buy the artifacts and where it is possible for tourists to take a "guided tour" of an "archaeological" excavation and purchase looted artifacts to take home (illegally). This is damaging in terms of the artifacts and sites and is also injurious to the professional reputations of archaeologists in the country. Custodians of cultural heritage legitimately decry such travesties. However, if we are going to change these situations, we need to understand the circumstances that produced them and provide alternatives that work for people on the ground. Using heritage values to develop the educational and tourism potential of cultural heritage sites, for example, is an important way of caring for heritage globally.

Heritage values are integral to national identity and to international perceptions of this identity. For example, the new coat of arms for South Africa launched in 2000 to celebrate a post-apartheid identity for the country includes images from San rock art, bringing Indigenous identity to the fore in the symbolic processes around nation building. In countries with clearly defined Indigenous populations, such as the United States, Canada, Australia, and New Zealand, Indigenous heritage is incorporated into national values and acts as a fundamental draw for international tourism. In Australia, around 80 percent of international visitors leave having had some kind of experience or interaction with Indigenous culture.

Often, heritage is a casualty of war. Throughout human history, victors have destroyed or diminished the heritage of the vanquished. Sometimes, this has involved transporting huge statues thousands of kilometers, such as with the Medusa heads that are now in the cisterns of Istanbul, or the Axum monolith that was taken from Ethiopia to Italy as part of the prelude to the Second World War. Other examples of strategic engagements which focused on cultural icons include toppling of the statues of Stalin in Eastern Europe in 1989 after the fall of Stalinist regimes and of Saddam Hussein in Iraq in 2003, after the invasion by the United States and her allies; the deliberate bombing of Dresden during the Second World War; the Taliban's destruction of the two Buddhas at Bamiyan, Afghanistan; the shelling of the 16th century Stari Most bridge at Mostar, as part of the cultural cleansing of Ottoman heritage in Bosnia—and the crashing of planes into the twin towers of the World Trade Center in New York. All of these attacks on material culture were simultaneously assaults on iconic cultural values and associated heritage values.

Then there is the matter of hidden heritage and its role in producing and reproducing structures of power. In the contemporary world, it is not enough to assume that the heritage one person values will also be valued by others. Throughout the world, societies are increasingly cosmopolitan, bringing together different kinds of heritage values. While there are some core commonalities, as with my opening anecdote, there are also examples in which one person's heritage is subsumed by another's. In my own country, Australia, for example, the population of the northern regions was largely Chinese until the beginning of the 20th century—yet the colonial history of Australia is one of British colonization and few Chinese sites have been preserved. Similarly, the Indigenous histories of countries such as my own receive little public recognition, even though these countries were once (and still are) Indigenous lands.

The discussion of heritage values in this book speaks to the socially responsible development of a global world. Accordingly, I commend this volume to students, teachers, practitioners, and members of the public. This book will assist professionals ranging from lawyers and anthropologists to cultural heritage managers and archaeologists as they grapple with the diverse ways that people value their heritage.

The world of big business is another, perhaps surprising, group that will benefit from this book. In top business schools in the United States, there has been a dramatic increase of interest in ethics courses and in discussions of personal and corporate responsibility. At Harvard Business School, a significant percentage of the 2009 graduating class signed "The M.B.A. Oath," a voluntary pledge that the goal of a business manager is to "serve the greater good." At Columbia Business School, all students pledge to an honor code. This student-led change speaks to an increasing concern about the impact corporations have upon communities, the lives of employees, and the environment. This book, with its many voices from around the world, will make a substantive contribution to ensuring that heritage values become an integral part of corporate ethics and social responsibility.

The nurturing and sustaining of our heritage is one of the major challenges facing humankind. To address this, we need to understand the structures of power that delimit the heritage values of diverse players, both big and small, within and across societies. This book plays a key role in a global conversation that will be ongoing throughout the 21st century. As I learned from my classes at Columbia University, heritage values span continents, cultures, and class. Heritage values are human values.

Claire Smith
President, World Archaeological Congress

Acknowledgments

This book would not have been possible without the support of a number of organizations and individuals. We would like to thank Jerre Brumbelow, Superintendent of Cumberland Island National Seashore, Georgia, United States and his staff for providing a stimulating environment in which to hold the 2007 Heritage Values Workshop that formed the basis for this book. Essential funding was provided by Kirk A. Cordell, Executive Director of the National Center for Preservation Technology and Training, National Park Service, Natchitoches, Louisiana, United States, and by the Halach-Winik Travel Agency, Cancún, Quintana Roo, México. Without their support, workshop participation and the range of discussion and perspectives in this book would have been reduced greatly. We are also grateful to Hamline University, St. Paul, Minnesota, United States for orchestrating workshop travel arrangements in addition to helping support and organize the workshop and book.

The Southeast Archeological Center, National Park Service, Tallahassee, Florida, United States contributed significantly to this project. For enabling the Center to participate, we owe a special thanks to former Center directors, John E. Ehrenhard and Dr. Bennie C. Keel. Exceptional logistical and other assistance for the workshop was provided by staff archaeologists of the Center. Charles F. Lawson and R. Steven Kidd organized the ground and sea transportation; Lawson, Meredith D. Hardy, and Jessica McNeil facilitated a permanent recording of the workshop proceedings; and, Guy Prentice and Charles F. Lawson helped with formatting. Archaeologists Bruce A. Ream's and Lewis C. "Skip" Messenger's contributions to the workshop's success are much appreciated, as is Skip's exceptional work on the index for this book.

Invaluable letters of support for this project were pledged by numerous universities and professional societies, including the Center for Heritage Resource Studies, University of Maryland; the Center for Science Teaching and Learning, Northern Arizona University; the Center for Tourism Research and Development, University of Florida; the Cultural Business Group, Heritage Futures, Glasgow Caledonian

University; the European Association of Archaeologists; the Higher Education Academy, Subject Centre for History, Classics, and Archaeology, University of Liverpool; the International Centre for Cultural and Heritage Studies, University of Newcastle upon Tyne; the Society for American Archaeology; the Society for Historical Archaeology; the United States Committee, International Council on Monuments and Sites (US ICOMOS); and, the World Archaeological Congress.

The editors wish to thank photographer Alex Messenger for the use of his image taken at the Phnom Bakheng Temple Complex in Angkor, Cambodia for the cover of this book.

A final expression of thanks is due to Paul Hartwig, the former Southeast Region Associate Director for Cultural Resources, National Park Service, Atlanta, Georgia, United States, for it was his encouragement that initiated this project.

INTRODUCTION

George S. Smith, Phyllis Mauch Messenger, and Hilary A. Soderland

Heritage is important to us. Our local, regional, and national identities are formed and defined by legacies from the past. They are reflected in the ways our predecessors have shaped the landscape, in the buildings and monuments and archaeological sites we know, as well as by the cultural and artistic practices and traditions we embrace and enjoy. Taken together, these tangible and intangible expressions contribute to our sense of belonging, of order and continuity, and of our collective meaning in the world. They inevitably lead to questions of, "What is it that people want to save?" (Howard 2006: 484).

The language used to label and describe objects, places, and ideas of heritage has changed over time. Archaeological sites or historic structures have been referred to variously as cultural resources, cultural property, cultural heritage, or heritage resources. Attempts to codify definitions of heritage have confounded scholars, lawmakers, and practitioners alike; some are perceived as too narrow while others so broad that they become meaningless (Ahmad 2006; Carman 2000; Harvey 2001). The 2005 Council of Europe Faro Framework Convention on the Value of Cultural Heritage for Society provides a reasonable definition with which to begin our discussion of heritage values: "Cultural heritage is a group of resources inherited from the past which people identify, independently of ownership, as a reflection and expression of their constantly evolving values, beliefs, knowledge and traditions" (Council of Europe 2005: Section I, Article 2(a)).

This volume explores the concepts and values inherent in consideration of cultural heritage, presenting perspectives from different geographic regions and frames of reference. It seeks to stimulate thinking within and beyond academia about the many questions and issues regarding heritage values.

As global pressures on the landscape have increased, threats to the places and practices related to heritage have amplified. Realities such as armed conflicts, illicit trafficking, and looting continue to escalate (although not explicitly addressed in this volume). International organizations such as the United Nations Educational, Scientific, and Cultural Organization (UNESCO) and the International Council on Monuments and Sites (ICOMOS) as well as many individual nations have developed charters, laws, and practices to protect heritage (e.g., ICOMOS 2009; UNESCO 1972). These protective measures have been adopted because of the enduring value that we place on heritage. What is it that we value about the past? What is its worth and meaning to us? What touches us? What guides our decisions?

Any discussion of values, including heritage values, begins in the realm of ethics and morals (Lipe 1974; Lowenthal 2004; Lynott and Wylie 1995; McManamon and Hatton 2000; Pluciennik 2001; Scarre and Scarre 2006; Zimmerman et al. 2003). For millennia, philosophers and other thinkers from both Western and non-Western perspectives have been captivated by the ethical complexities and conundrums inherent in the fabric of society. One classical line of reasoning considers value to be generated by individual actors in society whose free will creates and sustains a universe of actions and linked responsibilities (Tessitore 1996). Another approach comprehends value to be determined by the orientation of the will, not the consequences of acts. Value is thus based on the conception that freedom is the most fundamental element of human existence and the foundation for morals and ethics (Guyer 1993). Yet another line of thinking contends that acts are morally right or justified if they cause the greatest happiness to the greatest number. The value assigned to acts therefore corresponds to the resultant effect on quality of life and/or promotion of the greatest public good (Dinwiddy 1989).

In exploring the concept of values, a number of common themes have emerged with direct application to the underlying questions of how to define and apply heritage values in contemporary society. The themes include suppositions that value is assigned and influences the quality of life for individuals, communities, and nations and that choosing whether or not to value the past has important consequences. As such, the quintessence of heritage values could be defined in terms of freedom and responsibility as expressed in mores of duty, honor, personal responsibility, fairness, inclusiveness, stewardship, social obligations, and an extensive array of similar ideals.

It is clear that heritage values underpin the basis for management and policy formation relating to our collective cultural heritage. While many in the cultural sector—particularly those involved in heritage decision making—are just beginning to address how to define and apply heritage values in contemporary society, the effort to connect to the past in meaningful ways is nothing new (Fowler 1992; Hewison 1987; Lowenthal 1985; see also chapters in this volume by Altschul, Holtorf, Okamura, Russell, and Silberman). In some countries, how the past should be transplanted into the present or future has been debated for generations (Carman 2005; Messenger 1999), while in others such acute awareness of past manifestations is a more recent occurrence (Rowan and Baram 2004; Smith 2000). This process has not always been smooth or equitable, since many conflicting ideals influence the ascription of value in the realm of heritage.

Governments and international organizations struggle to balance heritage values with the needs of contemporary society (Fairclough et al. 2008; Hoffman 2006; see also chapters in this volume by Clark, Fleming, Lizama Aranda, and Morgan et al.). The perceived success or failure of these efforts depends on the perspective and relative position of those who are measuring. For example, there has been a long-established history of employing heritage values to establish rights to land. This can, and often does, result in the construction of national identities and pride at the expense of other claims. Such current practice, however, raises complex issues of land tenure, social conflict, and indigenous rights, reflecting the increasingly understood recognition that there are multiple perspectives on heritage values: that "no heritage derives from one pure source...[but from] a concomitant willingness to value heritage of patently mixed multiple origin and mixed character" (Lowenthal 2004:27). One of the stated goals of the 2006 ICOMOS Charter for the Interpretation and Presentation of Cultural Heritage Sites, commonly known as the Ename Charter, is to "ensure inclusiveness in the interpretation of cultural heritage sites, by fostering the productive involvement of all stakeholders and associated communities in the development and implementation of interpretive programmes" (ICOMOS, Ename Charter 2006: Principle 6 "Concern for Inclusiveness").

The inclusion of multiple stakeholders has emerged as one of the important themes in defining and applying heritage values (Meskell and Pels 2005; Watkins et al. 2000; see also chapters in this volume by Bruning, Soderland, and Yu and Foreword by Smith). The rights of stakeholders are inextricably entwined within discussions of codes of conduct and ethics, heritage tourism, site management, education, and professional outreach. The dialogue among stakeholders brings into focus fundamental and challenging questions. Whose heritage are we concerned with preserving? Who is allowed to have a voice, and who has the authority to make decisions? How should heritage be interpreted and presented when stakeholders' voices are in conflict? Does the past belong to everyone, or do some stakeholders have a stronger claim to particular pieces than others?

To compete with other public concerns and agendas, there must be a clear understanding of how heritage values influence our daily lives and how shared heritage connects us to our past as individuals and as communities and nations. But how do we measure this influence and what is the worth of this shared heritage? Knowing the price of something is not necessarily the same as knowing its value. In order to capture the full extent of heritage value, according to Clark (2006; see also chapter in this volume by Clark), it is necessary to examine *intrinsic value* (individual experiences of heritage), *instrumental value* (associated social or economic aspects of heritage), and *institutional value* (the processes and techniques institutions use to create heritage value). Heritage value differs from economic value, which assesses worth relative to other things as indicated by a financial price tag, not in relation to preferences and satisfaction associated with the moral and ethical sphere.

These concerns are representative of the variety of issues associated with value and heritage that formed the basis of the workshop Heritage Values: The Past in Contemporary Society held at Cumberland Island National Seashore, Georgia, United States, in November 2007. The workshop itself built upon a series of conferences and workshops on archaeological stewardship (SAA 1990), education (Bender and Smith 2000; MATRIX 2003; SAA 1995), public value (Clark 2006), and global issues (Smith et al. 2002).

Participants in the 2007 Heritage Values Workshop included anthropologists, archaeologists, heritage managers, lawyers, architects, and public policy experts from four continents. They engaged in discussion and debate on such topics as heritage decision making and the public; accountability and heritage; market forces and globalization; tangible and intangible heritage; community identity and heritage; social and economic benefits of heritage; articulation of heritage values; interpretation and public values; technology and heritage; and, the past and the power of place. Based on the 2007 Heritage Values Workshop, chapters in this book, previous conferences, workshops, panels, and associated publications, a number of critical needs and questions have been identified and are listed in the Appendix. We hope that this book will further discussion on these important topics with respect to heritage values in contemporary society.

Part I. Defining Heritage Values

Section 1. Heritage Values and Meaning in Social Context

Major Themes:

- What constitutes heritage values and who determines those values

- Caring for and caring about heritage values
- The impact of heritage values on group identity
- The dialogue between archaeologists and society regarding heritage values

In Chapter 1, Ian Russell discusses how and why people value the past from emotional, psychological, and intellectual standpoints both within the context of group identity and as affected by legislative and management structures. Next, Cornelius Holtorf discusses how heritage values are expressed in contemporary society and the corresponding impact on cultural policies and management. Katsuyuki Okamura's chapter approaches heritage values as public property within the context of individual and social values at various levels within Japanese society. He underscores the role of education in the dialogue between archaeologists and communities. Neil Asher Silberman situates heritage values within a constantly changing social context. He discusses the methods and effects of technically enhanced interpretation designed to increase heritage values as well as the need to establish public forums for reflection and dialogue on the value and meaning of the past. In the concluding chapter of this section, Jeffrey H. Altschul critically assesses the differences and common ground between those dealing with the built environment (historic preservation) and those concerned with archaeological resources. He addresses how the identity of those determining the value of archaeological sites affects what is valued, managed, and protected.

Part I. Defining Heritage Values

Section 2. Management, Policy Formation, and Heritage Values

Major Themes:

- Heritage values as applied to development and cultural resource management
- Public policy tools for development planning and implementation
- The role of cultural diversity and changing values in heritage management
- The impact of inclusive and exclusive cultural policies and practices on heritage values

Kate Clark begins this section with a focus on how development schemes for individual versus community values differentially impact value-based approaches to cultural resource management. In Chapter 7, Arlene K. Fleming addresses how historical and cultural continuity has been codified in many countries through public policies, laws, and regulations that reflect cultural heritage assets within social, economic, and biophysical environments. Then David W. Morgan, Nancy I. M. Morgan, Brenda Barrett, and Suzanne Copping deliberate on the consequences of establishing heritage lists such as the United States National Register of Historic Places. They highlight the growing recognition that such lists do not adequately represent cultural diversity, changing social context, and intangible values. In Chapter 9, using the legal structure in the United States, Hilary A. Soderland centers on the dynamic relationship between history and heritage to emphasize how laws are increasingly relied upon to structure and institutionalize heritage values within a national context.

Part II. Applying Heritage Values

Section 1. Teaching and Learning Heritage Values

Major Themes:

- The need for archaeology to consider wider publics and stakeholders
- The politics of identity as applied to the practice of archaeology including the manner in which it is taught
- The opportunity to build bridges with Native communities through curricula development
- The role of heritage values in teaching archaeology in higher education

In Chapter 10, Elizabeth S. Chilton discusses how post-processual archaeology, with its emphasis on multivocality, directs the discipline and teaching of archaeology to take into account wider publics and stakeholders as well as diverse applications. Joëlle Clark and Margaret A. Heath then convey how heritage values that reflect intrinsic ideals of Native Americans can be implemented in educational programs in collaboration with indigenous communities in order to engage Native students in their own language, cultural history, and identities. In the final chapter in this section, Karina Croucher underlines the role of archaeology in nurturing an understanding of the importance of the past and of heritage values in a curriculum that includes alternative narratives of the past.

Part II. Applying Heritage Values

Section 2. Stakeholders and Heritage Values

Major Themes:

- Experiencing heritage values of another culture and sharing indigenous heritage values in a way that is consistent with different perspectives of value
- The distinction between history and heritage and how the past is valued
- Legal mechanisms to address myriad interests when cultural heritage knowledge is disclosed, interpreted, and used
- The past as part of the contemporary culture of living indigenous people

Using the example of the Doro Ana Pumé of Venezuela, Pei-Lin Yu's chapter illustrates the consequences of outside influences on a community's values and its efforts to guard and propagate those values so that children learn them and outsiders understand their unique significance. In Chapter 14, Susan B. Bruning situates heritage values within the context of the 1990 Native American Graves Protection and Repatriation Act (NAGPRA) and probes how this law and others have attempted to define and manage interests in Native American cultural heritage. Turning to México, Lilia Lizama Aranda discusses how current policies marginalize and restrict the involvement of indigenous communities, private organizations, professionals, and the general public in the management and protection of cultural heritage.

Part II. Applying Heritage Values

Section 3. Heritage Values and World Heritage

Major Themes:

- Experiencing the past and its application to global heritage tourism
- Assessing the value of World Heritage sites for heritage management and cultural tourism in developing countries
- Protecting heritage values with respect to development and tourism while maintaining community integrity
- Using heritage values for educational, symbolic, political, and economic purposes

Ian Baxter opens this section by presenting pervasive trends in global heritage tourism data, the implications for heritage sites, and the need for the industrial sector to understand shared and divergent values. Then Chen Shen presents the role of heritage tourism in marketing China's rich heritage, particularly how its application to local economic development has resulted in support of previously overlooked heritage values issues. In Chapter 18, Roy Eugene Graham describes the conservation plans for two World Heritage site towns that employed economic development to protect heritage values through international marketing, increased tourism, new cultural industries, and rejuvenation of local businesses/industry. Finally, Thanik Lertcharnrit discusses how heritage is highly valued by contemporary Thai people and how it has been, and is being, used for educational, symbolic, political, and economic purposes.

In sum, these chapters provide a broad range of perspectives on the meaning of heritage and the many ways its value is assigned and understood in the world today. The authors confront issues of rapidly increasing significance in the interpretative representation of past material objects, landscapes, and cultures. They call to question lines of demarcation that narrowly position heritage values within contemporary society. We hope that the dialogue and diversity of approaches represented in this volume stimulate further scholarship, practical applications, and the ongoing global conversation about heritage values.

References

Ahmad, Yahaya
2006   The Scope and Definitions of Heritage: From Tangible to Intangible. *International Journal of Heritage Studies* 12(3):292–300.

Bender, Susan J., and George S. Smith, eds.
2000   *Teaching Archaeology in the 21st Century*. Washington, D.C.: Society for American Archaeology.

Carman, John
2000   Theorising a Realm of Practice: Introducing Archaeological Heritage Management as a Research Field. *International Journal of Heritage Studies* 6(4):303–308.
2005   *Against Cultural Property: Archaeology, Heritage and Ownership*. London: Duckworth and Company.

Clark, Kate, ed.
2006   *Capturing the Public Value of Heritage: The Proceedings of the London Conference 25–26 January 2006*. Swindon, England: English Heritage.

Council of Europe
2005   Faro Framework Convention on the Value of Cultural Heritage for Society. Electronic document, http://conventions.coe.int/Treaty/EN/Treaties/Html/199.htm, accessed January 11, 2009.

Dinwiddy, J. R.
1989   (John Rowland), Bentham. Oxford: Oxford University Press.

Fairclough, Graham, Rodney Harrison, John H. Jameson, Jr., and John Schofield, eds.
2008   The Heritage Reader. London: Rougledge.

Fowler, Peter J.
1992   The Past in Contemporary Society: Then, Now. London: Routledge.

Guyer, Paul
1993   Kant and the Experience of Freedom: Essays on Aesthetics and Morality. Cambridge: Cambridge University Press.

Harvey, David C.
2001   Heritage Pasts and Heritage Presents: Temporality, Meaning and the Scope of Heritage Studies. Journal of Heritage Studies 7(4):319–338.

Hewison, Robert
1987   The Heritage Industry. Oxford: Oxford University Press.

Hoffman, Barbara T., ed.
2006   Art and Cultural Heritage: Law, Policy and Practice. Cambridge: Cambridge University Press.

Howard, Peter
2006   Editorial: Valediction and Reflection. International Journal of Heritage Studies 12(6):483–488.

ICOMOS
2006   ICOMOS Charter for the Interpretation and Presentation of Cultural Heritage Sites, commonly known as the Ename Charter. Electronic Document, http://www.enamecharter.org/index.html, accessed July 30, 2009.
2009   Charters Adopted by the General Assembly of ICOMOS. Electronic document, http://www.international.icomos.org/centre_documentation/chartes_eng.htm, accessed January 19, 2009.

Lipe, William D.
1974   A Conservation Model for American Archaeology. The Kiva 39(1–2): 213–245.

Lowenthal, David
1985   The Past is a Foreign Country. Cambridge: Cambridge University Press.
2004   Heritage Ethics. In Interpreting the Past: Presenting Archaeological Sites to the Public. D. Callebaut, N.A. Silberman, A. Ervynck, and A. E. Killebrew,

eds. Pp. 23–31. Brussels: Institute for the Archaeological Heritage of the Flemish Community.

Lynott, Mark J., and Alison Wylie, eds.
1995 *Ethics in American Archaeology: Challenges for the 1990s*. Special Report. Washington, D.C.: Society for American Archaeology.

MATRIX
2003 Making Archaeological Teaching Relevant in the XXI Century (MATRIX). Electronic document, http://www.indiana.edu/%7Earch/saa/matrix/, accessed May 22, 2008.

McManamon, Francis P., and Alf Hatton, eds.
2000 *Cultural Resource Management in Contemporary Society*. London: Routledge.

Meskell, Lynn, and Peter Pels, eds.
2005 *Embedding Ethics: Shifting Boundaries of the Anthropological Profession*. Oxford: Berg.

Messenger, Phyllis Mauch, ed.
1999 *The Ethics of Collecting Cultural Property: Whose Culture? Whose Property?* 2nd edition. Albuquerque: University of New Mexico Press.

Pluciennik, Mark, ed.
2001 *The Responsibilities of Archaeologists. Archaeology and Ethics*. British Archaeological Reports International Series 981. Oxford: Archaeopress.

Rowan, Yorke, and Uzi Baram, eds.
2004 *Marketing Heritage: Archaeology and the Consumption of the Past*. Walnut Creek, California: AltaMira Press.

Scarre, Chris, and Geoffrey Scarre, eds.
2006 *The Ethics of Archaeology. Philosophical Perspectives on Archaeological Practice*. Cambridge: Cambridge University Press.

Smith, George S., Donald G. Jones, and Thomas R. Wheaton, Jr.
2002 Workshop Report: Working Together: Archaeology in Global Perspective. *International Journal of Heritage Studies* 10(3):321–327.

Smith, Laurajane
2000 'Doing Archaeology': Cultural Heritage Management and Its Role in Identifying the Link Between Archaeological Practice and Theory. *International Journal of Heritage Studies* 6(4):309–316.

SAA
1990 *Save the Past for the Future: Actions for the '90s*. Washington, D.C.: SAA.
1995 *Save the Past for the Future II: Report of the Working Conference*. Washington, D.C.: SAA.

Tessitore, Aristide
1996 *Reading Aristotle's Ethics: Virtue, Rhetoric and Political Philosophy*. Albany: State University of New York Press.

UNESCO
1972 Convention Concerning the Protection of the World Cultural and Natural Heritage. Electronic document, http://portal.unesco.org/en/ev.php-URL_ID=13055&URL_DO=DO_TOPIC&URL_SECTION=201.html, accessed January 19, 2009.

Watkins, Joe, K. Anne Pyburn, and Pamela Cressey
2000 Community relations: What the practicing archaeologists needs to know to work effectively with local and/or descendant communities. In *Teaching Archaeology in the Twenty-First Century.* Susan J. Bender and George S. Smith, eds. Pp. 73–82. Washington, D.C.: Society for American Archaeology.

Zimmerman, Larry J., Karen D. Vitelli, and Julie Hollowell-Zimmer, eds.
2003 *Ethical Issues in Archaeology.* Walnut Creek, California: AltaMira Press.

PART I

Defining Heritage Values

Section 1

Heritage Values and Meaning
in Social Context

1

HERITAGES, IDENTITIES, AND ROOTS: A CRITIQUE OF ARBORESCENT MODELS OF HERITAGE AND IDENTITY

Ian Russell

Introduction

Heritage is often understood as an exchange relationship (see the chapters by Holtorf; Okamura; Silberman; and Altschul in this volume). Most definitions of heritage elaborate on its quality as a thing (or those things) that are passed on to future generations. The difficulty in quantifying these exchange relationships is that they are negotiated and mediated, often imperceptibly, over long periods of time.

A series of institutional charters, policy documents, legislative documents, and national constitutions have developed a body of terms, policies, and social behavioral precedents for the management of the costs and benefits of the heritage exchange relationship (see the chapters by Fleming; Morgan et al; Bruning; and Soderland in this volume). Indeed, UNESCO has been taking steps toward the recognition of heritage as an inalienable human birthright (particularly in the case of genetic heritage and copyright law) relating to the dignity, identity, and integrity of the person and the group within which the individual participates (Kwak 2005). Although these steps should be applauded, some have also voiced concern over the "boom" in heritage law, stating that we are living in an "age of heritage," with ever more conservationist values creating an inexorable burden on those to whom we wish to bequeath our heritage (Cooke 2007). Simply put, it is a question of sustainability.

Heritage is, however, not a *de facto* somatic phenomenon or social behavior. It is constituted by willful acts of choice (ICOMOS 2007:1). The maintenance of heritage as a choice points toward beliefs in an image of time that has passed, that enriches and inspires a time that has yet to pass. Therein a value can be ascribed to the heritage relationship. This value can be best expressed as a constellation of negotiated and mediated sentiments—hopes, dreams, desires, and beliefs.

A sentiment is a complex mixture of intellectual and emotional perceptions. Thus, heritage can be described not simply as a series of things to be managed, but also as a capricious coalescence of intellectual thought and emotional responses to the negotiation of our material and temporally understood experiences. The importance of this reorientation in heritage studies was articulated recently at the Capturing the Public Value of Heritage conference in London. Deborah Mattison (2006:97) noted, "experts 'think' and 'know,' whereas people 'feel' and 'believe.'"

Although Mattison's comment creates a false dichotomy between an unfeeling expert culture and an emotionally motivated public, the rhetorical call to highlight the significance of emotive responses for determining and articulating value in heritage is critical. Heritage does not simply exist. It is something we have to care about and simultaneously care for. Unfortunately, the vast majority of heritage studies literature does not engage critically with how or why people "care" from an emotional, psychological, or intellectual standpoint. That we "care" or "should care" is assumed. This assumption is often founded in the conflation of the concepts of heritage and identity.

Heritage and Identity

> When it comes to defining heritage, the vast majority of people in Wicklow, Ireland (71 percent) equate protecting Wicklow's heritage with "protecting our identity" and this is closely associated with "protecting our roots," with almost eight out of every ten people expressing pride in their heritage. Wicklow Heritage Awareness Survey. (Wicklow County Council 2005)

In articulating the value of heritage in contemporary life, public surveys, such as the one quoted above from Co. Wicklow in Ireland, often stress the importance of heritage for "protecting our identity." In its 2007 educational initiatives about world heritage, UNESCO (2007) also affirmed this conflation, saying, "Understanding World Heritage can help us become more aware of our own roots, and of our cultural and social identity." Students and young people have arrived at the same conclusion:

> Cultural and natural sites form the environment on which human beings depend psychologically, religiously, educationally and economically.

> Their destruction or even deterioration could be harmful to the survival
> of our identity, our nations and our planet. We have the responsibility
> to preserve these sites for future generations. (World Heritage
> Pledge, World Heritage Youth Forum, Bergen, Norway [UNESCO
> 2007])

These views are not limited to public opinions or institutional policies.
Conflations between heritage and identity are also enshrined in legisla-
tion and national constitutions such as in the *Bunreacht na hÉireann*
(Constitution of the Ireland) (1937):

> It is the entitlement and birthright of every person born in the island
> of Ireland, which includes its islands and seas, to be part of the Irish
> Nation. ... Furthermore, the Irish nation cherishes its special affinity
> with people of Irish ancestry living abroad who share its cultural
> identity and heritage. Article 2, *Bunreacht na hÉireann* (1937)

Such a conceptual basis for asserting the value of heritage is advantageous to the heritage sector as it defends the sector's role as caretaker
for an inalienable human right—identity. Operating within the structures of the state, the sanctity of individual and group identity creates
both a civic responsibility and social entitlement to recognition of group
identities. The vast majority of legislation and policy relating to heritage
and identity is the result of discourses of national identity manifestation.
Although nation-states provide a strong ideological defense of the heritage sector, their ideological foundation can also reduce the complexity
of choices in the manifestation of heritage to "either/or" decisions relative to national consciousness and identity.

For example, in Ireland where immigration and economic development has dramatically changed the demographics of the state in recent
years, debates over competing values between heritage and development concerns are often couched in reductive, romantic, and essentialist
language (Russell 2007). A recent example of this has been the debate
over the construction of the M3 motorway in the so-called Tara-Skryne
valley in Co. Meath. In an article entitled "Is nothing sacred?" by Eileen
Battersby in *The Irish Times*, the sacred, national qualities of the site of
Tara and its landscapes were appealed to in order to support a preservationist position as a "national obligation": If Ireland has a heart, it beats
here at Tara and throughout the dramatic hinterland that surrounds the
complex, with its monuments, earthworks, and cohesive record of settlement (Battersby 2007).

Such a perspective is not limited to nationalist ideologies. International
opinion regarding the Tara debate has also highlighted the fundamentalist

positions which the heritage sector can sometimes espouse. Prof. Dennis Harding (2004:16) of the University of Edinburgh stated in relation to the then-proposed M3 motorway that, "Carving a motorway through such a landscape is an act of cultural vandalism as flagrant as ripping a knife through a Rembrandt painting."

Pat Cooke, Director of the MA course in Arts Management and Cultural Policy at University College Dublin, has argued that this vein of debate in the heritage sector has much to do with the historicity of the sector itself which sees itself as a universal given. In suggesting some points for critical reflection on heritage in Ireland, Cooke (2008:5) suggested that, "A place to begin might be to develop some sense of the historical nature of this heritage argument. One of the ironies of heritage is that its advocates fail to see the historicity of the thing itself; where history's stock is relativity, heritage deals in absolutes."

Adherence to a reductive, essentialist interpretation of heritage which is based on ethnic or national structures can result in an Orwellian struggle. A heritage sector based on intractable absolutes may lead more toward the fragmentation and ghettoization of the heritage sector, with multiple identities competing for limited resources relying on arguments for *de facto* authenticity.

With increasing concern over civic apathy, heritage, when phrased as intrinsically linked to group identity, allows for the statutory recognition of a personal ideological stake in the manifestation of governance. This stake has dangerous potential as has been witnessed in the ethno-nationalist heritage and archaeological programs of European nation-states in the early 20th century (Galaty and Watkinson 2004; Kohl and Fawcett 1995). The Orwellian overtones of the state affirming civic stake through the sentiments of heritage and identity are well rehearsed (Díaz-Andreu and Champion 1996). Focusing solely on the politics of ethno-cultural entitlement to heritage such as citizenship based upon genetic inheritance (e.g., *jure sanguinis* in the Republic of Italy) can cause heritage to play an exclusive rather and inclusive role in the manifestation of civic co-presence and cooperation in the constitution of a state or community.

Rather than ownership, the language of trusteeship and stewardship should be preserved (Blaug et al. 2006). Heritage as civic cooperation and participation should be maintained as a forum for mediation, negotiation, and comprise over competing values in the spirit of equal civic partnerships (ICOMOS 2007:1). Perhaps what we are experiencing today is a convenient appropriation of heritage as an unquestionable ideology for the dictates of modern reactionary identity politics. Considering this, there is an opportunity for critical reflection on some of the fundamental conceptions of what heritage is.

Heritage and Group Identity

The link between heritage and identity has been expressed psychoanalytically by Vamik Volkan (2001, 2003) as "transgenerational transmission." Through the passing on of shared identifications with stories, objects, symbols, performances, and other aspects of heritage, one generation of a group can instill the values of the group's identity in the subsequent members of a group. Younger members can then remediate and carry on the emotional responses through both positive and traumatic commemorations. For example, an "apology" issued by the British Prime Minister, Tony Blair, (June 1, 1997) to Ireland for the "Great Famine" and the subsequent reactions in Irish society illustrated that such chosen narratives have residual potency in both Irish and British society as a result of transgenerational transmission (Holland 1997). In his statement, Blair noted:

> [That] one million people should have died in what was then part of the richest, most powerful nation in the world is something that still causes pain as we reflect on it today. ... Those who governed in London at the time failed their people through standing by while a crop failure turned into a massive human tragedy. We must not forget such a dreadful event. It is also right that we should pay tribute to the ways in which the Irish people have triumphed in the face of this catastrophe. (*Irish Times Reporter* 1997)

The transgenerational transmission of the trauma of the "Great Famine" is today commemorated worldwide not only as an aspect of heritage in Ireland but as world heritage, with farm cottages from rural Co. Mayo being transported as far as New York City as monuments (New York State Education Department 2002).

The power of the transgenerational transmission of experiences is that it can provide a historical lineage for the declaration of authentic identities. A conflation between authentic heritage and authentic identity can be used to create a stake for those who profess a specific identity and steward a specific heritage within a social power structure. Heritage and identity are not, however, things that simply exist as resources for the cohesion of communities. Founding heritage on such a psychological process can serve to exclude other manifestations of heritage through spontaneous interpersonal creation or discover (e.g., archaeology).

Heritage and identity are not essences within any single person. They are manifested and performed through interpersonal relationships and behavior. They are phenomena that we actively and continually must choose to constitute (ICOMOS 2007:1). Their constitution is in the form of agencies, perceptions, conceptions, mediations, performances, and materializations. UNESCO classifies the phenomena of heritage into two types, tangible and intangible. Though there is a perceptual difference between the two categories (i.e., perception of permanence and tangibility), tangible things (i.e., buildings and sites) are only materialized as heritage through human agency, choice, and will (Russell 2006). Thus, the underlying quality of heritage is as a set of interpersonal relationships.

Considering the above argument, justifying either heritage or identity through the deployment of the other is a tautology. Both are mutually-enmeshed phenomena of human interpersonal and group psychological dynamics. Neither is *a priori*. It is through the shared willful act and choice of humans to participate in negotiation and mediation of shared self and group images and in compromising over competing valuations of roles and terms of encountering the world that the co-creation of both heritage and identity as phenomena can be constituted. To abbreviate, both heritage and identity are the constellation of sentiments within the becoming of modern groups.

Undercutting the Roots of Heritage and Identity: Trees, Rhizomes, and Mycelia

Heritage is traditionally understood as a linear exchange relationship between two parties where there is a passing on of the role of trustee. Although the growing global market of heritage has increased the complexity of this web of networked relationships, the core concept is of preservation and sustainability of lineages—paths upon which things are passed to future generations. Fixing identity as a main determiner of heritage authenticity and value is part of a modernist Western arborescent paradigm (Deleuze and Guattari 1980). The arborescent paradigm pictures knowledge in the structure of a tree, where there is linear growth and progress (e.g., time), binary relations (e.g., inside and outside), and dualistic modes of thought (e.g., self and other).

Picturing arborescent heritage, the roots ground the structure of the relationships in the matter, ideas and images of the past, and the structure grows upward into complex hierarchies of social relation deriving their inheritance from the roots. Hierarchies of both temporal age and social position allow for power dynamics and competitions over authenticity of agency. Although the rationale of pluralism might lead us to plant many different trees, this would only effect a proliferation of rationalized hierarchical systems of control, entitlement, and power that reify the Western linear temporal paradigm. Despite the pragmatic usefulness of linear and arborescent models for power hierarchies in governance, the recent theoretical pressure to move away from modern bifurcations of self and other (us/them) suggests that new models for understanding the sentiment of heritage should be considered.

An alternative to the arborescent model was described by Carl Jung and further developed by Gilles Deleuze and Félix Guattari (1980)—the rhizome.

> Life has always seemed to me like a plant that lives on its rhizome. Its true life is invisible, hidden in the rhizome. The part that appears above the ground lasts only a single summer. Then it withers away—an ephemeral apparition. When we think of the unending growth and decay of life and civilizations, we cannot escape the impression of absolute nullity. Yet I have never lost the sense of something that lives and endures beneath the eternal flux. What we see is blossom, which passes. The rhizome remains (Jung 1962: Prologue).

In Jung's metaphor, the rhizome (e.g., ginger root) is a capricious, undulating coalescence of existential possibility from which our perceptible phenomena emanate and return. The Jungian rhizome allows us to leave behind linear logic and arborescent knowledge structures and instead suggests that heritage is a rhizomatic constellation of sentiments.

Turning toward heritage and identity, a different image may be more apt. In conversations with Andrew Cochrane, the metaphor of mycelia has been developed. In mycology (the study of fungi), the mycelium operates very similarly to the rhizome. It is more complex though since the fruit that appears on the surface (the mushroom) as distinct and separate is still part of a collective mycelium—the network of white filaments that make up the vegetative part of a fungus. Relating to heritage, it is an apt metaphor as the fruits of the system feed directly on decaying matter to grow.

For heritage and identity, sentiments emanate from the mycelia of social and interpersonal relations. Thus, the roots of heritage or identity are not in the things or materials of the past but rather are in the mycelial qualities of human phenomenological perception mediated through interpersonal relations. Thus, if we would wish to preserve heritage as an opportunity for dialectical mediation of perceptions of being and thinking, it is the opportunity for free social interaction and open mediation that should be preserved. It is not enough to simply preserve the dwelling places of humanity. This is only one part of the preservation of the opportunity to dwell and the multiple possibilities for dwelling. To simply preserve the buildings or structures or sites defined as tangible heritage (though this is a necessary and pragmatic endeavor) only stewards the symptoms (branches, blossoms or fungi) of heritage and identity.

In this model, we are not called to preserve or celebrate any singular phenomenon (branch, blossom, or fungus) as heritage but rather to nurture, steward, and cultivate the mycelium as space for negotiation and mediation from which heritage phenomena fruit. This removes the strain of the binary logic of the preservationist discourse in heritage—to preserve or to destroy—and allows for multiple possibilities for remediation of heritage. Even through the decaying of one conception of heritage, a new heritage could grow.

Cultivating Mycelial Sentiments

A policy structure that addresses the mycelial qualities of heritage and identity begins with an appreciation of emotions, sentiments, and psychological qualities of human responses to contemporary experience. Thus, policy can seek not only to save things from oblivion, but also to encourage the preservation and development of sentiment (caring about the past) by creating and stewarding open spaces for negotiation and mediation of heritage (ICOMOS 2007:1).

Acknowledgment of the importance of such open and diverse spaces has been noted publicly. The Nara Document on Authenticity (1994) stated: Cultural heritage diversity exists in time and space, and demands respect for other cultures and all aspects of their belief systems. In cases where cultural values appear to be in conflict, respect for cultural diversity demands acknowledgment of the legitimacy of the cultural values of all parties (Nara Conference on Authenticity 1994).

The Nara Document also stated that the underlying quality for the determining of value was "authenticity." Authenticity was defined as: the knowledge and understanding of … sources of information, in relation to original and subsequent characteristics of the cultural heritage, and their meaning.

Though a sound practicable basis for constructing a management system for evaluating competing claims, authenticity understood purely as data constructs a hierarchy of values, where some heritage claims are less authentic than others. Authenticity should be located not in data and information alone, but in human sentiment and choice. Such an understanding of authenticity is based on consensus, on human choice to come together and profess an identity or celebrate a heritage. There are no social relationships that can be said to be more authentic than the next. It follows then that there are no identities or heritages that are more authentic than others. All are deserving of equal recognition and protection as acts of human will and choice (ICOMOS 2007:1).

This is the most essential and precious resource we have—that we care about who we are and how we express both who we were and where we wish to go. Who is to say that humanity will always care about the past, heritage or identity? Is it enough to simply preserve the things of the past? Or is it equally important to preserve desire and opportunity for emotional responses to the past?

Some Limitations of Arborescent Identity for Heritage

There is currently a strain put on limited resources for preservation and conservation in some parts of the world. In an arborescent model of authenticity, it is difficult to articulate an acceptable method of deacquisitioning previously deemed authentic items worthy to be preserved. Mycelial heritage allows for a more open acceptance of the possibility of deacquisitioning collections and sites and demobilizing certain aspects of the heritage sector if it is deemed to be appropriate through consensus. The current arborescent analytical framework for heritage based on modern identity results in a sector that responds more to modernist structures of knowledge than to manifested human choice and consensus. Reducing heritage to a product whose authenticity is verifiable only through quantifiable scientific research reduces the emotive desires of humans for recognition, identity, and cultural expression to a tautological proof for modern ethno-national state systems. Such an unquestioned arborescent tautology of heritage preservation is potentially unsustainable and could prove to become a burden rather than a benefit for future generations (Cooke 2007).

A recent challenge to the arborescent understanding of heritage based on identity is the acknowledgment of digital heritage and digital lifeworlds. In 2003, UNESCO (2003:1) adopted a Charter on the Preservation of Digital Heritage, stating, "The digital heritage consists of unique resources of human knowledge and expression. ... Where resources are 'born digital,' there is no other format but the digital object."

As an open space, digital lifeworlds (especially open-source programming) are founded on the acceptance of anarchic expression of self and group. Knowledge bases such as wiki's rely upon participation, will, and choice to generate consensus on authenticity. The chosen authentic resources do not, however, supercede the awareness, or acknowledgment of other resources. All are equally accessible. In such a digital age, an arborescent conception of identity as a basis for the preservation of digital heritage is untenable as its epistemological foundation runs counter to that of the form of human digital expression.

Cultivating the Mycelia of Heritage

In an arborescent model of identity and heritage that creates a power structure of entitlement, often the identities and heritage that are celebrated are overly positive. What of the darker side of humanity? In the process of development and social recognition, identities can become sanitized and justified through the commemoration of positive actions of a group. Volkan's (2001, 2003) research reminds us of the importance of the transgenerational transmission of experiences of traumatic events in the formation of group identities though these events are often perpetrated by a conceived "other." Dino Domic's (2000) research on the role of heritage and identity in post-war Croatia has illustrated that there are complex group psychological dynamics that respond to traumatic events. These responses can turn toward nostalgia or idyllic mythologies to sanitize a group's identity and manifest a positive reflection of a group's identity in their heritage. Domic's research reminds us that heritage should not be seen as something that is essentially a reflection of good reified by the projection of evil. A mycelial conception of heritage undercuts such dualistic thought and allows for a myriad of heritage experiences that celebrate and commemorate human choice in all its manifestations however it is subsequently valorized.

Turning toward a language that seeks to preserve the mycelial emotive basis for human choice to participate in heritage can allow for productive reconceptualizations of heritage projects. The research of Jenny Blain and Robert Wallis (2006) on the enhancement of heritage projects through the inclusion of contemporary heathen spiritual groups in the management of such sites as Sutton Hoo in the United Kingdom has illustrated that an embracement of human desire rather than an enforcement of scientifically founded conceptions of authentic heritage can produce dynamic and positive social projects where new stakeholders and stewards can be found in previously excluded communities.

To return to the Tara/M3 controversy in Ireland, a mycelial conception of heritage would help alleviate anxieties about the complete loss of heritage through change and development of the Tara landscape. Though the building of the motorway has resulted in the destruction of some archaeological sites and has altered portions of the landscape, these acts in themselves create energy for new conceptions of heritage to be produced. The mycelium of heritage in Co. Meath or in Ireland can not be destroyed by a single motorway, and the more debate and sentiment created through such action as laying a motorway only nurtures the mycelium of sentiment and debate—encouraging a richer fruiting of heritage.

Heritage and Identity: The Future

Identity as a core aspect of human psychological behavior will not cease to be a useful concept in discussing heritage policy. It offers a way of recognizing and including diverse voices in the manifestation of heritage. It facilitates bringing new stakeholders into the management of social, cultural, and environmental resources. The limitation of identity is, however, its basis in arborescent models of human knowledge. These arborescent models facilitate power structures and exchange relationships that can seek to reify contemporary ethno-national entitlements and market economics. As boundaries between identities blur and a capricious array of identities manifest themselves in a globalizing world, a language of inclusiveness through civic agency and choice should become the basis for determining values and strategies for stewarding heritage. It is suggested that mycelial understandings of identity and heritage will help follow Ricardo Blaug, Louise Horner, and Rohit Lekhi's (2006) call to provoke the sector to refine its construction of valuation procedures in the development of a more democratic conception of heritage value. Rather than exploring heritage management as choices of either/or, heritages as mycelia allows for both/and.

Acknowledgments

The research for this paper was undertaken while I held the NEH Keough Fellowship of the Keough-Naughton Institute for Irish Studies at the University of Notre Dame. I would like to thank Pat Cooke, Director of the MA course in Arts Management and Cultural Policy at University College, Dublin, and Dr Andrew Cochrane of Cardiff University for their help and guidance through the development of this chapter.

References

Battersby, Eileen
2007   Is Nothing Sacred? *The Irish Times*, May 26, http://www.irishtimes.com/
        newspaper/newsfeatures/2007/0526/1179498835274.html

Blain, Jenny, and Robert Wallis
2006   Representing Spirit: Heathenry, New-Indigenes and the Imaged Past.
        In *Images, Representations and Heritage: Moving beyond Modern
        Approaches to Archaeology*. Ian Russell, ed. Pp. 89–108. New York:
        Springer.

Blaug, Ricardo, Louise Horner, and Rohit Lekhi
2006   Heritage, Democracy and Public Value. In *Capturing the Public Value of
        Heritage: Proceedings of the London Conference, 25–26 January 2006*.
        Kate Clark, ed. Pp. 23–27. Swindon: English Heritage.

Cooke, Pat
2007 Will Our Descendants Thank Us or Curse Us? *The Irish Times: Weekend Review* July 28:4.
2008 Plato's Landscape: The Quarrel over Lismullen and the Tara Skryne Valley. In *History Ireland* 15(5):5–6.

Deleuze, Gilles, and Félix Guattari
1980 *A Thousand Plateaus: Capitalism and Schizophrenia.* Minneapolis: University of Minnesota Press.

Díaz-Andreu, Margarita, and Timothy Champion, eds.
1996 *Nationalism and Archaeology in Europe.* Boulder: Westview Press.

Domic, Dino
2000 Heritage Consumption, Identity Formation and Interpretation of the Past within Post War Croatia (working paper). Management Research Centre, University of Wolverhampton. Electronic document, http://www.wlv.ac.uk/PDF/uwbs_WP005-00%20Domic.pdf, accessed October 1, 2007.

Galaty, M. L., and C. Watkinson
2004 *Archaeology Under Dictatorship.* New York: Springer.

Harding, Dennis
2004 Ripping a Knife Through a Rembrandt. *Sunday Tribune*, October 24.

Holland, M.
1997 Why Blair Deserves Bouquets for Famine Apology. *The Irish Times*, 5 June, http://www.irishtimes.com/newspaper/opinion/1997/0605/97060500100.html

ICOMOS (International Scientific Committee on Interpretation and Presentation)
2007 The ICOMOS Charter for the Interpretation of Cultural Heritage Sites, Proposed Final Draft, 10 April 2007. Electronic document, http://icip.icomos.org/downloads/ICOMOS_Interpretation_Charter_EN_10-04-07.pdf, accessed September 30, 2007.

Irish Times Reporter
1997 Blair Admits British Policy Failure Turned Famine into Massive Human Tragedy. *The Irish Times*, 2 June, http://www.irishtimes.com/newspaper/frontpage/1997/0602/97060200004.html

Jung, Carl G.
1962 *Memories, Dreams, Reflections.* London: Collins.

Kohl, P. L., and C. P. Fawcett, eds.
1995 *Nationalism, Politics and the Practice of Archaeology.* Cambridge: Cambridge University Press.

Kwak, Sun-Young
2005 World Heritage Rights Versus National Cultural Property Rights: The Case of the Jikji Human Rights Dialogue. In *Cultural Rights.* Electronic

document, http://www.cceia.org/resources/publications/dialogue/2_12/online_exclusive/5153.html, accessed October 4, 2007.

Mattison, Deborah
2006 The Value of Heritage: What does the Public Think? In *Capturing the Public Value of Heritage: Proceedings of the London Conference, 25–26 January 2006*. Kate Clark, ed. Pp. 86–91. Swindon: English Heritage.

Nara Conference on Authenticity in Relation to the World Heritage Convention
1994 The Nara Document on Authenticity. Electronic document, http://www.international.icomos.org/naradoc_eng.htm, accessed September 30, 2007.

New York State Education Department
2002 The Irish Hunger Memorial at Battery Park City: A Teacher's Guide. Electronic document, http://www.emsc.nysed.gov/nysssa/HungerMemorial/HungerMemorialCurriculumGuide.htm, accessed March 22, 2006.

Russell, Ian
2006 Freud and Volkan: Archaeology, Psychoanalysis and Large Group Identity. *Antiquity* 80:185–195.
2007 Romantic Notions Simply the Debate. *The Irish Times: Weekend Review* July 28:4.

UNESCO
2003 Charter on the Preservation of Digital Heritage. Electronic document, http://portal.unesco.org/ci/en/ev.php-URL_ID=13367&URL_DO=DO_TOPIC&URL_SECTION=201.html, accessed October 2, 2007.

UNESCO, World Heritage Education
2007 World Heritage and Education. Electronic document, http://whc.unesco.org/education/kit/kitengfl/whe1u3/whe1u3fra.html, accessed October 1, 2007 [now dead – but can also be found at: http://www.ukworldheritage.org.uk/documents/WHEducDevtProgv2.pdf, accessed January 5, 2008].

Volkan,Vamik D.
2001 Transgenerational Transmissions and Chosen Traumas: An Aspect of Large-Group Identity. *Group Analysis* 34(1):79–97.
2003 Large-Group Identity: Border Psychology and Related Societal Processes. *Mind and Human Interaction* 13(1):49–75.

Wicklow County Council
2005 Attitudes towards Heritage in County Wicklow. Electronic document, http://www.wicklow.ie/Heritage/Wicklow%20Heritage%20Awareness%20Study%202005.pdf, accessed October 1, 2007.

2

HERITAGE VALUES IN CONTEMPORARY POPULAR CULTURE

Cornelius Holtorf

Introduction

This chapter is about heritage values in contemporary popular culture. By popular culture, I mean the culture people make for themselves in their everyday lives. When I say heritage, I generally mean archaeological heritage such as sites, buildings, landscapes, artifacts, and so forth. My focus is on the so-called Western world, with most of my examples being drawn from Western Europe. This chapter is thus about the values of archaeological heritage in people's everyday lives in the Western world (see also Holtorf 2005).

To talk about the values of heritage for the public, or quite simply about "public values" of heritage, is currently fashionable among heritage professionals and politicians. In 2006, a high-profile conference in London was entitled *Capturing the Public Value of Heritage* (Clark 2006). The conference proceedings make frequent references to the heritage sector's need to increase democratic legitimacy by taking more into account what people actually value and what they want from government in terms of heritage. But the approach adopted is somewhat top-down and geared nearly exclusively toward professionals and politicians. There is very little (if any) discussion and analysis of the empirical phenomena in which the public values of heritage actually become manifest.

My argument in this chapter is that in popular culture, heritage is often not valued for its literal content, that is, the specific information it contains about the past, but for its metaphorical content, that is, the topics and notions it alludes to and evokes among people who encounter it in their lives. The argument will proceed in three steps. First, I will argue that heritage is appreciated because (a) it evokes stories about the visitors of heritage sites themselves, (b) it tells stories that reaffirm various collective identities, and (c) it is simply enjoyable to imagine traveling into the past. This argument is supplemented by a discussion of the important role of visitors' preconceptions about the past. After taking up the fact that heritage is often valued also as a backdrop for appealing stories about the professionals producing heritage (such as archaeologists and conservators), I will conclude with some thoughts on the possible consequences of my argument both for the heritage sector and for cultural policy.

Heritage Values and Tourism

It is probably fair to say that the most notable encounter people have with heritage is when they are traveling (Horne 1984; also see the chapters by Baxter; Shen; and Graham in this volume). As tourists, people travel the world to visit heritage attractions, but they also visit local heritage sites. One justification for visiting cultural heritage—especially when traveling with children—is that such sites have a particular "cultural" significance allowing visitors to learn more about the area. You have not visited a place properly, they say, until you have understood at least a bit of its history. Such choices and preferences for heritage are arguably a question of taste. Taste is however acquired and governed by social parameters like class and lifestyle. This is the main point of the French sociologist Pierre Bourdieu's (1984) famous "social critique of the judgement of taste." Tell me what you like and I tell you who you are!

The German sociologist Gerhard Schulze (1993) argued similarly that the Experience Society in which we are living is segmented and that customers demand experiences that correspond to one of several predefined schemes. Some people, who see themselves as particularly cultivated, enjoy culture that is consumed with the brain and does not stimulate extensive bodily reactions. Others will prefer cultural experiences that are unpretentious, embodied, and best consumed collectively. A final group prefers experiencing environments that involve the entire body and all the senses, and quickly change focus in order to avoid boredom. All these different groups may enjoy heritage, yet in distinctive ways that conform to the particular scheme with which they associate themselves. Whereas some can never have enough written information, others may primarily demand short and entertaining guided tours, and others again mostly want to engage themselves in exciting activities. Often heritage destinations now offer something for each of these (and other) prefer-ences. Significantly, in each case, one of the main aims of consuming heritage is in fact a confirmation of the visitor's own social milieu and lifestyle (see also Holtorf 2006:169–170).

The story people are perhaps most interested in when they choose to visit heritage sites is thus in part a story about themselves rather than one about the sites or objects they look at. It takes some education and class (!) to actually choose to look at ancient ruins at all, rather than lie on the beach or watch a blockbuster movie (Schulze 1993:145). Heritage is valued because it allows people to tell stories about—and thereby reaffirm—their own social contexts and lifestyles. These stories are best told at sites whose significance is widely recognized in people's own social context, which is why tourists always "must see" the same sites first. At the same time, it is often meaningless for tourists whether or not the heritage visited is unrelated or very different from the visit-ors' own collective heritage. The story about themselves matters, not the past. Tourists like to buy, and often treasure, tokens of their visits such as postcards, entrance tickets, and especially souvenir guidebooks. Although many such guides will remain unread, they will remind people for many years of their trip and that (rather than what) they have learned. In *The Great Museum. The Re-Presentation of History*, Australian writer Donald Horne (1984:10) argued accordingly that "what matters is what [tourists] are told they are seeing. The fame of the object becomes its meaning; what finally matters may be a souvenir postcard, perhaps even the admission ticket, kept for years afterwards with other mementoes of passing visions of how life might have been."

Heritage Values and Social Communities

Another reason why people are interested in the past and its remains is an interest in confirming their roles as members of larger communities (see also Russell this volume). All World Heritage sites and especially exhibits about human origins emphasize our identities as members of the same species and the fact that all people on this planet in fact belong to this same category. The new Origins Centre in Johannesburg, South Africa, is thus described as a museum "for the people of the world."[1] They offer workshops, the main objective of which is "to provide a space for renewal and inspiration—ways to open our minds and exchange ideas—to better understand what it means to be human."[2]

At the same time, heritage sites and many museums are managed as part of the collective heritage of a given nation state. They thus reify preconceived national identities. On a lower level, something equivalent might be said about regional and local heritage and the regional and local identities supported by them. In each case, the cultural heritage contributes to people's self-understanding as members of a local community, inhabitants of a region, or citizens of a nation-state. Such historic identities are often proudly presented to guests who visit these nations, regions, or local communities and its museums and heritage attractions. By appreciating the heritage of others, we become more aware of our own heritage for which we expect the same kind of appreciation by others.

Heritage can also create or strengthen shared social identities of people who have a common past beyond purely geographical parameters. Examples may be the heritage of the working classes, the heritage of African Americans, or the heritage of specific families. Here too, heritage serves to link people with each other and contributes to their collective identities in the present.

In all these cases, heritage is thus valued because it allows people to tell stories that can reassure them as members of a particular community. It is almost irrelevant precisely what kind of heritage is shared or how limited our knowledge about that heritage may be. The limited knowledge of our most distant ancestors during the Pliocene is as sufficient for collective human identity as the well-documented heritage of 20th century cities for collective urban identities. Germans are to the same extent in parts defined by the heritage of Nazi atrocities (or Beethoven) as are Russians by the heritage of Pushkin (or Stalinism). What matters is not so much the richness or character of the story being told, but that a story is being told at all!

Arguably, heritage functions less as a source of information about the past and more as a therapy for people uncertain about who they are. They need regular reminding and reaffirming of their own identities. These doubts about identity may have been caused (or amplified) by the rapid and comprehensive cultural changes during the past two hundred years, and especially by the consequences of recent globalization. The Swedish archaeologist Jes Wienberg (1999:197) stated accordingly that "the past functions as therapy for people who cannot cope with change." That inability to cope is partly about identity, but it is also about something else that Wienberg alludes to in the immediately following sentence: "The past becomes an escape to the exotic, to a 'foreign country,' from a grey everyday life." This brings me to the next value of heritage.

Heritage Values and Experiencing the Past

Heritage is valued even for the enjoyable experiences it provides for visitors. People love imagining life in a different period, quite irrespective of whether or not the period in question is one they themselves have memories from or own remains of. A nostalgic longing for experiences of the past is widespread in our age (Lowenthal 1985). Whereas such nostalgia is motivated by a desire to turn back the wheel of time and somehow access past realities, heritage can be enjoyable for visitors even without much commitment to any kind of historic realism. As the ethnologist Birgitta Svensson (1998:10) put it succinctly, "it is not the intrinsic historic value of ancient monuments that is important for today's tourists but their value as a leisure arena."

In recent years, an entire industry has developed around the notion of traveling to other places in time (Holtorf 2007a; Westergren 2006). An ever-growing number of people dream of alternative realities. They seek to realize such dreams by traveling to exciting heritage destinations linked with past worlds, by assuming alternative identities in role play or in computer games, or by enjoying the realities constructed in popular historical novels or TV docu-soaps. The Swedish author Jan Guillou's bestselling novels about the adventures of *Arn* in the late 12th century AD are to a large extent fictitious. Yet his readers are so impressed by their seeming historicity that they travel in large numbers to the Swedish sites where significant (fictitious) scenes in the novel are set. Time travel does not demand a particular intellectual attitude toward either past or present, but instead a readiness for an embodied engagement with different realities, involving both body and soul. Time travel is about imagining other worlds from the embodied perspective of somebody actually living in that world, involving all the senses. Some of the most significant aspects of time travel are based on knowledge that is next to impossible ever to be (re-)gained in a scientific way. Sensual perceptions, bodily experiences, habitual behavior, emotions, dreams, and not knowing what historically "came next" have been crucial to life in the past, but archaeologists and others cannot easily come to grips with these dimensions. Instead, they always run the risk of constructing the past as an extension of the present. Ironically, an extension of their familiar present may be precisely what people value most!

The popularity of time travel is indicative for the transformed society we have been living in for the past two decades. In his influential study about *Die Erlebnisgesellschaft* [The Experience Society], Gerhard Schulze (1993) argued that experience value is quickly replacing use and monetary values in significance. As people in affluent Western societies have become economically secure and possess all the tools they require, they are orientating their lives more and more toward other values. Sometimes you hear that a full life worth living is one in which the person concerned has seen and experienced a lot of different things. The market for experiences has thus been expanding fast. The American economists Joseph

Pine and James Gilmore argued in their book *The Experience Economy* (1999:25) that those "businesses that relegate themselves to the diminishing world of goods and services will be rendered irrelevant." Instead, businesses now need to offer experiences to people. These experiences consist of more than simply fun and are first and foremost about engaging people sensually, cognitively, socially, culturally, and emotionally.

Heritage Values and Visitors' Preconceptions

My argument thus far may imply that it is almost beside the point of heritage to convey to visitors any specific information about what actually happened in the past. If heritage is mostly about who the visitors are (or would like to be), and what stories they are telling about themselves while they are enjoying entertaining experiences, there is little need to get into intricate stories about a time long gone by. Whether or not this conclusion holds true in its totality, it is certainly the case that heritage managers are rightly careful to confirm certain preconceptions and not to deconstruct too many stories visitors tell themselves at heritage sites (e.g., about their own educational sophistication). For the motivation to travel and visit heritage sites is in many cases not a genuine experience of foreign places and their histories, but the realization of dreams and desires preconceived at the point of origin (Hennig 1999).

David Horne cited the telling example of the Stoa of Attalus which the American School of Classical Studies at Athens reconstructed during the 1950s in its original place on the Athenian Agora. Significantly, "they were faithful to every known detail except one—they couldn't bring themselves to paint it in red and blue as it had been in the original. To have been authentic would have made it seem untrue to the modern stereotype of the classical" (Horne 1984:29). In other words, the authenticity of a place is judged by the tourists' own preconceptions of the place. Preconceptions therefore need to be taken very seriously, and carefully managed by the heritage and tourism industries (Ooi 2005).

Do these trends amount to a "dumbing-down" of heritage? While not so long ago, positive references to entertainment values and stereotypical preconceptions among visitors would have amounted to sacrilege, the situation is different now. In the Experience Society (Schulze), the consumption habits of audiences have changed and cultural producers must quite simply adapt. As economist Richard Voase argued, a preference for sound bites, celebrities, and tabloid-style media formats does not necessarily represent an increasing lack of depth and sophistication which one must resist. Instead, it should be seen as representing "a lowering of the threshold of engagement" (Voase 2002:396) which ultimately enables more people to access cultural products and among them, the cultural heritage.

Heritage Values and Heritage Professionals

I still need to discuss a final reason why people value heritage. For much cultural heritage also alludes to and evokes stories about the professionals producing it. The aura of the genuine and authentic site or artifact puts even archaeologists and conservators (among others) in a special light. David Horne (1984:17) reasoned that precisely "the importance of the authentic can be so great that techniques of restoration may be more interesting to tourists than what has been restored." This was borne out, for example, in the extremely popular Vasa Museum in Stockholm where, for many years, the main display in a foggy hall were the partly covered remains of a 17th century warship regularly sprayed with water during the process of conservation.

Heritage also evokes stories about exciting exploration and discovery, and about meticulous documentation and analysis. This is mostly the domain of the archaeologist recovering cultural heritage on excavations. In popular culture, the archaeologist is often portrayed as a hero and role model, competent and resourceful, responsibly serving the interests of society and of humanity through careful management of the heritage and sometimes also through important revelations about the past and occasionally the future.

Many visitors are excited about the process of archaeological research and would like to get involved in archaeological excavations themselves. Many wish they could realize this childhood dream. The Canadian archaeologist Karolyn Smardz (1997:103) once speculated that it is precisely "the excitement and romance of archaeological discovery that makes people think archaeology is worth doing and learning about." This fascination with archaeological discoveries is an important dimension of the widespread archaeo-appeal that the subject enjoys in popular culture (Holtorf 2005, 2006). It is also part of what I have described as archaeology's brand value (Holtorf 2007b). Quite rightly, Smardz concluded from the popularity of archaeological digging that "it is not archaeology's ability to help all of us gain a better understanding of how people lived in the past that makes archaeology marketable, it is also that mysterious, romantic, exotic sense of delving into the unknown—ergo, the very process of archaeological research."

Throughout popular culture, archaeological heritage has come to be associated with an adventurous quest to exotic locations, hardship in the field, and spectacular recovery of treasures. What is more, the

archaeologist is also portrayed as a detective of the past, solving profound mysteries and revealing ancient secrets. As in forensic science and
criminology, archaeology draws on material evidence that is carefully
documented and, with the help of advanced technology, scrutinized for
clues as to what really had happened at the site under investigation. This
can lead to sensational revelations about the nature of human beings,
or the course of human history and evolution. Increasingly, the archaeologist is also seen as a caring specialist who, despite limited resources,
seeks to salvage valuable archaeological sites, or artifacts and the historical information they possess from decay, destruction, or the illicit
antiquities market.

People thus value heritage even because it evokes exciting stories about
archaeologists and conservators (among other heritage professionals).
Just as an adventure story is not characterized by precisely what the hero
accomplishes, a detective story does not rely a lot on what the solution of
the case eventually is, a great discovery can be great irrespective of what
it actually reveals, and professional care for archaeological heritage is
not about any specific site or artifact, the process of doing archaeology
seems in many cases more exciting than its results.

Conclusions: From Heritage Values to Heritage Policies

I have effectively argued in this chapter that, seen from the perspective of
popular culture, heritage today is not so much about education regarding
the past as it is about storytelling in the present. The stories told through
heritage are partly about the visitors themselves: their own social milieu
and lifestyles, their collective identities, and their preconceptions and
dreams about other periods. Partly, they are also about the professionals behind the cultural heritage, especially archaeologists and conservators. Crucially, all these stories are more about the present than about
the past. It is thus not the factual historicity and age of ancient sites or
artifacts that is the main property of heritage, but their capacity to tell
or evoke stories that appeal in the present. In this sense, an interesting
Medieval cathedral may be interesting because it reaffirms a social milieu
in which "you know your art history," and a precious Stone Age burial
may be precious because it marks the beginning of the story of your own
local community. Heritage is often less valued for its literal than for its
metaphorical content, that is, stories about remains of the past that are
much more so stories about the present. As a consequence, it matters
little for the story-telling potential if a heritage site has been meticulously
repaired, faithfully restored, or entirely reconstructed—as long as it gives
a believable total impression. I argued earlier that any expert activities

carried out can, if anything, suggest or tell memorable stories in themselves and thus further add to the value of the cultural heritage.

This does not make heritage any less important. If anything, experiencing heritage in terms of the stories it tells about the present increases its currency in the Experience Society. As many have argued, stories and experiences have become essential to peoples' social identities and often give inspiration, meaning, and happiness to their lives. It is the stories we tell that distinguish us from each other and make life enjoyable, maybe even worth living (Jensen 1999; Pine and Gilmore 1999; Schulze 1993). This is the larger social context within which the contemporary significance of heritage ought to be assessed.

One immediate implication is that heritage managers should, from the very start of their involvement, be actively engaging with all the people involved (the multiple stakeholders) and take seriously the stories about the present that are told through the cultural heritage (see also Clark 2001; and the chapters by Clark; Clark and Heath; Lizama Aranda in this volume). By the same token, in a major review of the Swedish heritage sector entitled "Putting People First," it was concluded that "we must make the public's involvement and participation our top priorities" and that "the motivation for preserving an object or an environment comes from the need and desire to tell a story" (Operation Heritage 2004:12–13). Not all such stories may, however, be equally acceptable in political and indeed ethical terms. Suitable forms of engagement may range from openly promoting and strengthening some stories that benefit society, to problematizing and undermining others that may harm it. In order to do so competently, a great deal of new research will be needed in order to better understand precisely how the cultural heritage is experienced and what stories are being told or appreciated by whom and in which contexts.

Moreover, cultural heritage is a part of the cultural sector at large and thus subject to cultural policies. If the aim in a given political framework is to improve society as a whole, the way the cultural heritage is managed and presented must not only reflect these aims, but also suit the specific conditions in that society. Professionals in charge of the heritage will need to be sufficiently flexible in order to address directly issues such as cultural prejudices, multicultural identities, social integration, or general health and well-being. The professionals' loyalties must lie with the living population, not a dead one.

Even when the stories told are mostly about the present, some historical information may be conveyed. But what is even more important than transmitting historical information is to improve society and to support people's own cultural ambitions and creative potentials. Heritage managers need to listen and respond to the stories that emerge in relation to

UNIVERSITY OF WINCHESTER
LIBRARY

the cultural heritage. For heritage matters when the stories about heritage matter.

Acknowledgments

I am extremely grateful to all the participants at the workshop for stimulating discussions during all hours of the day, and to Tony Axelsson, Bodil Petersson, and Jes Wienberg for comments on previous versions of this paper.

Endnotes

1. cited from http://rockart.wits.ac.za/origins/index.php?section=11
2. cited from http://www.originscentre.co.za/

References

Bourdieu, Pierre
1984 *Distinction. A Social Critique of the Judgement of Taste.* London: Routledge, Originally published 1979, London: Routledge.

Clark, Kate
2001 Preserving What Matters: Value-Led Planning for Cultural Heritage Sites. *Getty Conservation Institute Newsletter* 16(3):5–12. Electronic document, http://www.getty.us/conservation/publications/newsletters/16_3/feature.html, accessed July 14, 2009.

Clark, Kate, ed.
2006 Capturing the Public Value of Heritage. The Proceedings of the London Conference 25–26 January 2006. Swindon: English Heritage. Electronic document, http://www.english-heritage.org.uk/upload/pdf/Public-Value.pdf, accessed July 14, 2009.

Hennig, Christoph
1999 *Reiselust. Touristen, Tourismus und Urlaubskultur* (The Pleasures of Travelling: Tourists, Tourism and Vacation Culture). Frankfurt: Suhrkamp.

Holtorf, Cornelius
2005 *From Stonehenge to Las Vegas. Archaeology as Popular Culture.* Walnut Creek, California: AltaMira Press.
2006 Experiencing Archaeology in the Dream Society. In *Images, Representations and Heritage. Moving beyond Modern Approaches to Archaeology.* I. Russell, ed. Pp. 161–175. New York: Springer.

2007a Time Travel: A New Perspective on the Distant Past. In *On the Road. Studies in Honour of Lars Larsson*. B. Hårdh, K. Jennbert, and D. Olausson, eds. Pp. 127–132. Stockholm:Almqvist & Wiksell.

2007b *Archaeology is a Brand! The Meaning of Archaeology in Contemporary Popular Culture*. Oxford: Archaeopress; and Walnut Creek, California: Left Coast Press.

Horne, Donald
1984 *The Great Museum. The Re-Presentation of History*. London: Pluto Press.

Jensen, Rolf
1999 *The Dream Society. How the coming shift from information to imagination will transform your business*. New York: McGraw-Hill.

Lowenthal, David
1985 *The Past is a Foreign Country*. Cambridge: Cambridge University Press.

Ooi, Can-Seng
2005 A Theory of Tourism Experiences: The Management of Attention. In *Experiencescapes: Tourism, Culture and Economy*. T. O'Dell and P. Billing, eds. Pp. 51–68. Copenhagen: Copenhagen Business School.

Operation Heritage
2004 Putting People first. Agenda Kulturarv, Stockholm. Electronic document, http://www.agendakulturarv.se/opencms/export/agendakulturarv//dokument/Putting_people_First.pdf, accessed July 14, 2009.

Pine, Joseph, II, and James Gilmore
1999 *The Experience Economy. Work is Theatre & Every Business a Stage*. Boston: Harvard Business School Press.

Schulze, Gerhard
1993 *Die Erlebnis-Gesellschaft. Kultursoziologie der Gegenwart* (The Experience Society: A Sociology of Contemporary Culture). 3rd edition. Frankfurt and New York: Campus.

Smardz, Karolyn
1997 The Past through Tomorrow: Interpreting Toronto's Heritage to a Multicultural Public. In *Presenting Archaeology to the Public. Digging for Truths*. J. Jameson, ed. Pp. 101–113. Walnut Creek, California: AltaMira Press.

Svensson, Birgitta
1998 The Nature of Cultural Heritage Sites. *Ethnologia Europaea* 28(1):5–16.

Voase, Richard
2002 Rediscovering the Imagination: Investigating Active and Passive Visitor Experience in the 21st Century. *International Journal of Tourism Research* 4(5):391–399.

Westergren, Ebbe, ed.

2006   *Holy Cow—This is great! Report from a Symposium on Historic Environment Education and Time Travels in Vimmerby, Sweden, November 2004.* Kalmar: Kalmar läns Museum.

Wienberg, Jes

1999   The Perishable Past. On the Advantage and Disadvantage of Archaeology for Life. *Current Swedish Archaeology* 7:183–202.

3

A Consideration of Heritage Values in Contemporary Society

Katsuyuki Okamura

Introduction

The concepts of "heritage" and "value" often appear together, but the method by which we can increase the value of heritage materials for the public remains a concern for heritage managers, archaeologists, and others involved in heritage investigation, preservation, and education, and specifically for those directly involved in public archaeology.

When I am confronted with the notion of "heritage," I often wonder if the same concept applies internationally. For example, in Japan, terms such as *bunkazai* (cultural properties), *bunkaisan* (cultural heritage), *kouko-isan* (archaeological heritage) all carry significance, but are often applied with differing values in different socio-cultural contexts. Though the notions of these are similar, such notions are distinct in Japan but coupled together under the broader rubric of "cultural heritage" in other places.

To better understand the significant confusion of these notions, I will draw on more than 20 years of changes in the development of the notion of heritage as a "resource" to explore some aspects of the essence of "value" as applied to heritage. First, I will focus on the various social understandings of the value of heritage resources with respect to separation in time, space, and other aspects of the past. Second, I will explore the archaeologist's role in the valuation of heritage resources. Finally, I will explore issues related to archaeologists' presentation of the past to the general public as a means of increasing the general and universal value of such heritage resources.

Two Types of Value? "Invaluable" Heritage vs. "Valuable" Resources

Theoretically speaking, the value of objects of the past is immeasurable, but among individuals, each aspect of cultural heritage carries a different value. The expression, "one man's trash is another man's treasure," may be the best way to understand differing views of archaeological materials covered under the various notions of cultural heritage. These differences apply not only to the difference of opinion between professional archaeologists and the general public on the value of archaeological materials, but also to differences between people of different ages, communities, regions and nations, and even among archaeologists themselves. For example, gold and silver objects carry clear monetary value, and monumental sites such as Stonehenge and the pyramids of Egypt carry significant symbolic value. But seemingly insignificant potsherds can carry value for those who value "showy" heritage resources as well.

Furthermore, values in heritage can be considered in a social context of various levels as nations, regions, and communities. Some items of cultural heritage have come to generate local success through the specialized realm of cultural tourism that includes visiting historic and prehistoric sites. Furthermore, some items of cultural heritage have, in turn, come to generate local success through the specialized realm of cultural tourism that includes visiting historic and prehistoric sites. Sites such as Stonehenge and the numerous National Parks dedicated to archaeological tourism see thousands of visitors every year. Yet, despite this, the vast majority of sites are simply buried scatters of potsherds.

An Inclination to "Heritage" as "Resource"

In recent years, there has been a dramatic increase in the idea of "heritage" as an economic resource, in some ways above and beyond the more traditionally espoused values as a symbol of the past and a source of invaluable (and often intangible) research data. In Japan, as in other countries, there is a potent trend to label artifacts, buildings, monuments, and sites as "National Treasure," "Important Cultural Property," "Historic Site," and so on. It has become quite prevalent at the national level in Japan, but similar classifications have turned up in regional, prefectural, urban and even community organizations (Watanabe 2006). Management of these has been turned over largely to local authorities because such items have come to serve the interests of community and national self-image (Okamura and Matsuda, in press). However, it should be noted that the greatest appeal comes from visible monuments rather than deeply buried archaeological sites and other "invisible" remains. Thus, very few sites other than large tombs, stone structures and reconstructed sites receive much notice.

However, major changes have occurred that can give some hope for such elements of the past in Japan, for example, the Yayoi period palisaded village of the Yoshinogari site in Saga Prefecture (Okamura and Condon 1999:66–70) and the Sannai-maruyama settlement site of the Jomon period in Aomori Prefecture (Sannai-Maruyama Site Preservation Office 2004) excavated in the late 1980s and early 1990s. Such sites became sources of tremendous local fervor, with millions of visitors coming to them in their first year of public display. These sites also inspired the trends in management and reconstruction because they were viewed not as heritage for heritage sake, but heritage as a political, economic, and social resource to be used for local and national identity, growth, and expansion. In addition to these sites, the entry of UNESCO World Heritage sites in Japan in 1992 further drove tourism and the sense of national and local pride.

Since 2002, the "Visit Japan" campaign has further expanded the interest in developing heritage tourism to showcase Japan as a leader in management of cultural heritage for public consumption. However, such approaches can be a double-edged sword because although they have raised awareness of heritage values and sites, they have also led to a kind of "ranking valuation" which carries exceptional risks for the preservation of "minor" or "invisible" sites.

However, such sites and monuments are not so numerous, and the majority of archaeological sites—440,000 sites in Japan (Agency for Cultural Affairs 2001)—can be thought of as "ordinary" and not treated as cultural tourism locations. Attention to such sites is very important.

For example, there have been more than 160 named archaeological sites in Osaka City investigated at 1,600 locations yielding 60,000 containers of artifacts in the last 30 years, yet most of this great volume is "ordinary" material, not being granted labeled significance such as "Important Cultural Property." Yet, all of this material is an essential part of the cultural heritage of Osaka. With this in mind, and with the awareness that the situation in other regions is similar, it becomes clearer that the value of heritage is being discussed in two different ways in the contemporary cultural heritage management context.

The Archaeologist's Role in the Definition of Heritage Value

In contemporary society, the relationship between the archaeologist and cultural heritage has become far more complex. At this point, it may be useful to investigate the role that archaeologists have played in defining the value of cultural heritage and how differences between archaeological practices have served to muddy the waters of understanding the core value of heritage. Archaeologists are the principal advisors on the value of heritage items. Thus, as a profession, archaeology cannot escape this responsibility.

In the past, the traditional role of archaeologists led them to lurk in the realm of decoding the past and putting the materials in their proper contemporary context in a manner that comes close to wedding history and anthropology. However, as society has developed and changed to embrace larger social issues, archaeologists have also taken on the role of defining what cultural heritage is and imparting that knowledge on society at large.

Complicating this is the fact that heritage management and valuation is a job that has been taken on not only by archaeologists, but also museum curators, so-called "heritage managers," and others involved in dealing with materials of cultural-historical significance. However, archaeologists and other experts from all countries have the unique talent to extract information from heritage contexts, interpret that material, and present it in its broader historical and social context, thus adding value to the materials they are investigating for the public in the modern context.

This implies that archaeologists continue to have some influence on the value of heritage, due in part to their abilities in analysis for "research," but also due to their evolving role as educators and the increased interaction between educators and archaeologists. But the problem remains that there is a distinction between the interests of the archaeologist and those of the public. Further, there are differences in the "personal distance" between the archaeologists and their object of study. The meaning of heritage varies not only between professional archaeologists and the public due to their perception of distance in space and time, but also among archaeologists due to their unique interest and valuation of heritage resources.

As an example, the largely anthropology-influenced processual archaeological approach differs from the Japanese approach that emphasizes a strong slant toward culture-history. To this end, two such archaeologists would view the same artifact from the same site in very different ways. The same can be said, by way of extension, about the approach to heritage value as a whole. This further influences the public's understanding of archaeological work and its value for their lives.

Archaeologists are people with unique access to the materials of the distant past. They have professional and social obligations to report on and explain the materials discovered through the course of their work. At the same time they must excite and invite enthusiasm from the public to share in the fun of solving complex "intelligent puzzles." Such demands on an archaeologist create considerable pressure. However, contemporary situations are usually based on value for money. It is a path that archaeologists will face sooner or later.

Illusory views? New World vs. Old World, East vs. West

So many conflicting views of archaeological practice and (to use the popular post-modern term) praxis exist (e.g., East vs. West, culture history vs. processual), that it is easy to become lost in the quagmire. But from a heritage management point of view, there is one key difference I would like to explore.

There seems to be a growing gulf of understanding between approaches to heritage in places like Australia and the US versus places like Japan. This may be due to the perceived differences in the nature of archaeologists themselves. Particularly of note is the difference that most archaeologists in Japan are Japanese, whereas in the New World, the majority of archaeologists do not belong to an indigenous group. It is commonly perceived that in Japan, where its historical roots heavily define national character, public interest in heritage is great, as there are frequent television news programs and newspaper articles related to archaeological discoveries (Fawcett 1990:263; Okamura 2000:62). However, this is not necessarily the case. With as many as 9,000 salvage excavations a year (Watanabe 2008:39), most are never known and even those appearing in the news are quickly forgotten by the general public.

The reality is that with increased emphasis on personal interests and freedom and greater decentralization of national and local interests, people have lost sight of the significance of heritage as adding value to national and local image. Of 10 people on a local commuter train during rush hour, at least 8 will likely be using a cell-phone for talking or e-mail, playing with a Nintendo DS, or listening to an iPod, while ignoring the rest of the world. This is a symptom of the decreased emphasis on group identity that is so vital to increasing the value of heritage. With a decline in public concern, there is an increased need for heritage managers to draw attention to the value of heritage, both within the nation and on the international stage.

However, there are cases in which tragedy can sometimes reveal the nature of the relationship between heritage and the public. Following the Great Hanshin Earthquake of 1995, archaeologists from the region and throughout Japan descended upon the affected areas to perform a large number of salvage investigations preceding the reconstruction of the nearly 250,000 structures that were destroyed. In the wake of this great loss and the loss of 6,500 people, communities in the region took comfort in their past and, even if temporarily, vastly increased the value of heritage in the region (Fawcett and Okamura 1995; Okamura 1997). It is remarkable that such a strong outpouring of emotion served as a tremendous catalyst for increased valuation of the cultural past. Not only was the effect local, but it drew conscientious archaeologists from all over Japan, and those in affected areas were very deeply interested in the work being conducted at each site. It was a moving experience to see the outpouring of personal attachment to local history by residents and concerned archaeologists from all over the country. It is interesting that it sometimes takes a great event to encourage people to engage in a dialogue with the past and actively engage in its preservation (Okamura 1997:32).

Prospects: Exploring the Potentiality of Heritage Values

It is likely that heritage resources will continue to be developed for tourism giving them continued presence in contemporary society. However, there is greater hope if archaeologists can balance between research and public education and elevate the understanding of the importance of even "ordinary" heritage materials. It seems necessary to draw out the value of heritage through careful re-examination of the methodologies of archaeology in order to develop a more value-conscious approach to heritage issues.

It seems particularly important for archaeologists to understand and educate people in the notion that archaeology equals material, which equals local history, *our* history, and that heritage serve the goals of regionalism for the general public based on a cultural historical approach so the heritage can be shared with members of the local area. At the same time, archaeologists must continue to understand the material they are investigating through continued development and application of anthropology and other disciplines to archaeology (a processual approach) to encourage more a "universalist" understanding of local and regional archaeology in the broader global context. This will allow such heritage to have meaning not only for those locally, but it can have real meaning for those around them as well. For instance, in Osaka where I live, it might be useful to find a way to apply a processual approach to presenting the heritage of Osaka to the rest of the world, while keeping the Osaka "flavor" that comes from the rich local heritage.

Heritage issues are a concern about which the public should be educated and informed just as global warming and other environmental problems. As citizens of the world, we are bound to consider the significance of our efforts in both the context of localism and of universalism to preserve our heritage for the future. Integration of heritage studies into archaeology is essential for archaeology to become a fully matured discipline in the 21st century.

References

Agency for Cultural Affairs
2001   Maizou Bunkazai Hogo Taisei Ni Kansuru Chousakenkyuu Kekka No Houkoku Ni Tsuite (Report of Results of The Research on The System for The Protection of Buried Cultural Properties). *Gekkan Bunkazai* 459:20–44.

Fawcett, C.
1990   A Study of the Socio-Political Context of Japanese Archaeology. Ph.D. dissertation, Department of Anthropology, McGill University, Montreal, Canada.

Fawcett, C., and K. Okamura
1995   After the Earthquake: An Examination of the Implications of the Kobe Earthquake for Japanese Archaeological Heritage Management in Japan. Paper presented at the 1995 Chacmool Conference (11 November), Calgary.

Okamura, K.
1997   Shinsai Go No Maizoubunkazai No Chosa (Archaeological Excavation after the Hanshin-Awaji Earthquake). *Asu Eno Bunkazai* (Heritage for Tomorrow) 39:19–34.
2000   Conflict Between Preservation and Development in Japan: The Challenges for Rescue Archaeologists. In *Cultural Resource Management in Contemporary Society: Perspectives on Managing and Presenting the Past.* F. P. McManamon and A. Hatton, eds. Pp. 55–65. London: Routledge.

Okamura, K., and R. Condon
1999   Reconstruction Sites and Education in Japan: A Case Study from the Kansai Region. In *The Constructed Past: Experimental Archaeology, Education and the Public.* P. G. Stone and P. Planel, eds. Pp. 63–75. London: Routledge.

Okamura, K., and A. Matsuda
In press A Consideration of Heritage Values in Contemporary Society. In *Cultural Heritage Management in Global Perspective.* Phyllis Mauch Messenger and George S. Smith, eds. Gainesville: University Press of Florida.

Sannai-Maruyama Site Preservation Office
2004   *The Sannai Maruyama Site: An Extraordinarily Large Settlement in Prehistoric Japan.* Electronic document, http://sannaimaruyama.pref. aomori.jp/english/image/english-pamph.pdf, accessed July 14, 2009.

Watanabe, A.

2006   The Japanese System for Safeguarding Cultural heritage. In *Proceedings of the International Conference on the Safeguarding of Tangible and Intangible Cultural Heritage: Towards an Integrated Approach*. UNESCO, ed. Pp. 74–97. Paris: UNESCO.

Watanable, K.

2008   Maizou Bunkazai Kankei Toukei Shiryou No Kaisetsu To Bunseki: Heisei 19 Nendo Ban (Statistical Data on Buried Cultural Properties in 2007: Commentary and Analysis). *Gekkan Bunkazai* 535:36–42.

4

TECHNOLOGY, HERITAGE VALUES, AND INTERPRETATION

Neil Asher Silberman

Introduction

If the aim of public heritage presentation and interpretation is to communicate both information and values, to what extent and by what methods is that dual objective now being achieved? In recent decades, there has been increasing worldwide interest and investment in public heritage interpretation in schools, sites, archives, libraries, and museums in which the new digital technologies have played an increasingly prominent role (MacDonald 2006; also see the chapters by Altschul; Chilton; Clark and Heath; Croucher; and Okamura in this volume). In the interactive touch screens of national museums and local visitor centers, in the interpretive applications at archaeological sites and monuments visited by school groups and tourists in their millions, and in countless websites and on-line archaeological databases, the past has become an ever-present reality that is simultaneously more real and more virtual than ever before. No longer the exclusive domain of specialized scholars, the past is now seen as a resource for the economic development of local communities and regions, a medium for cultural identity and cross-cultural communication, an edifying destination for cultural tourists, and a focus for educational enrichment (see the chapters by Baxter; Bruning; Fleming; Graham; Lizama Aranda; Russell; and Shen in this volume). Indeed, the digital technologies have already provided a compelling range of interpretive tools of far-reaching potential. In their interactivity and flexibility, these technologies can provide vivid visualizations and immersive experiences as well as immediate access to immense collections of data, offering anyone with a computer and an internet connection a direct link to historical monuments, archaeological sites, and laboratories all over the world.

In this chapter, I would like to focus on on-site interpretive technologies since heritage places (such as listed monuments, archaeological sites, cultural landscapes, and historic urban districts) represent a unique nexus of scholarship, public administration, tourism, town planning, and community activities quite distinct in their use of digital technologies from museums, classrooms, and cyberspace. By their very context and setting, these places are not only the venue for digital presentations; they are often the reason for the interpretation itself. Museums can be moved, rebuilt, redesigned, and reconfigured. Websites can pop up and disappear everyday. But heritage places are the tangible embodiments of our collective legacy from past generations, and as such, should they be altered or misrepresented by the use of technological applications and infrastructure, a part of their essential value would be permanently lost.

In discussing the relationship of technology, interpretation, and heritage values, it is important to make a clear distinction between the terms "Presentation" and "Interpretation." During the six-year review and revision of the ICOMOS Charter for the Interpretation and Presentation of Cultural Heritage Sites (Silberman 2006), it was evident just how confused and unclear two distinct approaches to communicating information about the past to the public—namely "Presentation" and "Interpretation"—have become. The essential functional meaning of "Presentation" is collection and transmission of condensed, comprehensive, systematic information; a summary or synopsis—a digest—and that is how Heritage Presentation has traditionally been done. On the basis of scholarly research and expert opinion, a carefully planned arrangement of information and physical access to a cultural heritage site is designed and presented to the public, usually by scholars, designers, and heritage professionals. Heritage Presentation in that sense is a largely one-way mode of communication in which scholarly or officially sanctioned perspectives are presented to the public in the form of physical and virtual reconstructions, historical narratives, and systematically arranged collections of facts. The "values" conveyed by this method are therefore exclusively those facts or conclusions identified by the presenters as important or relevant.

In contrast, "Interpretation" places the stress on the understanding of the receiver of the message as much as the content of the message conveyed. In that sense, interpretation is not complete or successful until some channel of communication has been established. It should have the active sense of sharing a personal sense of understanding, and that process of reflection and association can be accomplished by anyone who experiences a heritage site. Thus interpretation must, or should, include the full range of activities, reflection, research, creativity, and creative associations stimulated by a cultural heritage site. Although heritage professionals and scholars play important roles and often initiate this process, it continues and matures only with the input and involvement of visitors, community groups, and other stakeholders of various ages and educational backgrounds. For every generation's view of the past is a common, composite creation—a shared recognition of the burdens, the pleasures, the achievements, the legacies—and of course the values— inherited in many different ways.

Digital technologies have now become major elements in the contemporary shaping of our perceptions of the past and our understanding of its values, in both presentation and interpretation modes (Hemsley et al. 2005). Never before, have so many people in so many walks of life and in so many places been offered so many avenues to the past. But do these avenues all lead in the same direction? Should they? And what is the larger role in helping to promote productive, socially inclusive and constructive heritage values that the digital technologies can most effectively play?

Creating a Common Information Infrastructure for Cultural Heritage?

There is no question that the new digital technologies have already greatly enhanced public heritage and archaeology programs, becoming integral components of contemporary heritage activities (Evans 2005). Remote imaging, field data recording, database construction, the analysis of subtle statistical patterns, and the creation of dynamic visualizations have all profoundly altered the very character of heritage documentation and archaeological research. The enormous data processing power of the digital technologies now make recording much more precise and flexible. They also possess an unprecedented ability to detect subtle patterns in the material record through both space and time.

Yet, as we all know, the digitization of heritage is, if not in its infancy, then at least in its youth. It faces a wide variety of technical challenges (Addison 2003) whose ultimate practical solutions will determine what kind of heritage values these technologies may consciously or unconsciously convey. The present range of applications and data formats in which archaeological, architectural, environmental, and other types of heritage information are currently collected and processed results in isolated clusters of data and visualizations that are not easily transferable or even comparable. Yet is the digitization and networking of all heritage information a positive value? That certainly is the position of the

European Commission, one of the main international sponsors of the development of interpretive technologies. The mandate and challenge of its EPOCH network (a so-called "Network of Excellence" of the EU Sixth Research Framework Programme) is to coordinate the research of dozens of institutions working on various aspects of Cultural Heritage digital technologies in Europe to forge a common information infrastructure for all of cultural heritage (EPOCH 2007a).

This has so far been conceived primarily as an engineering challenge. In EPOCH's original vision, the basic strategy to overcome the fragmentation of information is integration—the seamless merging and interchange of digitized data along a cultural heritage informatics production pipeline (EPOCH 2007b). At the start of this pipeline are the applications for data collection and documentation, followed by those for processing and archiving information, management, curatorship, and preservation, image processing and enhancing, reconstruction, and narration. At the very end, after the scientific work has been concluded and the scientific judgments formulated, come authoritative, accessible, and complexly hyperlinked dissemination, in the form of academic publications, closely followed by popularized presentations for the general public in the form of effectively crafted CDs, DVDs, websites, and multimedia applications for use in education, community edification, and the valorization of museums, historical monuments, and archaeological sites. The goal of EPOCH's integrated pipeline is thus "to provide a clear organizational and disciplinary framework for increasing the effectiveness of work at the interface between technology and the cultural heritage of human experience represented in monuments, sites and museums" (EPOCH 2007b).

Another ambitious initiative toward integration of Cultural Heritage technologies deals more with the centralization of content than the technological structure. It is the proposed SAVE Project, formulated by Bernard Frischer of the Institute for Advanced Technologies in the Humanities of the University of Virginia (Frischer 2005). SAVE, whose acronym stands for "Serving and Archiving Virtual Environments," is conceived as a global framework for creating, archiving, and distributing an online real-time visualization of the entire cultural history of humanity. Linking together digital reconstructions of scattered sites and periods, it would become the definitive archive, library, and showcase for all digital heritage.

Many obstacles remain to the achievement of this vision of an integrated cultural heritage information infrastructure, both in terms of the enormous computing power and capacity required for such a grand challenge and in light of the current fragmentation of information sources and types. It is important to note, however, that these digital technology projects envision heritage presentation and interpretation programs essentially as the endpoint of a production process. That is to say, the general public are seen as end-users of a global database of definitive scientific information about the past that is presented in increasingly vivid and realistic ways. Yet can we take this at face value without considering the implicit vision of the past that this approach to heritage promotes? Are the digital technologies essentially value-neutral recording devices that can powerfully capture the unambiguous essence of ancient societies? (Cameron and Kenderdine 2007). In fact, do ancient monuments and the societies that built them even have a single unambiguous essence—or value—that can be agreed upon by all researchers and digitally visualized that will survive into an indefinite future despite the inevitable, continuing evolution of historiography itself?

David Lowenthal put it best—and with characteristic frankness—when he wrote that "the more authentic [a historical re-creation] seems, the more it reflects the present" (1990:303). This is especially true of visualization, in which the digital technologies excel. Just compare an artist's rendering of a Pharaonic temple from the massive 18th century Description de l'Egypte, with an early 20th century Egyptologist's reconstruction, with the latest computer-generated imagery. The differences are not only due to the progressive accumulation of scientific data or increasingly advanced techniques of reconstruction. Each of them also embodies the deepest cultural sensibilities of the era in which they were made (Molyneaux 1997). That cannot be avoided; we can only see the past from the perspective of the present and that inevitably time-bound perspective is what makes every generation's vision of the past so valuable and unique. And so we must ask if the most important value of this digital vision is its scientific conclusiveness—which will surely be superseded by the research and insights of future generations of scientists—or is it its equally important value—the capacity to expand, revise, and update tightly interwoven digital content with new facts, new discoveries, and ever changing hypotheses, emphases, and ideas.

From Commemorative Values to Entertainment Values?

The contemporary European approach to heritage is in many ways a particularly clear example of a process of steady technological development that has occurred—and is still unfolding—in many places in the world. Many styles and techniques of public presentation still coexist across the continent, from a local priest with a rusty key to a dark medieval chapel, to an isolated ancient tomb in a deserted agricultural field, to technical informational panels, costumed interpreters, and more recently, multimedia digital technologies at the more popular and heavily visited cultural heritage sites. Yet over the last 25 years or so, as economic and political changes and waves of immigration have altered both rural and urban landscapes, an increasing number of relatively remote and little-visited heritage places have turned to the use of digital presentation technologies as an economic survival strategy (Briedenhann and Wickens 2004).

In recent years, heritage sites by the hundreds if not thousands have been valorised, glamorized, and relentlessly merchandised by regions, municipalities, local communities, and now even private management companies seeking to attract visitors and the prospects for economic development that they bring (Hall and McArthur 1998). Governmental authorities and international development agencies have made substantial investments to convert archaeological and historical sites into "sustainable" engines of local and regional economic development, in hopes of creating new "heritage attractions" that will offer local employment opportunities and stimulate interregional tourism and trade. Public funding programs like those of the European Commission's Interreg Programs and Culture 2007 and the World Bank's "Framework for Action in Cultural Heritage and Development in the Middle East and North Africa" (Cernea 2001) have set standards—and offer substantial economic incentives—for governmental investment in the form, structure, and even presentation design of major historical monuments and archaeological sites.

And here is the special (if problematic) connection between technology and heritage values: an increasingly significant proportion of public funding for the development of digital heritage is now motivated by these modern economic strategies, in which the creation of multimedia visitors' centers is often an essential element. Borrowing design concepts from theme parks and interactive museums, the planners of even modest cultural attractions now utilize traditional didactic, museum-type presentations only when budgetary constraints mandate only the cheapest, no-frills displays. More creative and energetic interpretive solutions, such as interactive applications, computer 3D reconstructions, and Virtual Reality experiences are now almost always utilized in the refurbishing of monuments and archaeological sites when the project budget permits (Seaton and Bennett 1996). Great efforts have been taken to create stunning historical environments with a wide enough range of vivid images and impressions to satisfy almost every visitor's taste (Leask and Yeoman 1999).

Yet it is a mistake to see the new information age "edu-tainment" tools of interactivity and virtual reality as merely technological enhancements of time-honored interpretive techniques. As in earlier eras of heritage presentation, today's interactive, multimedia site presentations offer carefully constructed narratives of images and impressions, but they are meant to communicate not so much with the mind as with the visitors' emotions and feet. Their narratives are carefully and consciously inscribed in the walking paths and in the circulation routes through ruins and exhibit spaces, through the painstaking planning of professional (and almost always non-local) site designers, whose expertise lies in state-of-the-art scenography rather than content. Through the shaping of the site's space and precise placement of informational panels and multimedia applications, a site visit consists of passage through a series of almost theatrical frames: from the parking lot, through the ticket booth, into the main reception and information area, along the marked or suggested paths of public interpretation with stops at informational panels and multimedia installations, then out to the shop and cafeteria, and then out to the parking lot again.

This increasingly standardized experience of cultural tourism, in which the use of multimedia and interactive digital technologies is often a prominent element, has little connection with the content. Sites with such different archaeological and historical significance as Knossos, Pompeii, Versailles, and Auschwitz share more than they differ in the parking lots filled with tourist buses, visitor centers, multimedia presentations, and above all, in the patterned behavior of visitation that this spatial arrangement creates. For in this age of increasingly self-supported culture, attendance figures and account books are the real tyrants. If the main objective of these development-oriented heritage presentations is to attract heritage consumers, interpretation can rarely afford to offer the kinds of serious and troubling historical reflections that are likely to drive holiday visitors away. Are we in danger of transforming heritage sites into just another leisure time product? What will be the social impact of a heritage that is designed primarily for income-generating entertainment, in which the digital technologies are designed to enhance the visitor experience? While some holiday makers may choose to escape the daily grind in the mountains or the seashore, the 21st century cultural tourist has merely learned to seek another pleasant and unthreatening destination: exchanging the uncertainties of the present for the comforting stability of a virtual past.

New Heritage and the New Technologies?

Digitized data and heritage theme parks are of course not the only possible interpretive uses of information technologies. We are confronted today with new kinds of heritage whose significance—and intangible values—defy analysis by traditional heritage standards and categories

(Peckham 2003). The historic districts of many cities have become home to struggling immigrant communities for whom the official epics presented by antiquities services and national monument administrations—and even the concept of a distinctive "national" identity—have sharply different interpretations and, all too often, little practical relevance. Official heritage is no longer seen in only stately buildings or prehistoric settlement levels, but in an increasingly broad and sometimes unpleasant sampling of the achievements—and failings—of human history. Waves of immigration, trading connections, and shifting networks of military alliances and commerce through the millennia have left a complex and multifaceted record of human interaction—and new understandings of what global, national, regional, and ethnic identity might include.

The UNESCO World Heritage List now includes, under its vaguely-defined Criterion VI of "associated values" the grisly remains of World War I trench warfare, concentration camps, colonial prisons, and rusting, crumbling 19th century factories. New data sources also have to be considered now; elements of intangible heritage such as continually evolving folk traditions, music, dance, literature, foodways connected (or unconnected) with heritage sites often defy standard digital documentation procedures. Indeed, the implementation of the 2005 UNESCO Intangible Cultural Heritage Convention has inspired some innovative experiments in dynamic online documentation that accommodates continually evolving cultural expressions rather than digitally fossilizing them (e.g., Université Laval 2007). These factors are relevant to the reshaping of the digital heritage production pipeline from a one-way process of production into an ongoing, multi-channel public discussion—informed by reliable and meticulous scientific investigation, but also enriched by the feedback of a wide range of contemporary perspectives about the value and significance of the past.

It is evident that digital technology has the potential of increasing public participation in heritage, not only through the development of ever more complexly created and scientifically documented presentations, but in the creation of frameworks for online exchanges and the accumulation of user-generated content in which questions of the relevance and significance of the past to the present can be broadly discussed by both specialists and the public at large (for some notable recent experiments, see Dicks 2003, Chapter 5; Giaccardi 2006). Interpretive technologies may benefit by becoming focused more firmly on the challenge of developing new forms of interactive cultural communication programs—in which success lies not only in the collection and processing of empirical data, but in the creation of lively local heritage institutions, not static monuments or entertainment venues—sustainable in the long run not only because of how they look or what information they contain, but for how effectively they function as resources and public platforms for common reflection, productive questioning, and historical awareness within every community.

Our digital imaginings of the past—both scientific and creative—can serve a vital role in shaping the future. The key linkage between interpretation and technology lies not only in technological expertise and rational planning, but also in the intensity and honesty of interaction with visitors and the local community and in the depth of commitment to creating a sustainable memory institution, rather than a "heritage attraction"—sustainable in the long run not because of how it looks or what information it contains, but for how it functions within the community. Just as it is no longer enough for scholars to excavate sites and make no effort to disseminate their results in some form to the general public; just as it is no longer enough for conservation experts and planners to deal only with abstract questions of original fabric or technical architectural history; it is no longer enough for digital heritage technologists to deal only with the technological challenge of developing more vivid and powerful presentations. The goal should now also be to use information and communication technologies to involve the wider public directly and personally with the remains of past cultures not only to convey scientific information, but also to enhance shared historical understanding and enrich contemporary identity.

That is the wider goal that cultural heritage technologists should aspire to—a social attempt to understand where we are in time, what brought us to this point both in tragedies and triumphs, and what parts of it we should pass down to our children as a link in a continuing chain. In a word, it is an overall understanding of why the past is important and the quest by digital technologies for ever greater precision and wider networks of data must be understood in its larger, less-formalized perspective as an act of collective memory.

For as we move through the early decades of the 21st century, in a world in which the remains of the past are subject to both unprecedented attention and unprecedented neglect and destruction, the use of digital technologies to foster usable, productive heritage values can be best encouraged by a commitment to inclusive, community-based interpretation, in which static presentations are only a part. The process rather than the product—the civic discussion rather than the formal presentation—should be the ultimate focus. It is the key not only to the goals of conservation and education, but to a broader understanding of who we are as a global community of cultures, where we are going, and from where we have come.

References

Addison, Alonzo
2003 Virtual Heritage: Technology in the Service of Culture. In *VAST 2001: Virtual Reality, Archaeology and Cultural Heritage*. David B. Arnold, Alan Chalmers, and Dieter W. Fellner, eds. Pp. 343–354. New York: Association for Computing Machinery.

Briedenhann, Jenny, and Eugenia Wickens
2004 Tourism Routes for the Development of Rural Areas: Vibrant Hope or Impossible Dream? *Tourism Management* 25(1):71–79.

Cameron, Fiona, and Sarah Kenderdine
2007 *Theorizing Digital Cultural Heritage: A Critical Discourse*. Boston: MIT Press.

Cernea, Michael
2001 *Cultural Heritage and Development: A Framework for Action in the Middle East and North Africa*. Washington, DC: World Bank.

Dicks, Bella
2003 *Culture on Display: The Production of Contemporary Visitability*. Maidenhead, United Kingdom: Open University Press.

EPOCH (European Network of Excellence in Open Cultural Heritage)
2007a EPOCH Homepage. Electronic document, http://www.epoch-net.org, accessed January 22, 2009.
2007b The European Network of Excellence on ICT Application to Cultural Heritage, Slide 11. Electronic document, http://public-repository.epoch-net.org/presentations/EPOCH-Presentation.pps, accessed January 22, 2009.

Evans, Thomas
2005 *Digital Archaeology: Bridging Method and Theory*. London: Routledge.

Frischer, Bernard
2005 New Directions for Cultural Virtual Reality: A Global Strategy for Archiving, Serving, and Exhibiting 3D Computer Models of Cultural Heritage Sites. Electronic document, http://www.iath.virginia.edu/~bf3e/revision/pdf/VR_Frischer2005.pdf, accessed January 22, 2009.

Giaccardi, Elise
2006 Collective Storytelling and Social Creativity in the Virtual Museum: A Case Study. *Design Issues* 22(3):29–41.

Hall, C. Michael, and Simon McArthur
1998 *Integrated Heritage Management: Principles and Practice*. London: The Stationery Office.

Hemsley, James, Vito Cappellini, and Gerd Stanke, eds.
2005 *Digital Applications for Cultural and Heritage Institutions*. Aldershot: Ashgate Publishing.

Leask, Anna, and Ian Yeoman, eds.
1999   *Heritage Visitor Attractions: An Operations Management Perspective.*
       London: Cassell.

Lowenthal, David
1990   Conclusion: Archaeologists and Others. *In The Politics of the Past.*
       Peter Gathercole and David Lowenthal, eds. Pp. 302–314. London:
       Routledge.

MacDonald, Lindsay
2006   *Digital Heritage.* Oxford: Butterworth-Heinemann.

Molyneaux, Brian L.
1997   *The Cultural Life of Images: Visual Representation in Archaeology.*
       London: Routledge.

Peckham, Robert S.
2003   *Rethinking Heritage: Cultures and Politics in Europe.* London: L.B.
       Taurus & Co.

Seaton, A. V., and M. M.Bennett
1996   *Marketing Tourism Products: Concepts, Issues and Cases.* London:
       Thomson Business Press.

Silberman, Neil
2006   The ICOMOS–Ename Charter Initiative: Rethinking the Role of Heritage
       Interpretation in the 21st Century. *George Wright Forum* 23(1):28–33.

Université Laval
2007   Inventaire des resources ethnologiques du patrimoine immatériel (IREPI).
       Electronic   document,   http://www.patrimoine-immateriel.ulaval.ca/,
       accessed January 22, 2009.

5

Archaeological Heritage Values in Cross-Cultural Context

Jeffrey H. Altschul

Introduction

For most of my professional life, I have been a cultural resource management consultant. Working within the confines of the United States, I developed a pretty good idea about how we go about valuing "things" made in the past. Or, so I thought. The chapters in this book have challenged many of these ideas and set my thinking on the subject of heritage values in motion. Questions that used to seem so simple are now difficult to answer. How do we define archaeological values? How do we measure them? And, how do we use them? There is little doubt that my line of thought, along with others, is still evolving. This chapter provides the opportunity to set down my current place on this evolutionary path.

Divides in U.S. Cultural Resource Management

Throughout my career, I have observed the two major fault lines in historic preservation as it is practiced in the United States. The primary professional divide is between those more concerned about built things (historic architects, architectural historians, landscape architects, etc.) than destroyed things (archaeologists)(see the chapters by Clark; Fleming; Lizama Aranda; and Morgan et al. in this volume). Over the years, it seemed to me that we developed some type of unholy alliance. To the outside, we were all historic preservationists, thanks in part to the U.S. Congress, which, in 1966, branded us together in the National Historic Preservation Act (NHPA). Although we come together in times of crisis, such as when historic preservation laws come under attack, for the most part, our professional lives are distinct. We view the common laws that bind us through the filter of our own disciplines, which makes the practice of "valuing" historic things quite different. As long as the two worlds of historic preservation are separate, however, there seems to be no harm in the marriage.

As an archaeologist who primarily worked out West, I experienced a second division in the valuing the physical remains of the past. Until the early 1990s, archaeologists were by and large the sole arbiters of determining the value of an archaeological site. The criterion used in this evaluation was the site's scientific significance, which for any particular project was determined by a small circle of archaeologists representing federal agencies, State Historic Preservation Offices, and consultants. Treatment of significant sites was always the same: avoid or dig them.

The sea change occurred with the passage of the Native American Graves Protection and Repatriation Act (NAGPRA), amendments to the NHPA allowing tribes greater influence in the Section 106 process, and the emerging concept of traditional cultural property (TCP). Now those of us trained as archaeologists had to somehow take into consideration other people's interest in archaeological sites when evaluating a property's significance. Many tribes in the areas where I work consider archaeological sites, features, and artifacts to be part of the fabric of their culture. They are sacred, and accordingly, tribes place a high value on their preservation. For the most part, archaeologists feel inadequate to the task of evaluating tribal claims. That is, when a tribe tells us something is sacred, we are not in the business of making them "prove it."

This practice is problematic on two scores. First, agencies get very nervous when tribes claim all archaeological finds, including isolated surface artifacts, as significant. Archaeologists are instructed that simply because something is sacred, it is not necessarily "significant." Significance in this context is narrowly defined by the four criteria established by the regulations implementing the NHPA. These situations always leave me uneasy as I parse the words of tribal elders to create a logical argument using a framework that seems so illogical.

The second problem is treatment. What are we going to do about all those sacred sites? Generally, we are not in a position to avoid them. Moreover, treating these sites by recovering their scientific value through archaeological excavation in many cases is viewed no differently by Native American groups than bulldozing them. In both cases, they are destroyed. Although much ink has been spilled on alternative mitigations, such as sponsoring rituals or paying for other tribal priorities, the truth is that in practice, we still have not developed any really good ways of treating archaeological sites for nonscientific values.

Much of the discussion about heritage values comes down to devising ways of bridging these two divides. Among qualitatively different types of historic properties—the built environment versus the archaeological record—we want to make sure that the properties being determined significant are roughly equivalent. It is not that we want the same number or proportion of buildings and sites to be treated or preserved, but we are concerned that historic preservation professionals have roughly the same "value" scale—that the cutoff between a significant and non-significant building is roughly the same as a significant or non-significant archaeological site. My sense is that things have gotten out of whack in the United States. In the West, only a fraction of historical buildings are considered significant, whereas almost any archaeological site that has not been totally compromised by modern disturbances is determined to be significant. In the East, the contrary often is the case.

Other parts of the discussion rightfully focus on how we measure, weigh, and consider the values from interested sectors of the public. The divide between Native Americans and archaeologists in the United States is only one example of historic preservation professionals having to integrate qualitatively different viewpoints on historic properties. Other situations may be more nuanced, but differences between different populations exist and must somehow be dealt with in our evaluation and treatment of significant properties.

The two divides discussed above—between historic preservation professionals and between groups that value the same historic resources differently—occur within national borders. These schisms exist between professionals in the United States, Britain, France, and so on, as well as between various segments of the public in individual countries. They generally do not, however, cross political borders. In that sense, discussions of heritage values among professionals from around the world works perfectly well; we all have the same problems, the only difference being our country of origin.

Over the last few years, I have become increasingly aware of a third level of complexity—a cross-cultural level—to the issue of defining and treating values. I have found that professionals from various countries use the same terms—significance, values, importance—but attach very different meanings to them. In Mexico, for example, there is no notion of significance (see the chapter by Lizama Aranda in this volume). All archaeological sites are equally important; they are considered national patrimony and cannot be individually owned. In contrast, archaeological sites in the United States are not distinguished from the land on which they are located. They are considered property that can be bought and sold; they only receive protection if located on land subject to federal, state, or municipal laws. When Mexican archaeologists speak of significance, they are not making a legal statement, but rather they are offering their opinion about a site's cultural worth. The term "significant" is reserved for sites considered to be of genuine national or international importance. Significance in the United States is a bureaucratic hurdle—a bar that must be cleared for a site to receive some form of protection. As in Mexico, an artifact scatter and Pueblo Bonito can be equally protected by the law. In Mexico, however, only Pueblo Bonito would be considered significant.

That different countries place different values on archaeological sites is not surprising. What interests me is how the core values of a country are translated into its historic preservation apparatus, and, in turn, how this apparatus influences the practice and thought of heritage professionals. As an archaeologist, I will limit my discussion to my field, though I suspect that similar experiences resonate throughout the historic preservation field (see the chapters by Shen; and Lertcharnrit in this volume).

The Education of a Contract Archaeologist

In 2005, I was asked to represent the United States at a conference on international rescue archaeology held in Pultusk, Poland (Altschul 2005). Representatives of many countries attended, though Europe was the best represented region. There were many lines of agreement. Yet, what caught my attention was the way Western and Eastern European archaeologists talked past each other when it came to the concept of significance. Everyone seemed to agree that excavating archaeological sites that would otherwise be destroyed by development was a good thing, a value we shared in common. Where the Europeans differed was how to put this value into practice. The Western Europeans, particularly the British and Germans, had clear processes for valuing sites, which rested solely on their scientific significance. In this model, a sort of cultural triage is performed by which sites are ranked in importance and sampled. Eastern European archaeologists simply would not accept the notion that archaeologists could value sites and insisted that all sites be treated equally and that all sites be excavated completely.

In my self-assigned role of participant observer, it seemed pretty clear that many of the statements were politically or culturally driven. It was not that the Eastern Europeans did not accept the scientific basis of sampling or the practical impossibility of excavating and analyzing the remains from entire medieval town sites. But in light of their recent history, in which power and decision making was centralized, archaeologists were not comfortable with the notion that they could pick and choose what is important from the country's past.

The following year, my company, Statistical Research, Inc. (SRI), helped prepare land use plans for two *municipios* in the state of Morelos, Mexico (Altschul et al. 2006; López Varela et al. 2007). For the first time, these plans were including cultural heritage in their five-year forecast. Based on our experience in the United States, we prepared cultural sensitivity maps showing areas where land planners could expect to find archaeological and historical sites. We also presented a process by which the *municipio* could ensure that land developers would look for suspected sites and adequately treat them. Our report generated interest but, for the most part, left the *municipio* leaders scratching their heads. They did not know how to incorporate our recommendations into the land-use plan. They well understood that other sites might be found and that these might be disturbed during land development. But it was not their place to acknowledge that archaeological and historical sites might be affected by future activities of the *municipio*. Instead of a process, *municipio* leaders wanted a list of the most important sites and their locations so that they could avoid them. *Municipio* leaders needed to show that they would leave the critical part of their patrimony intact.

About the same time that our work in Mexico took place, I assumed the post of president of the Register of Professional Archaeologists. The Register is a voluntary list of archaeologists who have an advanced degree, possess demonstrated research experience, and agree to abide by a specific code of conduct and standards of research performance (www.rpanet.org). The goal of the Register is the establishment and acceptance of universal standards in archaeology. As such, all archaeologists throughout the world are encouraged to register. Yet, of the 2,100 registered professional archaeologists (RPAs), more than 95 percent are from the United States, with the balance mostly from Canada. As president, I expected most of the problems and issues that I would confront to center on North American archaeology. It came as somewhat of a shock, therefore, that the crisis that landed on my plate on day one originated in Peru.

It appeared that many Peruvian archaeologists were fed up with the behavior of U.S. archaeologists working in their country. To their way of thinking, U.S. archaeologists commonly slighted their Peruvian counterparts; took credit for joint research; published in prestigious journals printed only in English; rarely, if ever, gave presentations at regional conferences; and did not speak adequate Spanish. In response to one perceived egregious slight, Peruvians archaeologists took the unprecedented step of changing the legal requirements for obtaining a permit to conduct archaeological investigations in Peru so that for all intents and purposes, most foreign archaeologists could not work in the country. Because the issues involved professional conduct, the Register was asked to intercede by the Society for American Archaeology. The goal was to find a way in which being an RPA would suffice for the condition that required a permitee to be a member of the Colegio Profesional de Arqueólogos del Perú (COARPE), the Peruvian body charged with enforcing archaeological ethics and standards.

At the outset, it did not appear to me that the negotiations would be difficult. The two bodies' codes of ethics are quite similar. As discussions progressed, however, it became apparent that we were using the same words to mean very different things. Behaviors viewed positively by Americans, particularly those associated with individual achievement, were considered to be negative attributes by the Peruvians. For example, grant research in which individual scholars demonstrate their own creativity to craft topics and select sites to pursue research goals is lauded in the United States, but viewed suspiciously in Peru. Peruvian archaeologists feel slighted that others chose the sites and the topics to be studied with their heritage. United States archaeologists I spoke with felt unduly attacked, as their projects not only funded many Peruvian archaeologists, but also protected Peru's cultural heritage. Few viewed their work as part of a long history of relations marked by imperialism and colonialism.

Valuing Value

I no longer find it surprising at international meetings to find archaeologists arguing past each other about the significance of archaeological sites. Many of these arguments seem more passionate than more traditional academic debates over method and theory. Though I have no evidence, it seems that positions on significance stem from a deeper place than more cerebral subjects. Archaeologists appear to be giving voice to the core values of their country's or culture's relationship with its past.

Where does this discussion leave the concept of significance? Archaeologists in the United States, Britain, and other parts of Western Europe use significance as some sort of invisible bar that must be cleared for a site to receive some form of heritage consideration. The bar may be set at a different height in each country, but the process is essentially the same. Using largely subjective measurements of scientific worth, a small group of archaeologists reach a consensus regarding the "importance" of a site. In other countries, significance is an inherent condition of all archaeological sites. Archaeologists in these countries may differ as to how to extract the significance from each site or even whether they have to extract the significance.

It strikes me that the concept of significance is not terribly useful. It leads to endless arguments about whether artifact scatters, for example, should or should not be considered important as a means of enlightening us about prehistory, often with different outcomes for different projects. In cases where significance is ascribed to all resources, there is a tendency to focus effort on making sure every site "gets touched" archaeologically as opposed to thinking hard about what this process is yielding in terms of knowledge of the past or any other possible benefit.

The problem as I see it is not whether or not a site is significant, but how we reach decisions about what to do with archaeological sites in heritage management contexts. Almost all countries now adopt some form of "polluter pays," which requires that the proponent of an action that disturbs an archaeological site assumes the responsibility of mitigating the adverse effect of their action, as the underlying touchstone of their heritage management programs. Archaeology in these contexts is performed because of actions that are independent of anything to do with the discipline. A project is undertaken, sites are found in the project area, their scientific importance is assessed, and, if deemed worthy, the sites are avoided or excavated. The process has a perverse relationship with research. Creative and innovative thought can make otherwise insignificant sites, significant. Although such innovation drives the science of archaeology, it also increases costs and therefore is not encouraged by the financial sponsors of archaeological investigations.

The dumbing down of archaeology also is encouraged by the ad hoc and service business nature of heritage management archaeology. It is extremely difficult to conduct innovative and creative research on the clock. It is much easier to place results within tried and staid research frameworks. The consequence is that the same types of research questions involving the same types of sites are asked over and over. Significance, then, is not a measure of research value. Instead, it is a consensus-driven assignment for which the agents—archaeologists, developers, regulators, and others—involved in heritage management have very little incentive to change.

Many have argued that the way around this problem is to define significance within regional frameworks. Instead of deciding the fate of an artifact scatter, pueblo, Bronze Age site, or Roman aqueduct each time a new development project comes up, archaeologists should develop regional contexts or research designs that specify research questions, set research priorities, identify site types, assess the importance of each type vis-à-vis research questions, and guide the evaluation of site "significance." Many such historic contexts and research designs have been developed for small river valleys, entire states, even countries. By and large, they have not worked very well. In some cases, practicing archaeologists and regulators pay lip service to them; in most cases, they are ignored. Their failure is instructive for what it tells us about the core values of archaeologists.

Archaeology as a science is pushed forward by scholars and research teams that largely work independent of each other. Rarely do archaeologists working in a region agree to come together, agree on a research agenda, and organize themselves in a cooperative fashion to meet that agenda. Instead, research follows a competitive model in which individual scholars present ideas and results in publications and presentations, which are then accepted, challenged, and/or refined by others working on the same topic or in the same region. The positivistic tradition of archaeology assumes that better ideas will win out through scientific scrutiny, gain funding, and ultimately lead us to a greater understanding of the past. Heritage management regional research designs, which compile existing knowledge into general research avenues and goals, may bring order and consistency to the compliance process, but they do not comport well with the academic traditions of archaeology.

Given the economic pressures, academic traditions, and nationalistic core values associated with patrimony, it is not surprising that measuring the value or significance of an archaeological resource in any absolute sense seems a fool's errand. One possible avenue out of this morass is to disentangle archaeological heritage into two components. The first component consists of the physical constituents of the archaeological record—artifacts, tombs, ruins—the "things" of the past. The second component consists of our understanding of the past or our interpretation of how those "things" reflect human behavior. In some countries, archaeological sites are valued primarily for the information that can be derived from the study of their remains. Other countries place greater value on the cultural, artistic, and aesthetic merit of the artifacts and ruins themselves. Regardless of where the balance falls out in any particular country, it is important to recognize that managing "understanding" is very different from managing "things."

Managing physical remains is relatively straightforward. Surveys allow archaeological sites to be identified and mapped; sites with more "stuff" are more important than sites with less material. Survey data, then, generally provides archaeologists with all the information needed to make decisions about what to avoid and, if necessary, what to dig.

Managing the archaeological record for the information it contains is much more difficult. Observations about the archaeological record can be made at all sites. These observations in and of themselves are neither important nor unimportant. They only take on value in relation to questions that we ask about the past. It is for this reason that programs of systematic observation that characterize so much of heritage management—collection of 10 percent of all surface artifacts, excavation of 5 percent of all structures, analysis of 15 percent of all body sherds, analysis of 5 radiocarbon assays—generally produce descriptive results that rarely make substantive contributions to our understanding of the past. Fueling these formulaic practices is the assumption that even though we cannot think of important questions now, such questions exist. By systematically making observations, we are providing future archaeologists with the data needed to address these questions in the future. The problem, of course, is that there are an infinite number of possible observations we can make, and there is no guarantee that we are making the right ones.

Much of the problem in the use of the concept of significance for archaeological resources is that the proxy measure for knowledge is a site's physical constituents—its things. But to manage the archaeological record for its information requires that we have some measure of "knowledge gain." We have been asking, "What does the site contain and in what condition are the remains?" Instead, we need to be asking, "What will digging sites of this type tell us about the past that we didn't know 5, 10, or 15 years ago? What types of sites, excavation techniques, and analytical methods will yield the best return on knowledge?"

The shift from managing things to managing understanding returns heritage management of archaeological sites from a bureaucratic typological exercise, in which significance is a measure of site integrity and constituents, to an intellectual enterprise more in keeping with the historical traditions of archaeology. It fits comfortably within the culture of archaeology with a focus on the competition of ideas as opposed to the formulaic approach which appears to have flowed steadily from regulatory and economic pressures.

Conclusions

At professional meetings, I try to attend sessions on assessing the significance of archaeological sites. Generally, I hear the same passionate arguments between those who want all archaeological sites to be con-sidered significant and those who restrict significance to a smaller number of the larger and more intact ones. The lines are familiar: "We haven't learned anything from these types of sites, so why do we keep digging them?" "We don't have the money to dig everything; we must focus our effort on 'important' sites." And on the other side: "We don't know what we're missing." "Last year, officials wanted to destroy this small site without excavation, but we prevailed and upon excavating we found something totally new and unexpected."

As I listen to the arguments, it strikes me that as a group, we have fallen into a trap of our own making. As preservation laws have expanded to cover more of the archaeological record, we have allowed social, economic, and political forces to color our archaeological instincts. We continue to pursue archaeology as an intellectual enterprise in which dis-covery and new ideas are critical components, even as the results of our labor are co-opted into bureaucratic systems designed to bring order and predictability to decisions about what we can and cannot study. Pushing the debate forward will require us to move beyond using significance as a proxy for defending national bureaucratic apparatuses and finding ways of bringing decisions about archaeological resources back in line with the traditions of the discipline.

Acknowledgments

The thoughts expressed in this paper have been sharpened consider-ably by comments received from Richard Ciolek-Torrello, Carla Van West, Terry Klein, and Donn Grenda. Maria Molina assisted with technical edits. Errors are mine alone.

References

Altschul, Jeffrey H.
2005   When Rescue becomes Management: The History and Practice of Cultural Resource Management in the United States. Paper presented at the International Conference on Archaeological Rescue Research, spon-sored by the International Union of Prehistoric and Protohistoric Science, Commission for Salvage Archaeology, Pultusk, Poland, December.

Altschul, Jeffrey H., Christopher D. Dore, Stephen A. McElroy, Scott O'Mack, and Sandra L. López Varela
2006   *Estudio de Ordenamiento Ecológico y Territorial, Municipio de Jiutepec, Morelos, México: Recursos Culturales.* Technical Report 06–15. Statistical Research, Tucson.

López Varela, Sandra L., Christopher D. Dore, and Stephen A. McElroy
2007   *El Ordenamiento Ecológico y Territorial del Municipio de Cuernavaca, Morelos, México: Estudio sobre la Administración de Recursos Patrimoniales y Ambientales*. Technical Report 07–21. Statistical Research, Tucson.

PART I

Defining Heritage Values

Section 2

*Management, Policy Formation,
and Heritage Values*

6

VALUES IN CULTURAL RESOURCE MANAGEMENT

Kate Clark

Introduction

Try as we might, a concept of value lies at the heart of any cultural resource (or heritage) management (see the chapters by Altschul; Holtorf; Okamura; and Russell in this volume). Every time we protect a site, allocate public funding, or interfere with someone's ability to develop their own property, we are making a judgement that something is of value to a wider community (see the chapters by Bruning; Soderland; and Yu in this volume). Indeed, all heritage is based on the assertion of a public interest in something, regardless of ownership.

Apart from archaeologists, most heritage professionals have been reluctant to talk about values. But over the past few years there has been a growing willingness to talk about how and why heritage is valued. The move has been part of what we have called a values-based approach to culture resource management that is all about recognizing that what makes something part of the heritage and worth keeping is the value that is placed on it. But as soon as you do that, the inevitable questions arise—which values should we conserve?—and of course, whose values are we preserving?

A focus on values in heritage also takes you away from the traditional "rules" or recipe-based approach to conservation decisions (restoration, reinstatement, or repair) toward an approach that takes each decision on its merits, based on an understanding of value.

In this chapter, I want to briefly explore the move toward values-based conservation, to look at what it means for heritage, and then to look at how values have been categorized.

Values in Conservation Charters

The concept of value is not new in heritage, but although the idea is present in many conservation documents, the role of values in decision making is not explicit. Thus, in "The Manifesto of The Society for the Protection of Ancient Buildings," seen in the United Kingdom as one of the founding documents for conservation, the author William Morris notes,

> "If it be asked us to specify what kind of amount of art, style or other interest in a building, makes it worth protecting, we answer, anything which can be looked on as artistic, picturesque, historical, antique or substantial: any work, in short, over which educated, artistic people would think it worth while to argue at all." (Morris 1877)

But his focus in the document is the damage done by the process of restoration.

The Athens charter of 1931 (ICOMOS 1931) drawn up at the first international congress of architects and technicians of historic monuments, talks about "artistic, historic, and scientific interest" and about respecting the historic character of buildings, but the main focus is on processes and the damage done by modern materials. The Venice Charter (ICOMOS 1964) talks about the idea of "cultural significance" in conservation, implying that significance lies in the "interesting parts of the building, its setting, balance of composition and relationship to the setting." But again, significance is not given an explicit role in decision making. Instead, there are principles; "use must not change the layout or decoration of a building," the traditional setting "must be kept."

The Australia ICOMOS Burra Charter of 1979 (revised 1988 and again in 1999) was probably the first conservation charter to make explicit the role of significance in heritage conservation (Australia ICOMOS 1999). The charter defines cultural significance as the "aesthetic, historic, scientific or social value for past, present or future generations." Conservation involves all of the processes of looking after a place so as to retain its cultural significance, and that the aim of conservation is to retain the cultural significance of a place.

The charter also emphasizes the need for study and recording prior to intervention—a process that became the basis for the "Burra Charter Process," or Conservation Planning. This suggests that every decision needs to be based on an understanding of significance. Although the charter still mentions conservation "rules"—restoration, repair, preservation—it suggests that the choice of approach should be based on understanding significance.

The Burra Charter has no status outside Australia, but nevertheless, it has been influential in changing conservation practices. In the United Kingdom, for example, a requirement for conservation plans based on cultural significance was adopted by the Heritage Lottery Fund (HLF 2005), and more recently English Heritage has drafted a series of conservation principles based on values (English Heritage 2007). The National Trust has been using Statements of Significance as part of its property management procedures for many years and China has also adapted a series of conservation principles based on the Burra Charter (China ICOMOS 2002).

Which Values?

But what values should we protect? There is an extensive literature on this subject, including Bruier and Mathers' (1996) annotated bibliography of trends in cultural heritage significance, the papers by Timothy Darvill, John Carman, and others in a book devoted to ideas of significance in archaeology (Mathers et al. 2005) and Randall Mason's review of the values in conservation planning (2003). Broadly, most systems of heritage value involve a relatively narrow set of values—artistic or aesthetic, historical (usually in the sense of being associated with important people or events), and scientific or technical (examples of innovative technology). In Australia and United Kingdom, "evidential" values—sometimes described as the ability to demonstrate—are important, given a strong tradition of the archaeological analysis of fabric. Uniquely, Australia also identifies "social" value as important, which can be taken into account in protecting sites (Byrne et al. 2001).

It is worth noting that the archaeological fascination with value contrasts with a general lack of interest from other sectors of the heritage conservation world where the conservation literature has been largely focussed on the issues and ethics of restoration (Price et al. 1996).

Whose Values?

Behind the question of "what values?" lies that of "whose values?." Heritage protection is usually based on the idea of common or shared values—seeing heritage as a public interest in property, regardless of ownership (English Heritage 2007:15). That public interest is assumed to operate at different levels—thus in the United Kingdom, scheduled ancient monuments are of national importance, but it is also possible to recognize buildings of local importance in local planning policies; in Australia as in the United Sates, sites of national importance are on the Federal register, but there are also state registers based on sites of state importance. The World Heritage Convention is based on the concept of "Outstanding universal human values" (UNESCO 1972, Article 1).

But however hard you look at this, it is difficult to see how values can transcend cultural perspectives. In those countries where there is a significant indigenous minority, such as Canada, the United States, and Australia, heritage practitioners often work with people with very different cultural perspectives from their own[1]. Debates over the treatment of human remains have forced people to think about traditional community values, as well as architectural and historical values. The importance of such values in cultural resource management has been recognized for some time (e.g., Moratto and Kelly 1976) and writing more recently about the controversy over Native America sacred sites, Sherene Baugher describes how archaeologists and Native Americans see sites very differently—archaeologists looking for quantifiable data about the past, the Hopi and Zumi seeing sites as living places not conceptually different from the present (2005:251). As a result, there has been a move toward much greater indigenous involvement in cultural resource management through, for example, the co-management of parks or management planning that explicitly recognizes the rights, interests, skills, and knowledge of the traditional owners. Such values are also explicitly recognized in the "Convention for the Safeguarding of Intangible Cultural Heritage" (UNESCO 2003).

But values in heritage are often contested, whether or not there is an indigenous minority. This was very apparent in the case studies from the recent Getty Conservation Institute initiative on values, which looked at heritage sites in four different countries—Grosse Ile in Canada, Chaco Canyon in the States, Hadrian's Wall in the north of England, and Port Arthur in Tasmania, Australia. The study put the process of site management planning under the spotlight, looking at who was involved, what values were covered and then how decisions were actually made. At Hadrian's Wall, for example, it was critical to understand the values and interests of the large number of farmers through whose land the wall passes; at Chaco, the values of archaeologists, two different indigenous groups, and people with "new age" beliefs all seemed to be in conflict, while at Port Arthur, conflicting values emerged from a recent tragedy at this difficult convict site (de la Torre et al. 2005).

The study showed that site management involves a much more complex process which involves taking into account both the values for which the site was designated, and the values and interests of different communities associated with the site, and began to take the debate on values in heritage beyond the classification of values in designation into the area of discussing the management of value in practice. It introduced the concept of "values-based management," which involves recognizing and articulating the different values of a site as part of the planning process and using those—as the Burra Charter recommends—to decide the right approach (Clark 2005; Mason 2003).

Public or Cultural Value

But understanding how people value places is only part of the problem in cultural resource management. One of our biggest challenges is to communicate the wider value of protecting cultural resources to skeptical audiences—in particular governments, funding bodies, and developers, who frequently caricature heritage as a backward-looking drain on the economy. Arguments about the wider economic, social, and environmental benefits of heritage are far more likely to carry weight than debates about significance.

During the Getty project on values, it became clear that in heritage practice, there is a distinction between two kinds of value—the significance that is attributed to a site, and the benefits that flow from investing in that site. For example, a landscape may be important to the heritage for its design qualities, but it can also provide health benefits to users as a place to exercise or economic benefits to neighbours as their house prices rise. While this is not a hard and fast distinction, it is one that is proving useful.

One organization that has been using this distinction to explore the debate over heritage values in more detail has been the Heritage Lottery Fund (HLF) in the United Kingdom. Set up in 1994 to distribute funding from the national Lottery to heritage projects, it has now given nearly £4 billion to heritage. The Fund manages a program of impact research into that funding, looking at the difference those projects have made to the heritage and to people. It includes economic impact studies, neighbourhood surveys, surveys of project participants, and a wide range of other studies (Clark 2004). HLF needs to understand the impact and benefits of its funding, both in order to make the case to government and others for the value of investment in heritage, but also to become a better funder. The Fund has a lot of data, but the problem was how best to interrogate that data.

The HLF approached the think tank Demos, which suggested looking at the "Public Value" model put forward by Mark H. Moore (Hewison and Holden 2004). Moore (1995) points out that private sector organizations measure value in financial terms for shareholders, but asks how the public sector should capture value. He is interested in how public sector organizations legitimize themselves with their political masters, their employees, taxpayers, and service users. Bringing Moore's work together with heritage ideas about significance and benefits, Demos identified three kinds of value that heritage organizations might create for the public:

- The conservation of things that are significant to people (so-called "intrinsic values");[2]
- The economic, social and environmental benefits created through policy or investment in heritage ("instrumental benefits"); and
- The values demonstrated by heritage bodies themselves ("institutional values").

They suggested that HLF might analyze its data using more specific values under each of these headings. Under the first, they suggested the Fund should look at stewardship and what it had achieved in terms of the range and number of heritage assets that were conserved; under the second, they suggested that the Fund should look at prosperity, well-being, learning and strengthening local communities. Under the heading of "institutional values," they suggested that HLF look at equity and fairness, trust, value for money and resilience in the organizations that are funded (Hewison and Holden 2006).

These ideas were presented at a conference in London in January 2006, which brought together a range of people from government ministers to young people who had taken part in heritage projects. It looked at the wider issue of the public value of heritage, and debated how heritage organizations might develop this (Clark 2006).

Public Views on the Value of Heritage

At one of the conference sessions, members of the public who had been involved in "Citizen's Juries" spoke about their reactions to heritage. They had taken part in a series of events organized by Opinion Leader Research for the Fund. The aim of the project was to enable members of the general public with no specific interest in heritage to consider the value of heritage, and in particular, to test the public value model. Juries were held in the East Midlands and in Wales. Sixteen participants, randomly selected to fit the demographic profile of the area, reviewed a series of projects such as a restored park, a church, a mining museum, and several heritage activity projects. Although public value was used as a framework for the research design and interpretation, the participants were allowed to develop their thoughts spontaneously.

In terms of the significance or "intrinsic" value of heritage, four key priority values emerged from participants:

- Knowledge value which places heritage as central learning about ourselves and society;
- Identity value delivering a sense of identity on a personal, community, regional, and national level;
- Bequest value—heritage should be cared for in order to hand things on to future generations;
- Distinctiveness value or what makes somewhere special—important because it is closely linked to personal and cultural identity.

The four priority instrumental benefits for the groups were:

- Regeneration and economic growth in areas;
- Benefits to the area where the project took place, including the profile and reputation of the area, safer environment, improved leisure, and reduction in anti-social behavior;
- Benefits to the community affected by the project, including greater public spirit, mutual understanding, and pride in the local area; and
- Benefits to individuals, such as learning skills and confidence.

Although the Fund itself was not the focus of the work, there were some comments about the operation of the Fund. There was clear support for the very broad view of heritage adopted by the Fund, because, as one participant noted, "one person's definition of heritage is going to be different from another person's." They felt HLF had been right to fund the projects considered, and there was endorsement for the support given to applicants. Other issues that emerged were clear support for smaller projects, the importance of projects that involve the whole community, praise for the enthusiasm of project volunteers, but concerns about long-term sustainability. As a result of taking part in the process, the jurors had changed their own views of heritage and indeed some were inspired to think actively about taking up heritage-related activities (Mattinson 2006:88–91).

Conclusion

This chapter has taken us from a 19th century concept of value to a 21st century one. But both William Morris through his campaigning for heritage, and Mark Moore in his work on Public Value are doing the same thing—helping people to articulate the wider value of a public asset or service in a world which is often dominated by economic valuation methods. However, values are classified, the ultimate purpose of all of this is to help heritage practitioners to make better decisions; and to help articulate the case to skeptical politicians for the value of what we are doing.

None of this is without criticism. In the United Kingdom, there is genuine concern about the values-based approach to heritage. As Phillip Venning notes, "The great Victorian restorers, who did so much damage to our churches and cathedrals, could have used the 'significance' test with the greatest of ease to justify even their most destructive actions" (2007:2); while there is a sense that the role of state organizations is to identify established values on which everybody agrees (Jowell 2006:11). However, at the conference, Ricardo Blaug and others recognized the need for both expert and public views, advocating a constructive conversation between professionals and the public.

Historically, debates about values have been dominated by economic models based on concepts such as "willingness to pay" or other financial proxies for value (e.g., Eftec 2005). But the cultural economist David Throsby argues that it is possible to use economic concepts in a different way seeing heritage assets as cultural capital which, if we invest in it properly, will yield cultural value in addition to any economic value (Throsby 2006:40). Cultural value is distinct from but not unrelated to economic value and he argues that we need to appraise heritage projects in terms of both the economic and their cultural value.

In their review of the literature on significance, Bruier and Mathers noted that there had been a falling off of interest in significance in the mid-1990s (1996:11). A decade later, the topic has a new urgency and a much wider constituency through a combination of both debates over values-based cultural resource management and the wider debate on the public or cultural value of heritage. But however heritage is valued, and whatever categories of value we work with, the important thing is that there is an open, inclusive discussion about what matters and why, and a willingness on the part of heritage experts to engage in a wider debate about what matters. There will never be simple answers, but in the process, we may learn something new about heritage.

Endnotes

1. This is beginning to change as people from First Nations are playing a more active role in heritage management, for example, the New South Wales National Parks and Wildlife Service have a policy of co-management. http://www.nationalparks.nsw.gov.au/npws. nsf/Content/Aboriginal +co-management+of+parks.

2.   The term "intrinsic" has been used as a shorthand for significance because it is a term that is easy to remember when paired with "instrumental" and "institutional" values, but its use is not intended to imply that items have a value of their own rather than one that is ascribed to them.

References

Australia ICOMOS
1999   Burra Charter—Australia ICOMOS Charter for the Conservation of Places of Cultural Significance. Electronic document, http://www.icomos.org/australia/burra, accessed October 12, 2007.

Baugher, Sherene
2005   Sacredness, Sensitivity, and Significance: The Controversy over Native American Sacred Sites. In *Heritage of Value, Archaeology of Renown.* Clay Mathers, Timothy Darvill, and Barbara, J. Little eds. Pp. 248–275. Gainesville: University of Florida Press.

Bruier, Frederick L., and Clay Mathers
1996   Trends and Patterns in Cultural Resource Significance: An Historical Perspective and Annotated Bibliography. *IWR Report 96-EL-1.* Washington D.C.: US Army Corps of Engineers.

Byrne, Denis, Helen Brayshaw, and Tracy Ireland
2001   *Social Significance: A Discussion Paper.* NSW: NSW National Parks and Wildlife Service.

China ICOMOS
2002   Principles for the Conservation of Heritage Sites in China. English-language translation, with Chinese text. Electronic document, http://www.unescobkk.org/fileadmin/user_upload/culture/cultureMain/Instruments/Principles_for_the_Heritage_Sites_Conservation_in_China.pdf, accessed October 12, 2007.

Clark, Kate
2004   Why Fund Heritage? The Role of Research in the Heritage Lottery Fund. *Cultural Trends* 52:65–85.
2005   Beyond Designation: The Role of Value in Cultural Resource Management. In *Heritage of Value, Archaeology of Renown.* Clay Mathers, Timothy Darvill, and Barbara J. Little, eds. Pp. 317–328. Gainesville: University of Florida Press.

Clark, Kate ed.
2006   Capturing the Public Value of Heritage. The Proceedings of the London Conference 25–26th January 2006. London: English Heritage.

de la Torre, Marta, Margaret G.H. MacLean, Randall Mason, and David Myers
2005   *Heritage Values in Site Management: Four Case Studies.* Los Angeles: Getty Conservation Institute.

Eftec
2005   Valuation of the Historic Environment: The Scope for Using Results of
        Valuation Studies in the Appraisal and Assessment of Heritage-Related
        Projects and Programmes. Report to English Heritage, the Heritage
        Lottery Fund, the Department for Culture, Media and Sport and the
        Department for Transport. Electronic document, www.english-heritage.
        org.uk, accessed October 12, 2007.

English Heritage
2007   Conservation Principles, Policies and Guidance for the Sustainable
        Management of the Historic Environment. Electronic document, http://
        www.english-heritage.org.uk/upload/pdf/Conservation_Principles_
        2.pdf, accessed October 12, 2007.

Heritage Lottery Fund
2005   Conservation Management Plans: Helping your Application. Heritage
        Lottery Fund, London. Electronic document, http://www.hlf.org.uk/NR/
        rdonlyres/F6B05389-9FF5-4565-800A-73439A7ABFDF/505/HLF Con-
        sPlan05.pdf, accessed October 12, 2007.

Hewison, Robert, and John Holden
2004   Challenge and Change: HLF and Cultural Value. A Report to the Heritage
        Lottery Fund. Electronic document, www.hlf.org.uk, accessed October
        12, 2007.
2006   Public Value as a Framework for Analyzing the Value of Heritage:
        The Ideas. In *Capturing the Public Value of Heritage*. Kate Clark, ed.
        Pp. 19–22. London: English Heritage.

ICOMOS
1964   Venice Charter. International Charter for the Conservation and Restor-
        ation of Monuments and Sites. Electronic document, http://www.icomos.
        org./docs/venice_charter.html, accessed October 12, 2007.
1931   The Athens Charter for the Restoration of Historic Monuments. Adopted
        at the First International Congress of Architects and Technicians of
        Historic Monuments, Athens 1931. Electronic document, http://www.
        icomos.org/athens_charter.html, accessed October 12, 2007.

Jowell, Tessa
2006   From Consultation to Conversation: The Challenge of 'Better Places to
        Live.' In *Capturing the Public Value of Heritage*. Kate Clark, ed. Pp. 7–
        13. London: English Heritage.

Mason, Randall
2003   Assessing Values in Conservation Planning: Methodological Issues and
        Choices. In *Assessing the Values of Cultural Heritage*. Marta de la Torre,
        ed. Pp. 5–30. Los Angeles: Getty Conservation Institute. Available at
        http://www.getty.edu/conservation/publications/pdf_publications/assess-
        ing.pdf.

Mathers, Clay, Timothy Darvill, and Barbara J. Little
2005   *Heritage of Value, Archaeology of Renown: Reshaping Archaeological Assessment and Significance.* Gainesville: University of Florida Press.

Mattinson, D.
2006   The Value of Heritage: What does the Public Think? In *Capturing the Public Value of Heritage.* Kate Clark, ed. Pp. 86–91. London: English Heritage.

Moratto, Michael J., and Roger E. Kelly
1976   Significance in Archaeology. *The Kiva* 42(2):193–202.

Moore, Mark H.
1995   *Creating Public Value: Strategic Management in Government.* Cambridge: Harvard University Press.

Morris, William
1877   Manifesto of the Society for the Protection of Ancient Buildings. Electronic document, http://www.spab.org.uk/html/what-is-spab/the-manifesto/?PHPSESSID=2c514b3df205, accessed October 12, 2007.

Price, Nicholas S., M. Kirby Talley Jr., and Alessandra Melucco Vaccaro, eds.
1996   *Historical and Philosophical Issues in the Conservation of Cultural Heritage.* Los Angeles: Getty Conservation Institute.

Throsby, David
2006   The Value of Cultural Heritage: What can Economics Tell Us? In *Capturing the Public Value of Heritage.* Kate Clark, ed. Pp. 40–43. London: English Heritage.

UNESCO
1972   Convention Concerning the Protection of the World Cultural and Natural Heritage. Electronic document, http://whc.unesco.org/?cid=175, accessed October 12, 2007.
2003   Convention for the Safeguarding of the Intangible Cultural Heritage. Electronic document, http://www.unesco.org/culture/ich/index.php?pg=00006, accessed October 12, 2007.

Venning, Phillip
2007   Prepare to be Baffled by the Buzz-Word in Heritage Funding "Significance": Significant? *Cornerstone* 28(1):2.

7

HERITAGE VALUES, PUBLIC POLICY, AND DEVELOPMENT

Arlene K. Fleming

Introduction

Infrastructure development is often regarded as the enemy of cultural heritage preservation, and there is copious evidence supporting this fact. Historic buildings, entire neighborhoods, and archaeological sites are constantly being demolished to make way for modern residential or commercial structures, for energy, transport, and other construction projects. Resistance to heritage destruction, and recognition of the importance of historical and cultural continuity, have given rise to countervailing forces throughout the world, at international, regional, national, and local levels. This opposition is codified in public policies, laws and regulations, as well as in standards issued by professional and voluntary organizations (see the chapters by Bruning; and Soderland in this volume). On occasion, the resistance comes from individuals and groups who rally around the cause of saving a particular structure or site from demolition.

In most countries, the emphasis is preponderantly on saving heritage marked for destruction by planned development projects. Cultural heritage proponents and government agencies responsible for the conservation and maintenance of heritage in most parts of the world have been slow to realize the necessity for their systematic and timely participation in the development process. Potentially powerful tools exist to enable such participation, beginning at the earliest stages of development planning, and to advocate for the value of cultural heritage assets within the context of social, economic, and biophysical facets of the environment. These tools include national and local laws and regulations, as well as

Environmental Impact Assessment (EIA) and Strategic Environmental Assessment (SEA).[1] EIA and SEA are increasingly mandated by national governments and international financing agencies, and a growing number of large commercial banks voluntarily require EIA under the rubric of the "Equator Principles."[2] Cultural heritage is an established component of both EIA and SEA—along with biophysical and social factors. However, it is generally the weakest of the three components.[3] In most countries, this weakness is due in large part to the fact that cultural heritage proponents, in both public and private sectors, are unaccustomed to participating as key players in development planning and implementation.[4]

The two following case studies illustrate the positive role that infrastructure development can play in identifying, conserving, and utilizing cultural heritage resources through the use of existing public policy tools and agencies intended for the purpose. In the first case, an urban renewal project in Ningbo, China, political will and adherence to established law facilitated beneficial results. In the second instance, the Baku-Tbilisi-Ceyhan pipeline project, implementation of the EIA process significantly increased knowledge of cultural resources and management capacity in Azerbaijan, Georgia, and Turkey.

Urban Renewal in Ningbo, China: A Case Study in Heritage Preservation through Adherence to Law and Exercise of Political Will

Ningbo is among many cities in China where rapid modernization threatens preservation of cultural heritage. Located on the Bay of Hangzhou, in the coastal province of Zhejiang, Ningbo was one of the first places in China to be legally designated a Cultural Heritage Protected City of national importance. Settlement at the site dates back to the 8th century BC, and the city contains cultural property built during the Tang, Song, Ming, and Qing Dynasties. Ningbo maintained active trade with Europeans beginning in the 16th century, became an official treaty port in 1843, and was named one of China's 14 open cities for direct foreign investment in 1984.[5]

Contemporary Ningbo is the second largest city in Zhejiang province, after Shanghai, with a metropolitan area population of over five million. It is a major transportation hub for railways, roads, waterways, and air traffic. The Master Plan for Ningbo, created in 1986, recognized that the development boom had left the old city center in need of upgraded housing, transportation facilities, roads, and basic services. Provisions for these improvements were included in the Ningbo Basic Urban Services

Upgrading component of the Zhejiang Multicities Development Project, financed in part by the World Bank during the 1990s.[6]

At the outset, the project design did not provide for heritage conservation. The proponents were entirely focused on civil works in the central city, which included widening eight principal roads, and constructing urban services within the road reserve, such as lighting, power cables, water and sewer works, and landscaping. The project also provided for demolishing structures not considered economically useful and for construction of modern housing for people who were to be moved from the old center of the city. The terms of reference for the engineering design were limited to transportation and traffic management objectives, and did not anticipate the impact of road widening on historic structures and neighborhoods.

But as planning progressed, the project staff realized that valuable historic property located along the road alignments would be sacrificed. Despite the designation of Ningbo as a national Cultural Heritage Protected City, the city officials were indifferent to the loss, maintaining that the threatened property was not more than 400 years old, and thus not worthy of conservation.[7] In an effort to explain the value of Ningbo's surviving heritage structures to the development project proponents, a small team of Chinese and international historic conservation experts called on Zhu Zixuan, an eminent Chinese professor from Tsinghua University in Beijing. He led the group in assessing the importance of the historic structures threatened by the project, and together they convinced the city officials that conservation was both feasible and advantageous. With the recognition that urban modernization and historic conservation were compatible objectives, a cultural heritage component was added to the project in order to protect and utilize historic properties along the roadways, and the World Bank loan was increased by US$2.3 million to finance the component.

The Bank agreed to provide conservation specialists to work with city agencies responsible for infrastructure development and maintenance, particularly the Planning Bureau and the Institute of Preservation and Administration of Cultural Relics. The challenges included: building political support and leadership; establishing inter-agency coordination; enforcing laws and regulations regarding cultural heritage and development; finding an economically viable use for restored historic structures; and working with the public to create awareness of their cultural heritage. In essence, the success of the conservation effort would depend on how effectively information on the character and importance of the heritage could be presented to a variety of interest groups. This diverse audience included: city administrators and developers interested in economic return on investment; local entrepreneurs looking for retail space; tourism agencies; and the population at large.

City officials, once convinced that their historic structures had value, acted as facilitators. The Mayor's office and the Ningbo Planning Bureau lent support by quickly approving adjustments to the original plans for road realignment, which allowed for relocation or restoration of historic property. A Municipal Cultural Heritage Protection Committee was established to serve as an inter-agency coordinating group. It included the heads of the Planning Department; Infrastructure Development Office; Engineering and Public Utility Bureau; and the Institution of Preservation and Administration of Cultural Relics. At regular meetings, the Committee set priorities, approved plans, discussed issues relating to urban development and historic property, and considered individual projects that would affect cultural sites. Specialists and citizens' groups participated in the meetings. Thus, historic preservation became a shared objective in Ningbo.

In China, there are national, provincial, and municipal laws for protecting cultural heritage. Ningbo, as a nationally designated protected city, is subject to both local and national laws.[8] However, in China, as in many other parts of the world, intense pressures for modernization and development often override preservation laws and regulations. The interest of Ningbo's public authorities in cultural heritage conservation led to a more careful adherence to national and municipal laws for protection. In one instance, in order to preserve scenic and historic features and provide space for leisure activities, the Planning Bureau decided to revoke a previous agreement allowing real estate developers free reign in building on a lake-front conservation area. Developers in the area were subsequently required to contribute toward general improvements, including construction of public areas and landscaping.

A fundamental concern in historic conservation is the practical consideration of economic feasibility, which involves finding appropriate contemporary uses for structures. Among several examples of restoration and adaptive reuse in Ningbo is the Fan Center, a complex of shops selling books, antiques, and art, which is located in an area of 15th century Ming Dynasty houses. Formerly a group of deteriorating buildings, with families crowded into unsanitary courtyards, this historic ensemble is typical of the traditional Chinese domestic architecture now being sacrificed to high-rise construction in numerous cities. In Ningbo, the historic structures were conserved and the families resettled into more modern and spacious housing. The Jun Temple, which had been converted to a machine factory, then used for shops, was restored to become part of a commercial complex containing a new department store designed to blend with the historic temple's exterior. The He Zhang Hall, built on an island in Lake Yue during the Ming Dynasty, had deteriorated into a poorly maintained residence for municipal employees. Following resettlement of the occupants, the building was restored to house the Ningbo Culture and Arts Association, its former quarters having been moved to the lake shore for use as a tea house. In Ningbo, attention was not limited to individual structures and small architectural ensembles, but also focused on the urban fabric, including demarcation of conservation zones, provision for pedestrian links between such zones, and regulations for new structures to ensure harmonious design.

Public support was essential for the conservation activities. An educational campaign accompanied the process of preserving historic structures and creating conservation areas. Through a variety of media, including brochures, audio visual materials, radio, scale models, dramatic presentations, and special cultural heritage days, the Preservation Institute stimulated interest and garnered public support. Specialists and the residents of Ningbo were invited to express their opinions on current conservation issues and specific places. This emphasis on public education, by drawing attention to the cultural and historic significance of structures and the urban landscape, has motivated citizens to demand more preservation work from the city and stimulated private groups to launch conservation projects. In turn, public interest encourages city officials to institutionalize a concerted approach to valuing, enhancing, and maintaining the cultural heritage. Observing the results of historic preservation in the city, the Vice Mayor commented: "Ningbo has one of the richest cultural heritages in the country and we have a responsibility to preserve this heritage for generations to come. By doing this we enrich the quality of life for our people, now and in the future."[9]

The Baku-Tbilisi-Ceyhan Oil Pipeline: A Case Study in Safeguarding Cultural Heritage through EIA and Environmental Management Plans

The Baku-Tbilisi-Ceyhan (BTC) pipeline is 1,737 km. long, built to carry oil from Sangachal, near Baku in Azerbaijan, through Georgia and Turkey to the port of Ceyhan on the Mediterranean coast. The project is managed by the BTC Consortium (BTC Co.), a coalition of 11 oil companies led by British Petroleum (BP). Following completion and review of an EIA in each of the three countries involved, the International Finance Corporation (IFC)—the branch of the World Bank Group that finances private sector development projects—together with the European Bank for Reconstruction and Development and several national export credit agencies, agreed to finance the project in 2003. The pipeline was completed in 2005 and the oil is flowing.

The BTC pipeline route, extending from the Caspian Sea to the Mediterranean, avoids the narrow, dangerous Turkish straits connecting the Black and Mediterranean seas, as well as the territory of Russia. The pipeline corridor and project impact area contain numerous prehistoric and historic sites, as the line traverses territory of ancient trade routes, including the Silk Road. The rich heritage of the area has been largely unexplored, and archaeological research, especially in Azerbaijan and Georgia, has been hindered by decades of isolation that has affected the capacity for survey, excavation, and analysis.

Participation of the IFC as one of the financial partners in the BTC pipeline project required compliance with the institution's safeguard policy. The policy requires that cultural heritage be covered in an EIA conducted during the project planning process, as well as in an environmental management plan which is in effect during project construction. National laws and regulations in Azerbaijan, Georgia, and Turkey contain similar provisions.

A separate EIA was conducted for each country, with cultural heritage specialists, including archaeologists, participating to identify cultural sites along the proposed pipeline route. In certain instances, modifications were made in the route to avoid damage to cultural sites. Based on findings of the EIAs and on national laws and regulations, a Cultural Heritage Management Plan was devised for each country that included instructions for handling cultural sites and artifacts discovered by chance during construction. Five steps were followed in the EIA and during construction of the pipeline. First, a baseline survey was conducted to document the location of cultural sites in the project impact area. Second, where warranted, test trenches were dug at sites. Third, sites deemed most threatened or valuable were fully investigated. Fourth, during construction, monitoring and necessary excavation were carried out. Fifth, during the post-construction phase, archaeological material was analyzed, conserved, and published.[10]

The research and activities undertaken during the preparation, construction, and operational phases of the BTC pipeline have yielded rich results and enhanced the capacity of archaeologists and cultural historians to manage their heritage. Important material documenting the record of human habitation has been discovered, recorded, retrieved, and conserved. Financial resources from multiple partners enabled the research, conservation, and analysis, while providing technical assistance and strengthening local capacity for managing cultural heritage. Professional relationships between cultural heritage specialists in Azerbaijan, Georgia, Turkey, and colleagues in the West are continuing following completion of the pipeline. Three major benefits—identifying cultural sites, fostering national and regional identity, and building management capacity—are illustrated in the following brief summary of activities in each of the three countries: Azerbaijan, Georgia, and Turkey.

Collaboration of the BTC Co. contract archaeologists with staff of the Azeri Institute of Archaeology and Ethnography has provided technical assistance and financial support for improving the Institute's capacity to manage the country's archaeological resources. In pipeline-related investigations, more than 60 new sites were identified, and excavations were conducted in nearly 50 of these. The sites dated to the Copper Age, Bronze Age (with remains from 1500 to 700 B.C.), Hellenistic Greek and Roman periods, as well as the Middle Ages. Approximately 1,500 complete pottery vessels and several bronze daggers were found in 230 graves excavated at two Bronze Age sites.[11] The BTC Co.'s investment in archaeology began with work in the Gobustan, a natural preserve of approximately 6,000 acres, west of Baku. Investigations in a corner of this preserve traversed by the pipeline, led to surveying a larger area, and to documentation of hundreds of unexcavated archaeological sites as well as about 4,000 panels of rock art. The preserve is slated to become a large national park, and to be nominated as a UNESCO World Heritage site.[12]

The combination of technical assistance and financial support, totaling approximately US$1.2 million, is assisting the Institute to enhance its facilities. A conservation laboratory to treat artifacts from pipeline-related excavations is being established with an investment of US$90,000 for materials, equipment, and training. An additional US$50,000 is enabling improved storage, documentation and management of collections by providing materials and training.[13] Training and technical assistance have also facilitated analysis and publication of excavation reports and underwater archaeological exploration, an important contribution as the Caspian Sea in the Azeri region is a rich and undocumented area. During the preparation and construction phases of the pipeline, the BTC Co. worked with some 11 non-governmental organization committees to evaluate the impact of the pipeline on communities, considering a variety of topics, including cultural heritage. For this purpose, the Soros Open Society Institute financed training that was provided by Catholic Relief Services, drawing on experience gained previously in the Chad-Cameroon pipeline project.[14]

In Georgia, BTC Co. contract archaeologists worked with the staff of the Center for Archaeological Studies to identify dozens of new sites before and during construction of the pipeline. Over a four-year period, excavations took place at more than 30 sites, documenting habitation from the Ice Age through the Medieval Period. Significant sites included burial mounds (kurgans) containing wooden carts, bronze and silver weapons and jewelry, and monasteries with early evidence of wine production. Work continues on a number of these sites.[15] In 2005, the BTC

Co. financed and helped to prepare a popular exhibition of archaeological discoveries from the pipeline project at the National Museum in Tbilisi. Interest among Georgians in their history and culture reinforces a sense of national identity in the post-Soviet era.

Turkey is extremely rich in archaeological sites and historical remains, but most of the country has not been surveyed systematically. Identification of cultural sites along the BTC pipeline route during the EIA involved archaeologists and cultural historians who walked the entire pipeline route of over 1,000 kilometers. They included BTC Co. consultants, as well as representatives of the Turkish government energy agency, and archaeologists from Gazi University, the Middle East Technical University, and the British School of Archaeology in Turkey. Documentation consisted of large maps with sites shown according to their priority and value, supplemented by detailed topographical maps locating each site, together with a written inventory statement.[16] Consultation with local communities assisted in the discovery of archaeological and historical sites.

A large number of sites were identified, mapped, and inventoried and 11 were intensively excavated. These ranged from the Bronze Age to the Medieval Period, and included cemeteries, an early Iron Age site, two Hellenistic Greek sites, a late Roman bath complex, and two Christian churches. Results of the excavations are being published in several monographs according to international scholarly standards. Objects discovered are displayed in museums in several cities within the pipeline region, including: Adana, Erzurum, Sivas, and Kars. Technical assistance to regional museums for improved exhibition and interpretation of cultural artifacts discovered in the pipeline-related investigations is intended to raise awareness of regional history and to instruct communities on the importance of their cultural heritage.

Conclusion

In each of the two case studies described above, an infrastructure development project set in motion a process that yielded substantial benefits for cultural heritage identification, conservation, and use. This process was facilitated by the interest, policies, and involvement of the development financing institution—in the case of Ningbo, by the World Bank, and in the BTC pipeline, by the IFC. National and local laws, regulations, and institutions in the host countries also provided a framework for action, but it is important to note that the initiative and support of the financial institutions stimulated adherence to existing laws and use of established institutions for the objective of safeguarding cultural heritage resources.

In Ningbo, cultural heritage proponents became involved after the initial planning phase, but in time to modify the project so that significant historic structures could be saved and restored for contemporary use. The process served to strengthen laws and institutions devoted to cultural heritage conservation and management, to stimulate local interest and support, and to realize social and economic benefits from the use of the heritage resources.

Adherence to the mandatory policy of the IFC for an EIA during the preparatory phase of the BTC pipeline, and formulation of a Cultural Heritage Management Plan to be in effect during construction, resulted in the discovery and investigation of many sites along the culturally rich territory of the pipeline route in Azerbaijan, Georgia, and Turkey. In the process, the BTC Co. provided manpower, supervision, technical assistance, and the substantial funding necessary to complete the work according to international standards. As a result, the historical and archaeological record of all three countries was considerably expanded and local populations became aware of past habitation in their regions. Cultural heritage management institutions were strengthened and the capacity for excavating, inventorying, analyzing, conserving, and publishing cultural artifacts was enhanced.

The framework and tools exist for safeguarding cultural heritage resources in the development process. They include national and local laws, regulations and agencies dedicated to heritage protection, as well as the safeguard policies of international and regional development financial institutions that mandate EIA in the process of preparing projects. The more comprehensive planning tool, SEA, is coming into increasing use, thus providing the potential for cultural authorities to participate in long-range development and land use decisions. It is time for cultural heritage professionals and advocates throughout the world to take advantage of the opportunities open to them for timely and effective participation in the development process. This requires becoming knowledgeable about the development agenda in their respective countries, following it closely, becoming acquainted with development proponents and EIA practitioners, intervening in a timely manner, and promoting the valuation of cultural resources as social and economic assets at every stage in the development process.

Endnotes

1. For general information regarding EIA, see International Association for Impact Assessment, "Principles of Environmental Impact Assessment Best Practice." For SEA, see Dalal-Clayton and Sadler 2005.

2. Commercial banks subscribing to the Equator Principles indicate the intention to voluntarily follow the *Environmental and Social Standards* of the International Finance Corporation (IFC), including *Performance Standard 8—Cultural Heritage*. For information regarding the Equator Principles, see: http://www.equator-principles.com accessed March 30, 2008. For the IFC standards, see: http://www.ifc.org/ifcest/enviro.nsf/Content/EnvSocStandards, accessed March 30, 2008.

3. Carys Jones, Paul Slinn, et al., *Cultural Heritage and Environmental Impact Assessment in the Planarch Area of North West Europe. Maidstone.* 2006. Pp. i–ii, and passim.

4. Information provided to the author during consultations with respondents in client countries of the World Bank, 2000–2008.

5. Katrinka Ebbe and Donald Hankey, *Case Study: Ningbo, China. Cultural Heritage Conservation in Urban Upgrading.* Washington, D. C.: The International Bank for Reconstruction and Development/ The World Bank, 1999, p. 4.

6. Project Information Document on the Zhejiang Multicities Development Project (2003) Washington, D.C.: The International Bank for Reconstruction and Development/The World Bank.

7. Ebbe and Hankey 1999 (see Note 5). *Case Study: Ningbo....,* p. 7.

8. Ebbe and Hankey 1999 (see Note 5), p. 9. Article 22 of the *Constitution of the People's Republic of China* (1882), states that: "The state protects places of scenic and historical interest, valuable cultural monuments and treasures and other important items of China's historical and cultural heritage."

9. Ebbe and Hankey 1999 (see Note 5).

10. Afig Safarov, Zemfira Budagova, Farida Huseynova, and Sayyaf Pashayev, *Report on National NGO Monitoring of Baku-Tbilisi-Ceyhan Pipeline Project by the Historical, Cultural and Archaeological Heritage Protection Working Group.* Baku, Azerbaijan. 2005, p. 6.

11. Safarov et al. 2005 (see Note 10), Pp. 17–32; and interview in April 2007 by the author with Christopher Polglase, Principal Archaeologist, URS, Gaithersburg, Maryland, USA.

12. Interview by the author in April 2007 with Christopher Polglase.

13. See Note 12.

14. Safarov, *et al.,* Safarov et al. 2005, p. 10 (see Note 10).

15. "BTC Section—From Pipedream to Reality," in *Azerbaijan International* 2003 11(4):6–7. See: http://azer.com/aiweb/categories/magazine/ai114_folder/114_articles/114_btc.html, accessed March 15, 2007.

16. Center for Research and Assessment of Historic Environment (TACDAM), *Archaeological Research and Assessment for Baku Tbilisi Ceyhan Crude Oil Pipeline Project: Final Report.* Ankara, Turkey: Middle East Technical University. December 2001. Unpublished.

References

BTC Company
2003   BTC Section—From Pipedream to Reality. *Azerbaijan International* (11)4:84–89. Electronic document, http://azer.com/aiweb/categories/magazine/ai114_folder/114_articles/114_btc.html accessed March 30, 2007.

Carroll, Barbara, and Nicholas Pearson
2002   Environmental Impact Assessment Handbook: A Practical Guide for Planners, Developers, and Communities. Reston, Virginia: American Society of Civil Engineers Publications.

Center for Research and Assessment of Historic Environment (TACDAM)
2001   *Archaeological Research and Assessment for Baku Tbilisi Ceyhan Crude Oil Pipeline Project: Final Report.* Manuscript on file, Ankara: Middle East Technical University.

Dalal-Clayton, Barry, and Barry Sadler
2005   Strategic Environmental Assessment: A Sourcebook and Reference Guide to International Experience. London: Earthscan.

Ebbe, Katrinka and Donald Hankey
1999   *Case Study: Ningbo, China. Cultural Heritage Conservation in Urban Upgrading.* Washington, D.C.: The International Bank for Reconstruction and Development/The World Bank.

Equator Principles
2008   Industrial Bank Co., Ltd Adopts the Equator Principles. Electronic document, http://www.equator-principles.com, accessed March 30, 2008.

International Association for Impact Assessment and Institute of Environmental Assessment
1999   Principles of Environmental Impact Assessment Best Practice. Electronic document, http://www.iaia.org/modx/assets/files/Principles%20of%20IA_web.pdf, accessed June 12, 2008.

International Finance Corporation
2006   *Environmental and Social Standards. Performance Standard 8—Cultural Heritage.* Washington, D.C.: International Finance Corporation, The World Bank Group.

Safarov, Afig, Zemfira Budagova, Farida Huseynova, and Sayyaf Pashayev
2005   *Report on National NGO Monitoring of Baku-Tbilisi-Ceyhan Pipeline Project.* Manuscript on file, Baku, Azerbaijan: Historical, Cultural and Archaeological Heritage Protection Working Group.

UNIVERSITY OF WINCHESTER
LIBRARY

Wood, Christopher
1997   What Has NEPA Wrought Abroad. In *Environmental Policy and NEPA: Past, Present, and Future*. Ray Clark and Larry Canter, ed. Pp. 99–111. Boca Raton, Florida: St Lucie Press.

World Bank
2006   Operational Policy/Bank Procedure 4.11: Physical Cultural Resources. Washington D.C.: The World Bank.

8

From National to Local: Intangible Values and the Decentralization of Heritage Management in the United States

David W. Morgan, Nancy I.M. Morgan, Brenda Barrett, and Suzanne Copping

"The soul of a community or region…is closely tied to its
tangible and intangible cultural heritage."
(Advisory Council on Historic Preservation 2007a:12)

Introduction

In the United States, the National Historic Preservation Act (NHPA; P.L. 89–665) established the National Register of Historic Places as the most successful and widely known framework in our country for evaluating the significance of heritage resources. Over time, it has proven to be an adaptable system capable of reconsidering and redefining heritage resource significance. Despite its potential flexibility, it legally dichotomizes "heritage" into things tangible and things intangible. Only the most tangible of things—real property with identifiable boundaries—can go on the National Register. In many cases, this has proven insufficient to capture that which should be part of its ultimate goal: preserving those resources and fostering those values that create a sense of place for our country's citizens (Morgan 2007, in press; Morgan et al. 2006).

As cultural anthropologists have long recognized, it is heritage in its most holistic of meanings, however ambiguous, that people use to create social and cultural identity at both the individual and corporate levels (see the chapters by Lertcharnrit; Shen; and Yu in this volume). It is a sense of culturally imbued geography, sometimes without real bounds, that tethers people to the places they repetitively use, in which they dwell, and in which their memories are made. Influenced by international approaches to heritage resources, other designation programs are developing that incorporate a more holistic notion of heritage values. These programs include a focus on greenways, blueways, scenic and historic byways, and geographic regions. National Heritage Areas (NHAs) are particularly notable because of their geographic expanse and their method of governance (Barrett 2003; Barrett et al. 2006; Daly 2003; Morgan et al. 2006; National Park Service System Advisory Board 2006).

What these alternate strategies have in common, and what distinguishes them from the traditional dichotomous perception of heritage imposed by the National Register (usually on the built environment), is what they mean to people. The practice of resource management suggests that what the American people value about the past is changing. Evidence may be seen in the explosive growth of NHAs, rising interest in historic highway corridors and historic trails, and professional discourse about heritage values.[1] From these, we glean a sense that what ordinary citizens value about the places they hold dear is much more expansive than what is currently encompassed by traditional historic preservation. That which is valued tends to include modified and unmodified aspects of the landscape; encompasses living and diverse communities, along with their cultural traditions; is centered on people and sense of place rather than historic "fabric" alone; and connects people through their heritage via the act of narration. In short, preservation is belatedly embracing its overlap with cultural anthropology as it shifts the locus of its efforts to contemporary communities of local people. Stakeholder participation must rest at the heart of any documentation and preservation system that tries to capture sense of place at a local level.

International Framework for Paradigm Shifts in the United States

The concept of emphasizing intangible values as core components of what makes a place special is not new outside of the United States. Indeed, these values have found their way into the formal documentation schemes employed to describe and classify heritage resources; international policy statements on resource management philosophy, ethics, and practices; and ways of recognizing and expressing heritage. It is useful to summarize some of the more visible international contexts in which intangible values are prominent considerations before discussing how the intangible significance of places is coming to be recognized in the United States.

Consider first some of the policies and standards espoused by multinational organizations. Perhaps the most well-known example of an international evaluation standard is the World Heritage List. The International Council on Monuments and Sites (ICOMOS) is an organization of professionals that serves as an advisor to UNESCO on World Heritage listings for historic places (International Council on Monuments and Sites 2005). Incorporation of the intangible values that give historic resources significance is most clearly visible in the way ICOMOS approaches cultural landscapes, a resource type whose recognition was first proposed in 1992. Landscape classifications include both traditional landscape types (e.g., gardens and parks) and those considered "associative" landscapes. The latter are valued for their powerful religious, artistic, or cultural associations with a natural element rather than for their ties to tangible material culture. Furthermore, a number of what are dubbed Category 2 landscapes—evolved relict or continuing-use properties—are mostly rural, primarily agricultural landscapes, but some are occupied places that reflect the combined interaction of humans and nature (Fowler 2003). Additionally, in 2006, UNESCO ratified the Convention for the Safeguarding of the Intangible Cultural Heritage, which is being implemented by a special intergovernmental committee.

The World Conservation Union (IUCN),[2] the organization that advises UNESCO on natural heritage listings, has attempted to bring order to the wide variety of protected areas that are found across the globe. These range from natural and wilderness areas that are strictly managed for environmental and ecosystem values (Category Ia and Ib) to protected landscapes and seascapes (Category V) that recognize the importance of the interaction of people and the land in creating a valuable resource. Category V landscapes have the virtue of recognizing the importance of places "where the interaction of people and nature over time has produced an area of distinct character" and incorporate in their recommended management objectives the need to support the social and cultural fabric of communities (World Conservation Union 1994). The conceptualization of a landscape as one of high scenic value—a purely intangible aesthetic sensibility—is what epitomizes significance in this context.

Also consider the Ename Charter first proposed in 2002 by the ICOMOS International Scientific Committee on Interpretation and Presentation and ratified in 2008 by the ICOMOS General Assembly (Ename Center for Public Archaeology and Heritage Presentation 2007). This charter begins with the precept that "every act of heritage conservation—within all the world's cultural traditions—is by its nature a communicative act" (2007:1), and its purpose is to "define the basic principles of Interpretation and Presentation as essential components of heritage conservation efforts and as a means of enhancing public appreciation and understanding of cultural heritage sites" (2007:2). To accomplish this lofty goal, it first establishes seven "cardinal principles" upon which interpretation and presentation should be based, and the third principle is that the charter shall endeavor to "safeguard the tangible and intangible values of cultural heritage sites in their natural and cultural settings and social contexts" (2007:4). Note, too, that the Charter goes on to explicitly place the locus of resource significance in the hands of the stakeholders.

In terms of individual nation states' concern for intangible heritage resource values, reflect on the examples of France, England, and Australia with regard to national documentation systems. Australian national policy has been shaped in recent years by the efforts of its indigenous community and their supporters. Consequently, the Australian National Heritage List, the national government's database of places with "outstanding heritage values," includes places with "natural, Indigenous or historic heritage value to the nation" (Australian Government n.d.). The government considers intangible values as minimally sufficient criteria for inclusion in several instances. These include resources that exhibit "particular aesthetic characteristics valued by a community or cultural group," places with "strong or special association with a particular community or cultural group for social, cultural or spiritual reasons," and if the place has "importance as part of Indigenous tradition" (Australian Government n.d.).

In France, special places where people live are recognized as Les Parcs Naturel Regionaux (Natural Regional Parks). These areas are managed to protect natural and cultural heritage, encourage economic and social community development, and to raise public awareness of the region. The program was established in 1967 and today recognizes 45 parks in France and also in Corsica, Martinique, and French Guiana (Fédération des Parcs Naturels Régionaux de France 2005). In describing the value of the program, Francis Leblanc, then president of ICOMOS Canada, described the parks as preserving precious heritage resources from the adverse impacts of the modern economic system. They were successful, stated Leblanc, because the resources represented by the parks are intangibles. The French Natural Regional Parks were an early expression of the managed landscape approach as defined by the ICOMOS Cultural Landscape Category 2 and the IUCN Category V protected area. They were also an early example of a protected area that was managed at the grassroots level by the people who occupy the landscape.

In the United Kingdom, a parallel is found in Areas of Outstanding Natural Beauty (AONB), a designation authorized by the 1949 National

Parks and Access to the Countryside Act as part of a larger scheme to designate both the country's national parks and the best of its rural landscapes. Both national parks and AONBs are living landscapes and examples of Category V protected areas. AONBs are designated by Ministerial Order empowered by the 1949 legislation, but the funding and planning for AONBs reflects strong local input and management. Historically, ministers have only been prepared to sign designation orders if there is strong evidence of support from the local authorities, local and national voluntary bodies, and community groups. Furthermore, the day-to-day responsibility for the AONBs lies with local governments, who share funding with the national government and other public sources, and since 2000 the areas have been required to complete a locally developed management plan.

What is apparent, at least in these few brief sketches, is that on the international level, concerns about the intangible values of heritage, national documentation systems, and stakeholder perceptions are inextricably entwined. The quirky and humble, the indigenous, and the living landscape that create a local sense of place are highlighted equally with the icons of national patrimony established on commemorative or protective lists. It is difficult to talk about valuing heritage without talking with those who do the valuing, and that conversation inevitably ranges into the terrain of the intangible, a domain that resource managers in the United States have only just begun to traverse.

Paradigm Shifts in the Valuation of U.S. Heritage

The role of sense of place in the documentation system of the United States has been discussed elsewhere (e.g., Barrett 2003; Barrett and Carlino 2003; Barrett et al. 2006; Daly 2003; King 2003; Mason 2006; Mitchell 2003; Morgan et al. 2006; Phillips 2003). In brief, the unique history of preservation in the United States has created a network of interrelated mandates that give legislative expression to sense of place and that form the cornerstone of historic preservation and cultural resource management in federal contexts.[3] Arguably, the most important of these mandates in terms of fiscal resources and land management impact is the National Historic Preservation Act of 1966. The NHPA, among other things, created the National Register and placed it in the administrative domain of the National Park Service (NPS). Language about intangible heritage values found in the associated NPS guidelines is expressed in greatest detail in the National Park Service's Bulletin 18, Bulletin 30, Bulletin 38, and Preservation Brief 36. These guidelines and the National Register itself have, however, at times proven problematic in terms of the intertwining of stakeholder consultation, community-level resource valuation, intangible resources, and national documentation (e.g., Brown 1997; Haley and Wilcoxon 1997; Kelley 1997; King 1998:557; 2003:37, 139; Mason 2006; Morgan 2007, in press; Morgan 2007; Morgan et al. 2006; Parker 1993:4; Winthrop 1998a, 1998b). Major preservation interests in the United States have in recent years begun to grapple with these problems, recognizing the need to reconcile national recognition systems with the humble resources and intangible values that create sense of place. Stakeholder participation in the preservation process is a key way to accomplish this. If representing community-level valuation of heritage resources by ordinary people is the goal, then it follows logically that ordinary people are of extraordinary importance in identifying the resources significant to them and why.

The call for an emphasis on community participation is being heard on a national level. For instance, stakeholder issues appeared as one of the central discussion areas of the Preserve America 2006 Summit, where it was highlighted in panel discussions on inclusive cultural representation and on greater involvement at the community level. This venue is particularly significant because Preserve America is a White House initiative, coordinated around the 40th anniversary of the NHPA, that is intended to chart "a future course for the national historic preservation program" (Advisory Council on Historic Preservation 2007a, 2007b). The initiative is being orchestrated in cooperation with the President's Advisory Council on Historic Preservation (ACHP), 12 major governmental agencies, and prominent non-profit preservation partners, like the National Trust for Historic Preservation. Stakeholders and intangible heritage values emerged most clearly in several formal "issue areas" around which discussion panels were formed. These included "Determining What's Important," "Protecting Places that Matter," and "Involving All Cultures." One of the other issue areas, appropriately enough, was "Participating in the Global Preservation Community," which specifically identified "our grassroots traditions" as a potential point of engagement (Advisory Council on Historic Preservation 2007a:17).

Some participants construed intangible values as indirect community benefits—usually economic—that occur because of the practice of preservation. Others, however, construed intangible values to be those nonmaterial considerations that make a place special, confer significance on its historic fabric, and drive choices about community planning and interpretation. For instance, the summit's Involving All Cultures panel reported to the ACHP two key summary findings:

(1) Diverse cultures must be empowered to use the process thus allowing recognition of their cultural resources. This will be

achieved by including people of diverse cultures and backgrounds on boards and panels as agents in the process and by educating and training cultural groups on the preservation process, benefits, and means to attain protection and recognition of properties they deem significant.

(2) There must be recognition of sites that reflect the cultural diversity of this nation, including natural and cultural resources that go beyond the built environment. Outreach is needed to bring places presently protected informally by cultural groups into the greater protection of the NHPA and National Register. The *evaluation of these special places should begin with stories of the people* and *then* progress to recognizing, preserving, and protecting their significant resources (Hutt et al. 2007:1, italics ours).

Moreover, the Determining What's Important panel stated that "we should recognize that there are other entities involved in the recording of non-material cultural heritage" and "we should be aware...of how we can utilize preservation to interpret this heritage in specific places" (Advisory Council on Historic Preservation 2007a:19). They urged expanding the use of Traditional Cultural Properties (TCPs) to place heritage resources on the National Register, and the Involving All Cultures panel echoed them by suggesting that NPS Bulletin 38 on TCPs be updated. These recommendations dovetailed with the suggestion that the evaluation criteria for listing a property on the National Register be reconsidered, especially those specifying that resources must be at least 50 years old and not associated with living architects, designers, and others.

Such suggestions might create ample room for the consideration and incorporation of intangible values into existing federal documentation and protection programs. One summit panel even proposed that communities should seek out artists and cultural institutions because of their economic significance (Advisory Council on Historic Preservation 2007a:21), a values-centric approach very different from that which is traditionally considered the "proper" domain of the National Register and its programs. By contrast, some summit panels suggested measures by which the federal government could expand extant programs (e.g., tax credits and Preserve America Community designation) to "increase synergy" between developers and public partners and to provide more technical assistance. These plans reflect a traditional approach to preservation, but the emphasis on local community involvement and empowerment again hints at the stakeholder emphasis characteristic of some international strategies for protecting both tangible and intangible resources.

Another sign that the mainstream preservation movement is beginning to consider heritage valuation as is done in international contexts can be found in the fact that issues raised by the Preserve America panels continue to be discussed in other venues. For example, the October 2007 meeting of the National Trust for Historic Preservation included a roundtable discussion aptly titled, "Valuing Heritage: Re-examining our Foundation," whose purpose was two-fold. First, the discussion sought to "continue, and broaden, the dialogue on defining what a heritage resource is and how tangible and intangible heritage values should be recognized and evaluated." Second, it attempted to "better define and understand the meanings that are ascribed to places by residents that live in or near heritage resources and those who are drawn to visit them." The session's standing-room attendance and diverse audience perspectives are anecdotal testimony to the round table's reception. The panelists' dialogue on the need to recognize multiple values with regard to heritage resources and on central narratives as key to bridging complementary heritage values resonated with the audience. They contributed their own examples to illustrate the discussions and called for additional discussions in the same vein. It bears pointing out that here, again, one sees the integral role of stakeholder dialogue in the valuation of resources, and one of the key action items to emerge from the meeting was the need to identify mechanisms for monitoring and recognizing values associated with intangible heritage resources.

Randall Mason (2006) places the impetus for this theoretical shift in what Andreas Huyssen (2003) termed "memory culture." The last decade, Huyssen asserts, represents a time of innovation in how society deals with memories of its past, a crisis response catalyzed by "deep, fundamental dislocations in society caused by mega-trends like globalization, regional economic transformations, post-colonial policy shifts, migration, and the influence and reach of the media" (Mason 2006:26). Memory culture, says Mason (2006:28), "demands a different sort of preservation practice, in which preservationists' traditional focus on materiality is augmented by means for dealing with different cultural interpretations, competing political demands, and economic influences," that is, values-centered preservation.

The U.S. National Heritage Area Movement

The ACHP and the NPS may be reticent to openly adopt values-centered approaches to intangible heritage resource signification, but the United States has in recent years moved closer to a value-centered practice through the precipitous growth of recognized NHAs and other regionally based designations. Specifically, the NPS is charged with assisting nationally important places through a program of Congressionally designated NHAs. In formal terms, the way the NPS defines these areas is based primarily on their physical resources, as NHAs are "places where natural, cultural, historic, and scenic resources combine to form a cohesive, nationally important landscape arising from patterns of human activity shaped by geography" (National Park Service System Advisory Board 2006). In practice, however, heritage areas are defined by people and ideas as much as by place. The heritage area movement tends to be a locally driven strategy by which a region identifies common values through its heritage. The strategy is distinguished by its interdisciplinary, non-political management approach, which enables residents to develop shared conservation and development priorities based on their shared heritage.

It is in the legislative arena where the tension plays out between the NPS' traditional emphasis on discrete, bounded, tangible places and the people and ideas that animate NHAs. The priority recommendation of the recent National Park System Advisory Board (2006) report was to establish a legislative foundation for a system of NHAs based on the following criteria: (1) the area must represent a story of national importance; (2) its heritage resources must contribute to the telling of that story; (3) the public must demonstrate strong interest and support; and (4) the area must have the capacity for leadership and management. Note that three of the four criteria address intangible factors about how a community values its heritage. What has bogged down progress toward this legal foundation, however, are traditional concerns over tangible real estate. Hypothetical concerns over impacts on private property rights have left the NHA program without a legislative foundation for almost two decades. It is informative, we think, that this legal concern has not discouraged communities nationwide from seeking the NHA designation. The NHA program remains one of the fastest-growing areas of the NPS, and at the time of writing, 13 new NHAs have been established since October 2006.

The National Park System Advisory Board (2006:7–8) report on the future of NHAs found that "National Heritage Areas reflect the evolution of our nation's thinking about how to best conserve revered and valued landscapes and cultures and make them available for the enjoyment of future generations." The report went on to find that NHAs offer "the National Park Service and the national parks a new strategy to meet their stewardship mission by engaging the public outside park boundaries." More pragmatically, the NPS has seen the designation as a cost-effective way to preserve nationally important resources and to tackle preservation initiatives that might otherwise be overwhelming, such as the industrial landscapes of steelmaking, coal mining, and automobile manufacturing; the vast rural landscapes around the Blue Ridge Parkway or the Great Basin; and, most challenging of all, the diverse cultural stories of such peoples as the Cane River Creoles of Louisiana, the Gullah/Geechee of the coastal Southeast, and the traditional Hispanic and Native American communities of the Northern Rio Grande.

Despite the NPS' recognition of the successes and the potential that NHAs offer for heritage resource preservation, the inclusive process by which NHAs are established and managed sets them disjointedly apart from the traditional park-focused mission of the NPS. This contradiction is visible in a measure of internal dissonance. For instance, the NPS is currently embarking on a major service-wide initiative—the Centennial Challenge—in preparation for its 100th anniversary in 2016. NHAs, however, are ineligible for direct project funding from the Centennial Challenge, even though their partnership style of management would be ideal for the matching fund requirements entailed in the funding requests (Certified Eligible Centennial Proposals for the Fiscal Year 2008, NPS August 2007).

Another example is the administrative disconnect involved in measuring and evaluating the success of NHAs and park units. The NPS, the Office of Management and Budget, and Congressional committees reasonably expect park units to have performance measures and to show progress toward conservation and public service goals— requirements implemented through the Government Performance and Results Act (GPRA). The difficulty is that such measures do not apply well and can be difficult to even identify for the large, complex initiatives typical of NHAs. This disconnect has serious implications for the longevity of individual NHAs, if not the entire heritage area movement. Most NHAs are created by statute in perpetuity, like park units, but, unlike their close NPS cousins, the funding provided for these "perpetual" NHAs is finite (usually $10 million over 15 years). Consequently, NHAs must justify seeking reauthorization of their funding from the NPS and thus must go beyond traditional value assessment schemes like GPRA in order to demonstrate their public value. Meanwhile, the public value and funding for traditional NPS units is not an issue.

The NPS, through the agency's Conservation Study Institute (CSI) and working with the Alliance of National Heritage Areas, has undertaken a series of three pilot projects to assess the progress of NHAs and to better understand the process by which they build partnerships and implement long range plans over a large region (Copping et al. 2006; Tuxill et al. 2005, 2008). CSI's research is interesting in the context of this chapter, because of what it is that the institute highlighted as the core value of an NHA: narratives and networks. CSI identified the central importance of the stories of a region—intangibles—in connecting local resources and integrating regional natural, historical, cultural, and economic values. The CSI projects also researched the partnership networks that are fundamental to carrying out the NHAs' mission. The studies point out that the success of the NHAs is built upon the management entities' ability to leverage and wield strong partnerships with the National Park Service, state and local governments, organizations, and communities. The CSI found that a prime contributing factor to success has been consensus-based planning and strong public involvement programs because they build a common vision and offer the opportunity for many groups to align their interests with the NHAs. NHAs, in short, seem to be successful precisely because their management and mission are oriented by stakeholders and the values they attribute to tangible and intangible resources that create sense of place.

Future Heritage Valuation in the United States

The Advisory Board report (2006:1) characterized the NHA initiative as "a citizens' movement," and it is an accurate description. NHAs' citizen focus is perhaps why the heritage area movement has the power to attract diverse proponents from across the country. Ironically, it is also what may draw the strongest antagonism from the traditional preservation communities as professionals and government agencies perceive this stakeholder emphasis as a threat to their power as stewards, gatekeepers, and decision makers. What is at stake, from their view, is not simply the body of nationally important resources in their care, but the ability to even define which resources are important and why. Their reluctance notwithstanding, there is a trend internationally to decentralize heritage resource management and to move management and valuation into the hands of stakeholders. This is happening in the United States with increasing frequency largely through grassroots initiatives, and NHAs are the most visible instance of a paradigm shift toward values-centered preservation, perhaps because of its juxtaposition with more traditionally managed NPS resources.

What does the future hold for heritage valuation? With regard to NHAs, the challenge is two-fold. First, the NPS must overlay these regions that are created through stories, memories, and personal connections with the more traditional cultural and natural resources programs. Second, they must strengthen the meaning, relevance, and viability of these initiatives through compatible best practices, guidelines, and legislation. In general, we must continue to learn from the way other nations treat and value their heritage. As professionals, we should recognize that preservation is not an end unto itself—we must recognize the historical trajectories of that which we seek to preserve, while simultaneously contextualizing our efforts in contemporary society. Our efforts as professionals to integrate funding and designation programs, and especially those of the NHA movement, with other local, national, and international designations and programs will, as Mason claims (2006:45), position "us best to make our work relevant to the rest of society." If we do, we will inevitably recognize that stakeholders, intangible resources, and the places of significance in our communities have always been inextricably connected. In whose hands shall we place our heritage resources if not in the hands of those who value them most through the process of daily life and interaction?

Endnotes

1. Recent examples of professional dialogue on heritage values can be seen in the Advisory Council on Historic Preservation Preserve America Summit proceedings (2007a, b), a round table discussion at the recent National Trust for Historic Preservation 2007 annual meeting, and at two related multinational policy workshops on heritage values convened by Hamline University and the National Park Service's Southeast Archeological Center in 2005 and in 2007 (Messenger and Smith in press). The publication of Randall Mason's (2006) discussion of a values-centered preservation ethos in the journal *CRM*, with its large National Park Service readership, also is indicative of the contemporary shift in preservation thought.

2. This organization was founded in 1956 as the International Union for the Conservation of Nature and Natural Resources. Since 1990, the organization has used the name the World Conservation Union, but it is still commonly referred to as the IUCN. It represents 82 states, 111 government agencies, and over 800 non-governmental organizations (www.iucn.org/gen/).

3. There are dozens of laws, regulations, guidelines, executive orders, and other mandates that form the legal framework for historic preservation in the United States. For further information, many of these may be found on the Internet at http://www.cr.nps.gov/linklaws.htm. Alternately, the National Park Service (2002) and National Conference of State Historic Preservation Officers have collaborated to produce a printed handbook of 23 federal laws and portions of laws relevant to historic preservation.

References

Advisory Council on Historic Preservation
2007a The Preserve America Summit: Findings and Recommendations of the Advisory Council on Historic Preservation. Advisory Council on Historic Preservation, Washington, D.C. Also available on the World Wide Web at http://www.preserveamerica.gov/docs/Summit_Report_full_LR.pdf, accessed January 9, 2009.
2007b The Preserve America Summit Executive Summary: Charting a Future Course for the National Historic Preservation Program. Advisory Council on Historic Preservation, Washington, D.C. Also available on the World Wide Web at http://www.preserveamerica.gov/docs/Executive_Summary_lr.pdf, accessed January 9, 2009.

Australian Government
n.d. Heritage List Criteria and Thresholds. Canberra: Heritage Division, Department of the Environment and Water Resources, Australian Government. Also available on the World Wide Web at http://www.environment.gov.au/heritage/about/national/criteria.html, accessed January 9, 2009.

Barrett, Brenda
2003 Roots for the National Heritage Area Family Tree. *The George Wright Forum* 20(2):41–49.

Barrett, Brenda, and Augie Carlino
2003 What is in the Future for the Heritage Area Movement? *Forum Journal* 17(4):51–56.

Barrett, Brenda, Nancy I. M. Morgan, and Laura Soullière Gates
2006 National Heritage Areas: Developing a New Conservation Strategy. In *Art and Cultural Heritage: Law, Policy and Practice*. B. Hoffman, ed. Pp. 220–233. Cambridge: Cambridge University Press.

Brown, Michael F.
1997 Comments: Anthropology and the Making of Chumash Tradition. *Current Anthropology* 38(5):777–778.

Copping, Suzanne E., Philip B. Huffman, Daniel N. Laven, Nora J. Mitchell, and Jacquelyn L. Tuxill
2006 *Connecting Stories, Landscapes, and People: Exploring the Delaware & Lehigh National Heritage Corridor Partnership. A Technical Assistance Project for the Delaware & Lehigh National Heritage Corridor Commission and the Delaware & Lehigh National Heritage Corridor, Inc.* Conservation and Stewardship Publication No. 9. Woodstock, Vermont: National Park Service, Department of the Interior, Conservation Study Institute. Also available on the World Wide Web at http://www.nps.gov/csi/pdf/BlackstoneReport.pdf, accessed July 20, 2009.

Daly, Jayne
2003 Heritage Areas: Connecting People to Their Place and History. *Forum Journal* 17(4):5–12.

Ename Center for Public Archaeology and Heritage Presentation
2007   *ICOMOS Ename Charter for the Interpretation and Presentation of Cultural Heritage Sites*. Oudenaarde, Belgium: ICOMOS International Scientific Committee on Interpretation and Presentation. Final Report, 10 April. Also available on the World Wide Web at http://www.enamecharter.org/downloads/ICOMOS_Interpretation_Charter_EN_10-04-07.pdf, accessed July 20, 2009.

Fédération des Parcs Naturels Régionaux de France
2005   Accueil. Fédération des Parcs Naturels Régionaux de France. Available on the World Wide Web at http://www.parcs-naturels-regionaux.tm.fr/fr/accueil/, accessed December 11, 2005.

Fowler, P.J.
2003   *World Heritage Cultural Landscapes 1992–2002*. World Heritage Series 6. Paris: UNESCO World Heritage Center.

Haley, Brian D., and Larry R. Wilcoxon
1997   Anthropology and the Making of Chumash Tradition. *Current Anthropology* 38(5):761–777.

Hutt, Sherry, Ruth Pierpont, and D. Bambi Kraus, eds.
2007   *Preserve America Summit Issue Areas Panel Report: Involving All Cultures*. Washington, D.C.: Advisory Council on Historic Preservation, Also available on the World Wide Web at http://www.preserveamerica-summit.org/pa/, accessed January 9, 2009.

Huyssen, Andreas
2003   *Present Pasts: Urban Palimpsests and the Politics of Memory*. Stanford: Stanford University Press.

International Council on Monuments and Sites
2005   ICOMOS and the World Heritage. International Council on Monuments and Sites. Available on the World Wide Web at http://www.international.icomos.org/world_heritage/index.html, accessed December 11, 2005.

Kelley, Klara Bonsack
1997   Comments: Anthropology and the Making of Chumash Tradition. *Current Anthropology* 38(5):782–783.

King, Thomas F.
1998   *Cultural Resource Laws and Practice: An Introductory Guide*. Walnut Creek: AltaMira Press.
2003   *Places that Count: Traditional Cultural Properties in Cultural Resource Management*. Walnut Creek: AltaMira Press.

Mason, Randall
2006   Theoretical and Practical Arguments for Values-Centered Preservation. *CRM: The Journal of Heritage Stewardship* 3(2):21–48.

Messenger, Phyllis Mauch and George S. Smith, eds.
In press *Cultural Heritage Management: A Global Perspective*. Gainesville: University Press of Florida.

Mitchell, Brent
2003 International Models of Protected Landscapes. *The George Wright Forum* 20(2):33–40.

Morgan, David W.
In press Descendent Communities, Heritage Resource Law, and Heritage Areas: Strategies for Managing and Interpreting Native American Traditional and Cultural Places. In *Cultural Heritage Management: A Global Perspective*. Phyllis Mauch Messenger, and George S. Smith, eds. Gainesville: University Press of Florida.
2007 The U.S. National Historic Preservation Act and Indigenous Heritage. In *Interpreting the Past: Who Owns The Past? Heritage Rights and Responsibilities in a Multicultural World*. N. Silberman, and C. Liuzza, eds. Pp. 234–245. Brussels: Flemish Heritage Institute.

Morgan, David W., Nancy I.M. Morgan, and Brenda Barrett
2006 Finding a Place for the Commonplace: Hurricane Katrina, Communities, and Preservation Law. *American Anthropologist* 108(4):706–718.

National Park Service
2002 *Federal Historic Preservation Laws*. National Center for Cultural Resources, National Park Service, U.S. Department of the Interior, Washington, D.C.

National Park System Advisory Board
2006 *Charting a Future for National Heritage Areas*. National Park System Advisory Board, Washington, D.C. Moore Langden, Indianapolis. Also available on the World Wide Web at http://www.nps.gov/policy/ NHAreport.htm, accessed July 20, 2009.

Parker, Patricia L.
1993 What You Do and How We Think. *Special issue, Cultural Resource Management* 16:1–5.

Phillips, Adrian
2003 Turning Ideas on Their Head: The New Paradigm of Protected Areas. *The George Wright Forum* 20(2):8–32.

Tuxill, Jacquelyn L., Philip B. Huffman, Daniel N. Laven, and Nora J. Mitchell
2008 *Shared Legacies in Cane River National Heritage Area: Linking People, Traditions, and Landscapes*. Technical Assistance Report for the Cane River National Heritage Area Commission, Cane River Evaluation and Visioning Project Final Report. Conservation and Stewardship Publication No. 15. Woodstock, Vermont: National Park Service, Department of the Interior, Conservation Study Institute. Also available on the World Wide Web at http://www.nps.gov/csi/pdf/cane%20river.pdf, accessed July 20, 2009.

Tuxill, Jacquelyn L., Nora J. Mitchell, Philip B. Huffman, Daniel Laven, Suzanne Copping, and Gayle Gifford
2005 *Reflecting on the Past, Looking to the Future. A Technical Assistance Report to the John H. Chafee Blackstone River Valley National Heritage*

Corridor Commission. Conservation and Stewardship Publication No. 7. Woodstock, Vermont: National Park Service, U.S. Department of the Interior, Conservation Study Institute. Also available on the World Wide Web at http://www.nps.gov/csi/pdf/BlackstoneReport.pdf, accessed July 20, 2009.

Winthrop, Robert H.
1998a The Making of Chumash Tradition: Replies to Haley and Wilcoxon. *Current Anthropology* 39(4):496–499.
1998b Tradition, Authenticity, and Dislocation: Some Dilemmas of Traditional Cultural Property Studies. *Practicing Anthropology* 20(3):25–27.

World Conservation Union
1994 *Guidelines for Protected Area Management Categories*. World Conservation Union, Cambridge.

9

Values and the Evolving Concept of Heritage: The First Century of Archaeology and Law in the United States (1906–2006)

Hilary A. Soderland

Introduction

Across the globe, law is the mechanism increasingly relied upon and utilized to determine the path of cultural heritage. Virtually every aspect of the past—from ownership and access to transfer and protection—has become governed by laws and regulations (see the chapter by Bruning in this volume). Whereas the present-day discipline of archaeology centers on the study of material remains that mark the course of past human existence, the meaning and inferences ascribed to the archaeological record by archaeologists and others intrinsically are influenced by contemporary social, political, cultural, and ethical values. Encapsulating bygone mores and situated within the context of cultural heritage, archaeology captures how the past—whether archaeological, historical, and/or legal—is constructed in the present. The process is shaped profoundly by law, for as society grapples with historical representation of the past in tandem with evolving cultural and ethical sensitivities, the law provides structure and institutionalizes contemporary values. Thus, the history of archaeology law identifies and traces the issues that law has circumscribed for archaeology: the creation of memory; the connection to past cultures through human remains and artifacts—what those are and who may claim them; how the past should be represented in the present; the role of custodians of that memory and representation—museums, governments, scholars, scientists, present-day descendants; the management of threats to preservation and protection such as looting, illicit trade, and fraud; and enforcement methods.

In the United States, the law pertaining to archaeology developed alongside the discipline itself. The professionalization of archaeology can be traced to the end of the 19th century. By the early 1900s, archaeology began to embody many of the professional attributes commonly associated with the modern-day discipline. In 1906, the Antiquities Act marked the initial intersection of archaeology and law. By providing unprecedented protection for cultural resources, the law bolstered the advance of professional archaeologists and of archaeology as an expanding field of science with adherence to methodological frameworks and theoretical bases. Since the turn of the 20th century, law—as a construct that accommodates and embodies social values—was the tool selected by Americans who first sought to effect change and influence the present and future of archaeology. For more than one hundred years, law has continued to be an influential instrument negotiated by various groups, individuals, and institutions representing a multitude of divergent interests, goals, and aspirations. Irrespective of ideological position, law has proved to be a means to an end. No matter which archaeological statute is examined, interest groups throughout the century have acknowledged (whether implicitly or explicitly) that not only does the path to effect change come through law but also the route to advance their particular interests is to acquire stakeholder status in the legislative process. Law is both a construct and a conduit and archaeology in the United States is partnered with, and inextricably linked to, law.

Law touches every aspect of archaeology from the conventional method of archaeological inquiry, excavation, to the manner in which unearthed artifacts are presented, interpreted, disposed of, and displayed, to the rights granted to certain stakeholders. The identities and positions of these stakeholders change over time as the legislative process accommodates the claims and interests of varying groups. Even so, it is more often than not the courts that must decide how the concept of archaeological heritage is to be interpreted under the umbrella of the law, and accordingly, which ownership claim or status is validated. The true practical nature of opposing cultural heritage claims is exemplified because the contested cultural heritage object(s) (such as ceramics, burial goods, or skeletal remains) effectively can be owned by one claimant only. Ownership determination grants title and/or possession. This simultaneously legitimizes and authenticates both the claim to the cultural property and the particular claimant(s) as stakeholder(s).

The discipline and practice of archaeology are inseparable from law, yet to situate the discourse of archaeology at the nexus of law, history, and heritage—to historicize archaeology through law—is far from traditional. This chapter focuses on the history of United States federal law governing archaeological heritage in order to explore the historical associations that have culminated in the archaeology of today and what that means in the context of heritage. In documenting the connection between archaeology and law, this chapter examines the changing concept of heritage as enshrined in the first century of archaeology law both in general and more specifically as it pertains to Native Americans. In so doing, the questions of "how," "when," and "why" archaeology and law have become linked come to the fore. This diachronic framework illustrates the impact of law on archaeology in order to assess how the historiography of archaeology law exhibits evolution in thought as to (1) what warrants protection; (2) who has legal standing to participate in that determination; and, (3) how the past is accorded a place in history. Such a legal-historical approach reveals the transformation of archaeology from a discipline focused on objects to one focused on cultures.

The Archive as Artifact: Positing the Legislative Archive as Archaeological Artifact

The mode of inquiry in tracing the historiography of the law of archaeology has been predominantly archival. The use of the archive as historical resource and object of study is common in the field of history, but is seldom the method enlisted in the domain of archaeology.[1] The methodological strictures curbing these two disciplines serve to entrench and perpetuate this divide. Consequently, there is often an undue distance and detachment between "history" and "prehistory." Nevertheless, archival material and archaeological artifacts can be congruent resources. Archives, like artifacts, are distinct records of the past, chronicling the materialization of past knowledge. In analyzing an artifact, an archaeologist strives to elicit information about the past just as does the historian analyzing text. Traditionally, archaeology has utilized any available written record as a supplement, secondary to the information gathered from material remains, which constitute the primary archaeological record. Archaeology, as a discipline that examines the pre-recorded human past does not depend on a written record. For the historical period, the textual record customarily has been regarded as adjunct rather than as the primary archaeological resource: translations of cuneiform, Egyptian hieroglyphics, and Mayan glyphs and codices have complemented hypotheses and conclusions made from the scrutiny of physical objects and artifacts.

In contrast, this approach asserts that material vestiges of the past do not always comprise the primary element composing the archaeological record. That record is also captured in text. Thus, the written record can be positioned as primary resource and object of study. The archives of the United States government housed at the Center for Legislative Archives at the National Archives and Records Administration (NARA) that record the procedures through which federal legislation is enacted provide such a textual record. This body of legislative archival material documents the law-making process that produces each federal statute governing archaeology and, in so doing, evinces the societal and historical associations that have culminated in the archaeology of today. Such a legal-historical methodological approach using archival legal text as artifact, as object of study, and as *the* archaeological record provides a diachronic framework from which to examine the historiography of archaeology law.

Positing the legislative archive as archaeological artifact thus captures the changing conceptions of heritage during the first century of law regulating United States archaeology (1906–2006). This structure does not map the developing technical protocols of archaeology (its advancement in techniques of discovery and preservation), but rather presents the study of archaeology as a construct of a century of laws and values that have dictated the manner in which—how and by whom—the physical manifestations of Native American cultural patrimony are to be used and studied. The ascription of such value to the corpus of federal law is assessed through a critical examination of four significant statutes: the 1906 Antiquities Act, the 1916 National Park Organic Act, the 1979 Archaeological Resources Protection Act (ARPA), and the 1990 Native American Graves Protection and Repatriation Act (NAGPRA). The legislative history of each statute was constructed from both published Congressional sources and unpublished archival documents by plotting the course of the bills that became law and related bills introduced in the same Congress that did not become law.[2] Thus, the development of federal law becomes situated in a dialectic among the broad conceptions of historical heritage that produced the impulse to legislate in a particular Congress, the specific legislation that resulted, and the contemporaneous social, political, and ethical milieu. The interplay among these factors reveals the process through which the concept of heritage is expressed as well as how it is sustained in law.

As the legislative histories of these four 20th century statutes unfold, so too surface the corresponding multifaceted meanings—imbued, more often than not, with contradictions. By furthering the frame of analysis from one centered on individual and more temporally situated legislative measures to one focused on a century of efforts to regulate and protect archaeology, a greater understanding of the emergence, expansion, and intricacies of the concept of heritage is possible. Therefore, the chronological synthesis of these legislative histories provides the temporal contextualization required to probe how the interconnectivity among law, archaeology, and history engender heritage in historical and contemporary contexts, and how heritage in turn rebounds on archaeology, history, and law. The "archive as artifact" thus renders the socio-legal construction of archaeological heritage from both an historical and a contemporary perspective.

Changing Conceptions of Heritage: The First Century of Archaeology and Law (1906–2006)

In the decades between 1906 and the present, law developed as the constant regulatory apparatus, shaping the contours of archaeology and providing the foundation for change. Within this temporal framework, the enactment of statutes supplies broad chronological indicators, whereas the more extensive legislative histories gauge context to offer insight into consistencies and variations that provide the basis for comparison. Juxtaposing the four laws by examining and comparing their legislative histories underscores the shift in the balance of power that determines authority over the past and which subjects are positioned where within historical representation.

What Warrants Protection

With the 1906 Antiquities Act, the law protected "objects of antiquity" or relics of the past prized for their value and potential to science. Native American human remains were not legally distinguished from other artifacts. Native American graves became property of the federal government to be held in perpetuity in public repositories at the government's discretion.

> Beginning with the passage of the Antiquities Act in 1906, archaeologists (perhaps unintentionally) began to co-opt the American Indian's unwritten history and material culture. The United States government deemed archaeological and historical sites of past cultures in the United States as worthy of protection for the benefit of the public, but it ultimately developed a permit system that centered protection of the past within the scientific community rather than in the hands of those whose ancestors were responsible for its creation. (Watkins 2003:275)

The nucleus of the first national law, the Antiquities Act, was the ethos of safeguarding the past, spearheaded by science, for the "public good." This was still important a decade later but became subsumed within a wider focus. Opposition in 1906 to the removal of lands from the public domain was inverted by 1916 with the dawning of economic potential for development. The making of the 1916 National Park Organic Act was grounded in a conservation ethic to secure the natural landscape for future generations but was tempered by economic exploitation.

Although the focus shifted over the first ten years of legal regulation from solely protective legislation to law that also provided for regulation and administration for the future care of those resources, the effect on the material remains of Native Americans was the same. Federal policy controlled the disposition of Native American human remains and sacred items as archaeological material without reference to their significance to Native peoples until the Native American Graves Protection and Repatriation Act (NAGPRA) in 1990.[3] In 1979, the Archaeological Resources Protection Act (ARPA) provided an intermediate step. ARPA was an important addition to the legal scheme to combat new and unrelenting threats to the nation's archaeological heritage. The statute's focus was on protecting the resources for all Americans for their scientific and educational value. Sensitivity to Native American culture was peripheral, but ARPA did acknowledge that Native American interests in the material remains of the past may conflict with the larger societal outlook.

In stark contrast to all prior legislation, in 1990, NAGPRA granted protection to Native American archaeological objects and human remains as manifestations of culture. The law acknowledged that the indigenous peoples of the United States maintained a special cultural and spiritual connection to the material remains of their ancestors. At the heart of such a connection is the long overdue recognition of Native American religious beliefs and cultural traditions. The legislative process resulting in NAGPRA underlined this acknowledgment by citing the centuries of past injustices, including the denial of civil liberties, citizenship, religious freedom, and respect for customs and traditions of an historically marginalized population. NAGPRA is hailed by many as human rights law and "unique legislation because it is the first time that the Federal Government and non-Indian institutions must consider what is *sacred* from an Indian perspective" (Trope and Echo-Hawk 2001:32). In granting protection to the sacred as a manifestation of culture, NAGPRA forever altered the course of archaeology by reversing the "commonplace [practice of]...public agencies to treat Native American dead as *archaeological resources, property, pathological material, data, specimens,* or *library books* but not as *human beings*" (Trope and Echo-Hawk 2001:13). Nonetheless, NAGPRA's application and adjudication have exposed limitations and ambiguities that in fact entrench some inequalities and power imbalances the law was enacted to amend.[4]

Who Has Legal Standing to Participate in the Determination of What Warrants Protection

Exactly who had legal standing to participate in the determination of that which warrants protection thus has shifted dramatically over the century. In 1906, there was no recognition that material remains originated from any particular Native American culture group (or ancestors of any living culture group). They were simply ancient. It was their age and the potential insight and knowledge they could provide to the scientific world that granted them special status and warranted their protection as national assets. Since there was no specific group associated with the remains, they were preserved in public trust, for "the people," protected (in theory) from private collection and trade. While ownership was solely in the hands of the federal government, which controlled permits to explore, excavate, and access resources and sites, expertise lay solely with scientists.[5] Authority over the past in the making of the Antiquities Act was vested in science, more specifically in archaeology, as a reputable, although relatively new, scientific discipline. As expert witnesses, who testified to the loss of scientific knowledge resulting from the lack of legal protections, archaeologists were the legitimate and dominant interest group enjoying absolute entitlement.

As the emphasis on scientific knowledge waned somewhat from the Antiquities Act to the broader National Park Organic Act, so did scientists' superior influence. Testimony of scientists was outweighed by that of government officials, representatives of preservation societies and associations, as well as those with ardent interest in the economic development of National Parks. The preservation concept espoused by the scientific community that had been so fundamental in underpinning the call for legislation in 1906 remained important, but, by 1916, was joined by other stimuli as antiquities became only a part of the overall picture. The economic opportunities that the systematization of National Parks presented dominated the legislative accounts. This emphasis on the hitherto unexplored financial capacity of National Parks accorded legitimacy to those whose motivations were to capitalize on such development. The potential for profit in the creation and operation of a National Park Service lay primarily in the creation of facilities, infrastructure, and services that would generate revenue by attracting, accommodating, and catering to tourism. Railroads were one of many commerce-driven enterprises that sought to stake a claim in what was envisioned as a limitless tourist industry. On offer was the railroads' commitment to invest substantial resources both in laying line (providing access) and in attracting (advertising/publicizing) visitors. This secured advantageous positions in obtaining contracts and in shaping how access to and among National Parks was to be developed. The result streamlined public access to the National Parks. Thus, with the National Park Organic Act, the exclusive focus of expert testimonies widened as the realm of preservation expanded from that of the solely protective to that which encompassed economic elements. Even with this transition, the National Park Organic Act was extremely important to the safeguarding of cultural heritage in the United States (albeit in a relatively hidden way). In establishing the framework for vast areas of federal land to remain more or less undisturbed for decades, the statute precluded destruction of many (still unknown) archaeological resources and Native American remains and cultural objects.

The sentiment that the enactment of legislation was for the greater "public good" persisted still, and mirrored that of 1906. However, *who* determined the "public interest" had changed over the decade. While the great reaches of the American landscape were to open to the nation's citizens, economic promise had become the foremost rationale that impelled the new authoritative cohort of businesses, entrepreneurs, and economic opportunists. Thus, in the interim between the Antiquities Act and the National Park Organic Act, the "public" for whom legislation ostensibly was enacted remained in the background—an amorphous and vague entity—whose interest was determined again by expert testimony. Although the predominant expert voice was not the same, it was nevertheless experts who decided and whose voices dominated the legislative process, formulating the law steering America's archaeological heritage.

In 1979, the shaping of ARPA was strongly influenced by an urgency to protect the nation's archaeological heritage, although this time protection was needed from modern depredations and destruction. The beneficiaries of the legislation were the public, the nation, and scientific inquiry. The focus of economic exploitation was no longer tourism and infrastructure but wholesale looting for the international market. Penalties and deterrence were the watchwords. Testifying before Congress at this time, scientists, politicians, academics, and public interest groups were joined by attorneys and a single Native American in examining and setting parameters for the new law. All were united in their support of law to preserve the non-renewable archaeological resources of the United States.

By 1990, the once homogeneous public had become fragmented within a pluralistic society. In the formulation of NAGPRA, scientists were now just one claimant group among many vying for the right to own and interpret the past. The railroads of 1916 were replaced by other corporate entities with interests in profit, development, and exploitation. Economic development, once an ally of preservation, had now become an incompatible collaborator as the repercussions of decades of development and tourism became transparent. The prized "objects of antiquity" were threatened by destruction, looting, and illicit trade. The past had become a much more complex phenomenon as the law embraced, rather than eschewed, cultural distinction and difference.

Why a Particular Representation of the Past is Accorded a Place in History

Little or no debate exists within the heritage paradigm that the past is a dynamic construct that changes over time. Yet, archaeologists have not regarded the dynamic nature of the historical record that documents, records, and captures the past, particularly as to the place and effect of law. An examination of the history of legislation, however, opens a window to the changing conceptions of what warrants protection and who has legal standing to participate in that determination. This, in turn, manifests why a particular representation of the past is accorded a place in history.

Throughout the first century of the legal direction of archaeology in the United States, the law has defined the place of indigenous peoples—and their heritage—in history. It was not until the making of NAGPRA that their inclusion in the legislative process resulted in significant proprietary rights. In 1990, NAGPRA conferred upon Native Americans a special stakeholder status in a manner that had never before been done. In expanding the legal arena, NAGPRA substantially changed how the past is accorded a place in history. It signified the transfer of ownership, or trusteeship, from the public, professional, and federal to the cultural, which in turn transferred authenticity, authority, and legitimacy to Native peoples. This incorporation extended the platform upon which power dynamics and the politics of participation/representation are determined. Moreover, it legalized many rights of indigenous peoples in the participation, expression, and representation of their cultures. NAGPRA is frequently considered landmark legislation for archaeology and for Native American rights.[6] In stipulating certain cultural property rights to Native peoples, NAGPRA integrated in law the concept that much of the archaeological past is part of a cultural continuum of living indigenous societies.

As the process of legislating has become more encompassing, multivocal, and less reliant upon one authoritative, expert opinion, it must be negotiated among many conflicting voices in a politicized social context. The legal process and law itself are marked by compromise. As NAGPRA attests, law is an instrument—not an automatic solution or remedy for conflicting ideologies and complex questions. Limitations exist for any legal apparatus to protect and manage tangible material and intangible values. This is clearly evident in NAGPRA's already contentious 19-year history. Since its passage, the law has been attacked from all angles, criticized as vague, or for not doing enough, or for going too far. The notoriety of Kennewick Man's[7] discovery and the subsequent protracted legal battle[8] "over...control [of] historical narrative and hence...power over the categories of identity that dominate and control the present and the future" (Crawford 2000:229–230) demonstrated NAGPRA's limits.[9] Yet as NAGPRA continues to be tested and tried in court, its precepts will guide the evolution of archaeology from now on. For all the advantages and disadvantages of law as a mechanism for regulating cultural heritage, the framework of law provides structure and continuity in the face of changing societal attitudes and sensitivities.

In the history of United States archaeology law, nationalism also played a significant role in encouraging the passage of statutes, although its direction shifted over the century as well. At the beginning of the 20th century, archaeology was recognized as a cultural resource with intrinsic value as a national asset, yet the protection and regulation of archaeology was not championed by law. To secure enactment of formative legislation, the scientific experts channeled nationalistic rhetoric. International comparison highlighted the absence of any American laws equivalent to European (or other) initiatives and kindled patriotic sentiments, which helped to propel the need for action into Congressional purview. This sentiment was harnessed to safeguard the nation's cultural and natural heritage, providing support for the action that culminated in the 1906 Antiquities Act and the 1916 National Park Organic Act. In 1979, legislators framed ARPA in terms of law to protect the nation's archaeological resources for Americans, present and future. The law to do so was no longer compared to other countries' codes. Instead, the call was to protect irreplaceable resources from the global illicit antiquities trade that was dispersing America's archaeological heritage to foreign collectors. By 1990, nationalism still featured prominently but was no longer framed in terms of some country or collector abroad. Now there was an internal focus. Native Americans were asserting rights to their culture as sovereign nations within the United States.

Historicizing Archaeology Law

[Archaeologists,] historians of archaeology [, and others] have yet to integrate fully the legal regulation of the archaeological record

and its political importance to the shaping of American archaeology.
(McLaughlin 1998:343)

The law of archaeology provides a mechanism to trace how the conceptions of heritage in the United Sates have changed through time. An
intrinsic component of and first step in creating law is categorization.
Classification and the necessity of defining terms in order to explicate
and clarify the object of the law are prerequisites to provisions concerning management, administration, and implementation. Thus, terms
for concepts associated with archaeology—even those that arguably defy
definition, such as those in the realm of intangible attributes—have been
classified, categorized, and defined in law. As the intangible has emerged
as a concept distinct from the tangible within the heritage discourse,
so has a recognition of the tensions and complexities inherent in a cat-
egorical division of the two concepts. Law the world over has been one
instrument that figures notably in this demarcation. There has been an
increasing need for both tangible and intangible archaeological heritage
to be defined in and by law in order for nations to implement protective and regulatory policies, prioritize rights to certain stakeholders, and
adjudicate conflicting claims.

As United States society has become more fragmented and, in the case
of Native Americans, as the law continues to be an avenue to right past
ill treatment, the need for precision in law has magnified. This becomes
transparent even with a cursory glance at the bookends of archaeology
legislation over the century: in 1906 and 1916, none of the four short
sections of either Act supplied definitions, whereas in both 1979 and
1990, there was a section devoted entirely to defining the terms utilized
in the Act. In 1979, this section defined 7 terms and in 1990, this number
more than doubled, with 19 defined terms. The continual increase in definitional specificity in the law of archaeology can be well documented.
An examination of the law's reflection of the contemporaneous societal
context that prompted this shift is new. The setting from which law
emerged and a critical examination of its making through legislative histories has not been conducted within the scope of archaeology.

Situated at the intersection of archaeology, law, history, and heritage,
this analysis is predicated on the fusion of issues not previously integrated in such a framework and time period. The law provides a lens
through which archaeology can be historicized by exploring the voices
through which heritage has come to be defined and redefined in law over
time as well as how legal classification engages our contemporary understanding of archaeological heritage. The historicization of archaeology
law has implications for the past, the present, and the future of archaeology. The legislative histories over the century have revealed numerous

themes. Law has clearly registered a movement toward the consideration of indigenous concerns. Most apparent however is the fact that law is integral not only to the past but also to the future of archaeology. Within heritage, law provides an order under which societal issues and contests are directed. Law in the United States positions the legal domain as an axis of articulation between the discipline of archaeology and the discourse of indigenous cultural heritage.

Throughout the first century of legal regulation (1906–2006), the corpus of law governing archaeological heritage has maintained consistency, yet also has experienced great change. The conception of heritage has embraced both "science" and "culture."[10] With NAGPRA, the law now has given special recognition and rights to the indigenous peoples of the United States. The recognition and equitable treatment of Native peoples is long overdue and the past injustices and failures have served to a large degree as one catalyst for legislating terms more open to their worldview as distinct from that of larger society. Along these lines, NAGPRA has been credited with extending the concept of archaeological heritage. This counters the science/culture dichotomy and asserts that the interpretations of the past based on multiple ideologies and considerations (such as Native American oral history as well as scientific/historical research), are complementary and foster a more holistic perspective.

Regardless of how this science/culture dichotomy or broadening interpretation of the past will be defined in the future, it is clear that it will be negotiated in the legal sphere. The future discourse of archaeology, as a practice, as a discipline, and as a paradigm that engages with indigenous traditions cannot be separated from law. Native Americans gained a voice to their past when they became stakeholders in the law of archaeology. Many Native peoples and scholars assert that, with control of their past, their communities have regained a pride and dignity in their culture that had been almost destroyed, consistently marginalized, and always controlled by the dominant culture. In this way, NAGPRA cannot be disconnected from the historical context that played an important part in its making. It is a product of history, articulated in the modern times.

Archaeology is therefore more than sequestered relics of the past. As a discipline and as a practice, it is integrally connected to the law that governs it. Change to archaeology has come through legislation and law is the conduit for future protection, regulation, or modification to the landscape of American archaeology. It is not possible to grasp the full picture of what archaeology is today without understanding how law has permeated the discipline. Legal-historical inquiry documents law as the regulatory constant through time and attests to the fact that law is the instrument of change. In a field of nonrenewable resources and materials steeped with disparate ideologies, conflict is inevitable. At least in the United States, efforts to resolve that conflict have been through law. Nowhere is this more evident than in the historiography of archaeology law.

Endnotes

1. Using archival documents to anchor a research methodology—considering archival material as "artifact"—is unusual and under-explored in archaeology.

2. Each bill's development was charted from origination to termination or codification. This included documenting when and by whom each was introduced and whether the bill was considered by Congressional committees as well as inspecting any associated debates, reports, hearings, and/or unpublished material.

3. The terminological distinction between "Native American" and "Indian tribe" is significant. NAGPRA defines "Native American" however "Indian" or "Indian tribe" is the term used in United States law to connote legal rights. Thus, it is "Indian tribes" or, in the case of NAGPRA, "lineal descendents" or those with "cultural affiliation" that have formalized roles and vested rights under the law. This distinction is essential to understand the way in which indigenous peoples are classified in United States law. For the purpose of this chapter, however, the term "Native American" is used broadly to encompass Native Americans as peoples, cultures, and stakeholders.

4. For example, NAGPRA is restricted in jurisdiction to federal agencies, federally funded institutions, and to federal and tribal lands. Likewise, the rights in NAGPRA pertain only to Native American tribes legally recognized by the federal government. This creates an inequitable division among Native peoples. NAGPRA also requires Native Americans to assert claims according to the rules and procedures of a Western judicial system. The statute stipulates that "oral traditional evidence" is admissible in court to support a claim of "cultural affiliation" yet the effectual role of introducing such evidence is far from crystallized (*Bonnichsen v. United States*, 367 F.3d 864, 882 (9th Cir. 2004); see the chapter by Bruning in this volume). In these ways, among others, NAGPRA has been criticized for privileging the Western legal system and perpetuating the dominance and ultimate control of the majority.

5.   In the early regulation of the natural and cultural environment, scientists were the dominant interest group, viewed by society as the sole experts. This attitude ceded supreme authority to science in the legislative process. The classification of archaeology as a scientific enterprise with systematized methods and theories gave it specialized status in the preservation effort and in the legal sphere. The official legal regulation of archaeology validated the relatively new scientific discipline, affording legitimacy and authority to its professional practitioners, a somewhat circular process.

6.   NAGPRA was greatly affected by social movements. Beginning in the 1960s, the Native American rights movement began to assert political influence and call for sensitivity to Native American culture and beliefs. NAGPRA marked a significant step in the legal recognition that not only were remains of the past made by, or composed of, the forebears of today's Native Americans but also because of that, Native Americans possessed special rights to such material. Science was no longer preeminent. Under NAGPRA, "lineal descent" or "cultural affiliation" premised on "shared group identity" took precedence. In this regard, the Native American perspective was accorded authenticity and legitimacy for meaning and appropriate disposition options of "human remains" and statutorily defined "cultural items" ("associated funerary objects," "unassociated funerary objects," "sacred objects," and "cultural patrimony").

7.   The 9,300-year-old skeleton was discovered in 1996 along the banks of the Columbia River near Kennewick, Washington. The Columbia, a navigable waterway, is federal land under the jurisdiction of the United States Army Corps of Engineers. Local archaeologist James Chatters obtained an ARPA permit to excavate the site. The recovery of more than 90 percent of the skeleton, made it remarkably complete for its age. Questions of ownership rights quickly emerged as scientists' initial examination revealed details of "Kennewick Man's"/"Ancient One's" age and life circa 7,200 B.C.

8.   The Kennewick Man case is the most notorious, and arguably the most important, NAGPRA litigation. The protracted court battle over ownership of the human skeleton involved a coalition of Native American tribes, scientists, and the United States government. Under NAGPRA, Native Americans claimed "cultural affiliation" to Kennewick Man. Scientists disputed this claim with its statutory right to repatriation, asserting the scientific importance of the human remains as one of the best preserved New World skeletons in a minute sample size that could shed light on humanity's past (and past human migratory patterns). After almost eight years

of litigation, in 2004 the United States Court of Appeals for the 9th Circuit affirmed the August 2002 findings of the United States District Court of Oregon that the Kennewick Man remains did not meet the definition of "Native American" under NAGPRA and that "cultural affiliation" to modern-day Native American tribes required by NAGPRA could not be established (*Bonnichsen v. United States*, 367 F.3d 864 (9th Cir. 2004)). Consequently, NAGPRA did not apply and the scientists were granted access to study the remains. The legal dispute polarized Native Americans and scientists/archaeologists and positioned "science" against "religion" once again in United States archaeology.

9. The final ruling has not resolved tensions or debate. Conversely, it has prompted many attempts in Congress to amend NAGPRA.

10. The construction of the "science" versus "culture" dichotomy is problematic even though it has been perpetuated in law.

References

The Antiquities Act of 1906, 16 U.S.C. §431.

The Archaeological Resources Protection Act of 1979, 16 U.S.C. §470aa–mm.

Bonnichsen v. United States, 367 F.3d 864 (9th Cir. 2004).

Crawford, Suzanne J.
2000   (Re)Constructing Bodies: Semiotic Sovereignty and the Debate over Kennewick Man. In *Repatriation Reader: Who Owns American Indian Remains?* Devon A. Mihesuah, ed. Pp. 211–236. Lincoln, Nebraska: University of Nebraska Press.

McLaughlin, Robert H.
1998   The American Archaeological Record, Authority to Dig, Power to Interpret. *International Journal of Cultural Property* 7(2):342–375.

The National Park Organic Act of 1916, 16 U.S.C. §1.

The Native American Graves Protection and Repatriation Act of 1990, 25 U.S.C. §3001.

Trope, Jack F., and Walter R. Echo-Hawk
2001   The Native American Graves Protection and Repatriation Act: Background and Legislative History. In *The Future of the Past: Archaeologists, Native Americans and Repatriation*. Tamara Lynn Bray, ed. Pp. 9–34. New York: Garland Publishing.

Watkins, Joe E.
2003   Beyond the Margin: American Indians, First Nations, and Archaeology in North America. *American Antiquity* 68(2):273–285.

PART II

Applying Heritage Values

Section 1

Teaching and Learning Heritage Values

10

Teaching Heritage Values through Field Schools: Case Studies from New England

Elizabeth S. Chilton

Introduction

While heritage protection and management are not new to archaeology, thinking about heritage values in the context of inter- and intra-cultural meanings is, especially in the United States (see the chapters by Altschul; Bruning; Holtorf; Okamura; Russell; and Soderland in this volume). As Smith (1994) argues, post-processual debates in archaeology have proven to be more introspective than productive when it comes to heritage. However, one could argue that in North American archaeology, post-processualism—with its emphasis on multivocality—paved the way for American archaeologists to consider the wider publics and stakeholders of archaeology. More recently, indigenous archaeologies and other theoretical developments worldwide have led to a greater consideration of the role of archaeology in the politics of identity—with the goal of "decolonizing archaeology" (Atalay 2008; Smith and Wobst 2005; Thorley 2002; Watkins 2000). These changes in theoretical positioning in archaeology have greatly affected the practice of archaeology as well—from the selection of projects and building of a research design, to things as traditionally unquestioned as field methods, disseminate of information, and curation (Chilton 2006).

I have been teaching archaeological field schools in New England, a sub-region of the northeastern U.S., since 1989. There are a wide variety of archaeological field schools taught all over the world, and these vary a great deal in pedagogy, philosophy, duration, and range of skills learned. The overarching and explicit goal of the field schools that I direct is to teach and promote heritage values and management to multiple stakeholders, including: (1) students; (2) research community; (3) landowners and local residents; (4) state and other government constituencies; and (5) Native American and other descendant groups. Of course there are unequal power and socioeconomic relationships among these groups, and in our case, the Native peoples are the central "ethic client" (Blakey 2008). While the often-cited goal of an archaeological field school is to teach archaeological field methods, we do a disservice to students of archaeology (and the community of stakeholders) if field methods are taught outside of the context of heritage values. Field schools are unlike other archaeological excavations in that one must try to balance what are often competing priorities among the stakeholders listed above, and all in the context of an educational experience. However, if promoting a community-based archaeology is kept at the core, balancing the needs of these stakeholders becomes part of the process of engaging multiple publics in preservation, site management, and public histories. Here I define a community-based archaeology as one that moves beyond consultation, and includes community members in decisions about research foci, sites, analysis, curation, publication, and dissemination of information (Clarke 2002:251; Hart 2006a). In this chapter, I discuss my experience working with each of these groups of stakeholders in turn, emphasizing the role of teaching and learning heritage values.

Field School Students

Field schools are not like other excavations in that I believe the needs of the students must come first. I have been criticized for saying this, but after all, students are paying what may amount to thousands of dollars, and they are expecting a degree of "credentialing" from the field school experience. Many an excavation has been funded by the tuition received from field school students, and many universities in the United States make a significant profit from all summer programs. This requires us to evaluate the student experience perhaps before all other considerations. Students often give up employment over the summer to take six or eight weeks out of their lives to participate as—sometimes—unpaid labor on an archaeological research project. Field schools include students who wish to become professional archaeologists, but many students are there to fulfill other degree or professional requirements, such that we often have a team of students with wide-ranging experiences and goals. Certainly there are other (and perhaps less time-consuming) ways to fund an archaeological excavation and research project, so one should consider first and foremost whether a particular site makes a good case for a field school. I believe strongly that sites should not be excavated as a simple educational exercise.

Field school students should be introduced to basic field and lab methods and obtain a wide range of archaeological skills. I take the responsibility of teaching methods very seriously, since many of my field school students are soon employed as professional archaeologists in a cultural resource management context. I typically have 4 supervisors for every 16 students. Students learn basic field survey (using total station) and mapping, test unit excavation, soils and stratigraphy (including the Harris Matrix soil recording technique), feature excavation, field recording, soil sampling, flotation, and identification of material culture. We also do a unit on glacial geology/geoarchaeology.

If teaching methods was the only goal, however, one could teach an archaeological field school in the classroom or in one's own backyard. Aside from field methods per se, students should learn about the political, ethical, and legal contexts of archaeology, which include public education, community relationships, and cultural resource management. In many field schools, students are sheltered from the "messiness" of landowner negotiations, disagreements with avocational archaeologists, the wishes of local Native American tribes, and the like. However, sheltering students does not provide them with the kind of mentoring that they really need to do or to understand "real" archaeology, whether they become future professionals or stakeholders in some other capacity. In the field schools that I direct, I distribute the research design and permit applications to all students before they arrive for the first day of class. During the first week, before we put a shovel in their hands, we discuss which archaeological site we will be working on, why we chose the site, who the landowner is and how they feel about our work, what the local residents or avocational archaeologists know or don't know about the project and why, and which Native American descendant communities have been involved, how, and why. These are important preparations, but, as I will discuss below, community archaeology needs to go beyond the academic and into practice.

Another aspect of my approach to teaching students about the importance of heritage is that I only choose archaeological sites for field schools that are threatened in some way, either from erosion, construction, farming, or avocational digging, and I choose sites for which there is a group of stakeholders that is more or less involved in or concerned about these particular archaeological sites. That way the students' work takes on a practical and serious implication: they are participating in community archaeology and not simply reading about it. Readings and weekly discussion are, nevertheless, important ways that we keep students engaged in the bigger questions and implications of our work—reminding them why things like line levels and mesh size matter in the bigger picture.

Students are also involved in producing knowledge that is brought forth to these larger constituencies through our public field lab (discussed below). This opportunity and their reflective journals oblige them to be self-reflexive and think critically about how knowledge about the past is produced and how it is used.

Research Community

Aside from the students' educational needs, another important stakeholder is the archaeological research community. Field schools are not necessarily the most efficient or technically excellent way to excavate a site. Thus, while directors of field schools often try to combine their research with field school teaching, as I do, sites must be chosen that balance ethical and professional responsibilities with the needs of the students and with the needs of other stakeholders (discussed below). By working on threatened sites that would not be excavated otherwise, the research value of field school sites is greatly enhanced. Even if one is not working on a threatened site per se, educating students about cultural resource management is critical—even in the context of what might otherwise be a "purely academic" excavation.

Another aspect of research that might appropriately be called professional ethics is the treatment of lab work and curation in the context of field schools. Many field schools in the past—and some today—did not adequately train students in responsible excavation from the perspective of the proper analysis and care of collections. Many a field school student has the impression that archaeology is primarily about digging and has not given a thought as to how the artifacts will be used and cared for by archaeologists after the field schools ends. About ten years ago, I decided to incorporate more lab work into the context of the field school itself, in part to provide an opportunity for students to learn more about material culture, but also to be able to have a complete inventory of all materials before the end of the excavation. I also teach a follow-up laboratory methods class each fall following the field school. Thus, many field school students are also engaged in the dissemination of the research results, either through their individual analysis projects, by taking photographs of artifacts, or otherwise contributing to the final report or publications. But since not all students take this follow-up class, the lab experience during the field school is critical. In that lab context, we discuss proper curation and storage of artifacts as well as the importance of accessible digital inventories. Because the lab is open to the public, these messages are then communicated to the broader community (see below).

Landowners and Local Residents

For those of us who conduct archaeological fieldwork in a particular town, valley, or region over many years, building strong relationships with local residents and landowners is critical to building a larger heritage management community. In the United States, not only are archaeologists legally dependent on landowners for permission to conduct archaeological field schools, we are also dependent on local communities to help build networks of stakeholders committed to preserving and protecting heritage properties and teaching these values to others. Developing and maintaining such relationships take an inordinate amount of time and energy and cannot be taken for granted. Community residents will not "naturally" understand or agree with the value of archaeology or heritage, and this is where the relationships among the stakeholders become the most complex. As an aside, academic institutions do not always recognize and reward this type of engaged scholarship and instead see this as "public service"—something not all that important in most tenure reviews, for example. Thus, it is imperative for us to educate our institutions about the importance of building these relationships as a way to produce ethical scholarship and valuable teaching.

State and Other Governmental Constituencies

In virtually every part of the world, field schools take place in a context where there are laws or local statutes protecting at least some archaeological sites and there are often procedures for applying for permission to conduct an excavation. Because I work at a state-funded institution, I am especially self-conscious about following all state-level protocols for conducting archaeological fieldwork and for curating collections. However, in the United States, archaeological standards and review vary a great deal from state to state. Archaeologists often forget, too, that the people in state agencies that review archaeological project have their own priorities. These priorities by their very nature will not be exactly the same as someone conducting a field school, nor will they be static over time or across geographical areas. It has been important and rewarding for me to discuss potential field school projects with state and local officials (and federal officials if appropriate) well before beginning a field project. This, again, builds stronger and broader heritage management communities with shared interests.

Native American and Other Descendant Groups

Because my fieldwork and field schools have focused on pre-Contact and colonial sites, the descendant communities I have worked with have been largely Native American tribes and individuals. When I directed a field school project on Martha's Vineyard, Massachusetts, as part of the Harvard Archaeological Field School in 1998 and 1999, I worked with the Wampanoag Tribe of Gayhead (Aquinnah) more than a year before the field school began. The Aquinnah are a federally recognized Tribe, and the archaeological site was already well known to them. A few years prior to my beginning the project, two late prehistoric human burials had been discovered to be eroding out of a cliff face overlooking the ocean. In both cases, the state archaeologist's staff excavated the remains, and they were eventually repatriated to the Aquinnah. However, because this site is on a town beach, the location is not secure, resulting in a great deal of anxiety for the town, the state, and the Tribe. Thus, I undertook the project to better identify site function, site, integrity, and to work with the Tribe on either a salvage or preservation plan (Chilton and Doucette 2002a, 2002b).

I directed two field schools on Martha's Vineyard, as well as two other salvage excavations at the site. In all cases, the Tribe evaluated our research design. I appeared before the Tribal Council on a few occasions to answer questions about the research design and to seek their support before beginning excavations. My position was that, regardless of cultural resource laws and protocols, I would not participate in the project without the full support of the Tribe.

Field school students learned about this consultation and collaboration throughout the field schools in 1998 and 1999. Harvard University gave an Aquinnah student a full tuition waiver for the field school each year. The participation of these students, as well as field visits from Tribal members, made this particular stakeholder group both highly visible and clearly central in the minds of the students.

Field schools do not and cannot always have a direct relationship with descendant communities. Due to the diasporic nature of New England Native communities after the 17th century, not all sub-regions of New England have clearly defined descendant communities. I have been directing and co-directing an archaeological field school in Deerfield, MA, since the late 1980s. Siobhan Hart, a doctoral candidate at University of Massachusetts Amherst and the co-director of the project, has made community archaeology in Deerfield the subject of her dissertation (Hart 2006b). Deerfield, and the middle Connecticut River Valley in general, is a region where there are no resident, federally recognized tribes, tribally held lands, or sole descendant communities; descendant communities are dispersed, but nevertheless maintain connections to ancestral homelands (Chilton and Hart 2009). Thus, we work with representatives of descendant communities through the Massachusetts Commission on Indian Affairs (MCIA). The Commission was created by the Commonwealth of Massachusetts (Massachusetts General Law Chapter 6A: Section 8A) in 1974 to assist Native American individuals and groups in their relationships with state and local government agencies and to advise the Commonwealth in matters pertaining to Native Americans (Chilton and Hart 2009). Among many other responsibilities, the Commission represents Native communities with interests in archaeological sites in the Commonwealth (Chilton and Hart 2009). For decades, the Commission has played an important role in archaeological projects and repatriation efforts in the Commonwealth, particularly in areas where there are no resident descendant groups, such as Deerfield (Chilton and Hart 2009). Similar to the work that I did with the Aquinnah, the MCIA reviewed and discussed our research design well in advance of any archaeological field school. Representatives of MCIA have also visited the site and lab several times and we have kept in close communication throughout the project.

In this case, no tribal members participated in the field school directly, and our meetings with MCIA were primarily limited to before and after the field school session. Thus, field school students felt their presence as stakeholders primarily through reading our research design, through assigned readings and discussion, and through our informal discussions during the field school itself—not through direct interaction. Nevertheless, my sense from their journals and from conversations is that students come away with a sense of the importance of Native American communities as stakeholders.

Public Education

Public education has always formed a major component of all the archaeological field schools that I have directed. In part, this is because I was taught that this is what you do in field schools: you have students talk to the public about what we are doing and what we have found as part of "teaching" students to talk to the public. If the project is sensitive, and if some of the stakeholders do not support media coverage, then this type of public education can become difficult, or at least minimal. However, if it is supported by the above-mentioned stakeholders (particularly descendant communities, landowners, state officials, and sponsors), then "public education" can become part of the core mission and learning experience for students. It also has the potential to teach local residents about the importance of heritage management and build stronger community archaeology. For example, in the case of the Deerfield project, historical writings have essentially erased Native American history from the Connecticut River Valley or at least seriously underplayed it. For the past several years, we have had an open field lab in Historic Deerfield, Inc., a large history museum, which also helps sponsor our annual field school. Students rotate through the public lab each week and talk to visitors about archaeology, the general overview of the project, and about site preservation and stewardship. Students process and inventory artifacts and samples, and small displays are assembled for lab visitors. Each year we advertise this "open lab" through the museum's newsletter, local newspapers and radio, and through our field school website. Having field school students essentially run this open lab serves two main purposes: (1) it prompts students to think about clear messages and to learn how to communicate them effectively to the public, and (2) it helps build supportive community relationships and (we hope) builds new communities of stakeholders. For example, many lab visitors have reported previously undocumented archaeological sites, many of them threatened. An added bonus to having a lab open throughout the field school is that most years we have a complete and accurate inventory and basic analysis of all artifacts by the end of the season. Personally, I think it is important to teach students what happens after the digging, especially if this is the last archaeology class they take before being employed as a professional archaeologist, or if they decide not to go on any further in archaeology.

Field Schools and Community Service Learning

Over the past two years we have incorporated the pedagogy of community service learning (CSL) into the field school (Chilton and Hart 2009). The main principle of CSL is that the service needs are defined by the stakeholder communities. CSL has served as a useful pedagogical tool to approach archaeological field schools in the context of community archaeology, stakeholders, and heritage values (e.g., Nassaney 2004), and to move beyond public education to scholarly engagement. In our case, students carry out their service in the context of a cycle of reflexive writing and reevaluation. Students keep a journal throughout the field school, and the field school staff reads these journals each week and asks further questions for reflection the following week. These journals have been enormously helpful to us as teachers and as archaeologists because they allow us to continuously reevaluate our pedagogy, our field methods, relationships with community partners, and our public education efforts throughout the six weeks of the field school—while we still have the chance to make changes that will positively affect the educational experience of the students and the larger stakeholder context of the fieldwork.

Conclusions: De-Centering Archaeology

In sum, by choosing projects that are part of building a community-based archaeology, one can better teach heritage management to students because: (a) the project itself embodies the message, (b) their work is embedded through the praxis of building stakeholder groups, (c) the students themselves are integral to the process, and (d) they are asked to reflect and in turn, educate others about it. This is not to say that opening the door to stakeholders is easy or that all of its consequences are predictable.

Whenever one engages in community archaeology, indigenous archaeology, or community service learning, there is a certain a loss of control over every detail of the project. Being sensitive and responsive to community needs and wishes means that "pure archaeological questions" need to be rationalized and contextualized. In some cases, I have not been able to do everything I wanted to in terms of field testing, and in some cases I was deterred from working on particular sites because of stakeholder objections. McDavid (2003:57) suggests de-centering archaeology and archaeologists, along with historians and government employees, as the sole authorities on Native pasts and presents and the sole stewards and interpreters for archaeological sites (see also Trigger 2008). The process of "de-centering archaeology" is also much more time consuming than traditional (colonialist) archaeology. If you want to properly engage multiple stakeholders, you must organize many meetings, be available to talk on the phone, answer more emails and consider more opinions. This takes a considerable amount of time above and beyond the typically intensive preparation for a field project and a field school.

So if archaeology (as a profession and a type of inquiry) is de-centered, then what is at the center? The answer to that question will depend on who initiates this kind of community archaeology. In my case, the silent partner at the center of my field schools is the archaeological record itself, and the goal of ethical and responsible heritage management. That is at the core of what I try to teach to my field school students and that is a major part of the mentoring process of the graduate student teaching assistants (TAs). It is also at the core of all of the interactions we have with the wide variety of stakeholders we have invited into this project.

Nevertheless, not all of the stakeholders necessarily hold preservation as their central priority as concerns archaeology. Tensions can, and do, arise between avocational and professional archaeologists, between landowners and archaeologists, between landowners and historical societies, and the like. In the 1980s, when I was directing field schools, we would shelter students from much of this messiness. Now we discuss these tensions openly and involve students in problem solving. In this way students learn, perhaps, the two most important lessons concerning heritage values and archaeology: (1) not all stakeholders share the same values and priorities even as concerns the same archaeological project; and (2) archaeo-logical methods are only a toolkit—they are not a cookbook for archaeological practice. That is, no two archaeological projects are exactly the same when it comes to field methods, lab methods, ethical concerns, stakeholder groups, or the process for navigating all of these interests. Learning that heritage values and the role of archaeology in those values is situational and ever changing is perhaps the most important lesson that can be taught through an archaeological field school.

References

Atalay, Sonia
2008   Multivocality and Indigenous Archaeologies. In *Evaluating Multiple Narratives: Beyond Nationalist, Colonialist, Imperialist Archaeologies.* Junko Habu, Clare Fawcett, and John M. Matsunaga, eds. Pp. 29–44. New York: Springer.

Blakey, Michael L.
2008   An Ethical Epistemology of Publicly Engaged Biocultural Research. In *Evaluating Multiple Narratives: Beyond Nationalist, Colonialist, Imperialist Archaeologies.* Junko Habu, Clare Fawcett, and John M. Matsunaga, eds. Pp. 17–28. New York: Springer.

Chilton, Elizabeth S.
2006   From the Ground Up: The Effects of Consultation on Archaeological Methods. In *Cross-Cultural Collaboration: Native Peoples and Archaeology in the Northeastern United States.* Jordan Kerber, ed. Pp. 281–294. Lincoln, Nebraska: University of Nebraska Press.

Chilton, Elizabeth S., and Dianna L. Doucette
2002a   The Archaeology of Coastal New England: The View from Martha's Vineyard. *Northeast Anthropology* 64:55–66.
2002b   Archaeological Investigations at the Lucy Vincent Beach Site (19-DK-148): Preliminary Results and Interpretations. In *A Lasting Impression: Coastal, Lithic, and Ceramic Research in New England Archaeology.*

Jordan Kerber, ed. Pp. 41–70. Westport, Connecticut: Praeger Publishers.

Chilton, Elizabeth S., and Siobhan M. Hart
2009 Archaeology and Community Service Learning in the "Pioneer Valley." In *Archaeology and Community Service Learning*. Michael S. Nassaney and Mary Ann Levine, eds. Pp. 168–182. Gainesville: University Press of Florida.

Clarke, Anne
2002 The Ideal and the Real: Cultural and Personal Transformation of Archaeological Research on Groote Eylandt, Northern Australia. *World Archaeology* 34(2):249–264.

Hart, Siobhan M.
2006a A Stack of Hats: Exploring the Roles and Responsibilities of Archaeologists in Cross-Cultural Community-Based Archaeology in New England. Paper presented at the Institute of American Indian Studies Archaeology Round Table, "Identity and Community in Native Southern New England: Archaeology's Role and Responsibility in Contemporary Politics," Washington, Connecticut, October 26.
2006b High Stakes: An Archaeological History and Community Archaeology of the Pocumtuck Fort. Dissertation prospectus, Department of Anthropology, University of Massachusetts Amherst.

McDavid, Carol
2003 Collaboration, Power, and the Internet: The Public Archaeology of the Levi Jordan Plantation. In *Archaeologists and Local Communities: Partners in Exploring the Past*. Linda Derry and Maureen Malloy, eds. Pp. 45–66 Washington, D.C.: Society for American Archaeology.

Nassaney, Michael S.
2004 Implementing Community Service Learning through Archaeological Practice: Program Design and Preliminary Assessment. *Michigan Journal of Community Service Learning* 10(3):89–99.

Smith, Laurajane
1994 Heritage Management as Postprocessual Archaeology? *Antiquity* 68(259):300–309.

Smith, Claire, and H. Martin Wobst, eds.
2005 *Indigenous Archaeologies: Decolonizing Theory and Practice*. New York: Routledge.

Thorley, Peter
2002 Current Realities, Idealised Pasts: Archaeology, Values and Indigenous Heritage Management in Central Australia. *Oceania* 73(2):110–125.

Trigger, Bruce G.
2008 "Alternative Archaeologies" in Historical Perspective. In *Evaluating Multiple Narratives: Beyond Nationalist, Colonialist, Imperialist*

Archaeologies. Junko Habu, Clare Fawcett, and John M. Matsunaga, eds. Pp. 187–195. New York: Springer.

Watkins, Joe
2000   Indigenous Archaeology: American Indian Values and Scientific Practice. Walnut Creek, California: AltaMira Press.

11

Native American Heritage Values: Building Curriculum, Building Bridges

Joëlle Clark and Margaret A. Heath

Introduction

Heritage values represent the intrinsic (emotion, intellect, and spirituality), institutional (process and policy), and instrumental (social or economic) ideals of people (see the chapter by Clark in this volume). These values are often intangible when conducting typical archaeological endeavors as they reflect individuals, communities, and broader audiences (Clark 2006). Groups of people often value heritage places and objects differently. Archaeologists follow ethics and guidelines for professional practice that include values of preserving and learning from the past. When planning to teach archaeology, these values are important to include as part of a curriculum; but should expand to include answers for the following questions: How is heritage defined? Whose heritage is being valued? Who makes heritage decisions on behalf of the people? Are all heritage values included? (see the chapters by Bruning; Soderland; and Yu in this volume) In the case of Native American populations in the Southwest United States, the answers to these questions vary and often include ideals of preserving language and culture. For the past decade, Crow Canyon Archaeological Center, the Bureau of Land Management, the Society for American Archaeology Public Education Committee, and Northern Arizona University have each collaborated with indigenous communities in formal heritage education efforts to engage students in their own language, cultural history, and identities through archaeology. For heritage educators, the goal is to build bridges with native communities through curriculum development efforts.

Research on effective education for American Indian and Native Alaskan and Hawaiian learners advocates a community based, culturally responsive approach to curriculum planning and development (Cleary and Peacock 1998; Gilliland 1988; Nelson-Barber and Trumbull Estrin 1995; Rhodes 1994). Educators of Native American students often recognize that their students demonstrate a lack of enthusiasm for the traditional school experience (Kawagley and Barnhardt 1999); and that they respond favorably to learning at the local level. Teachers engage the learners' interest and increase their achievement on standardized tests by connecting classroom materials with the students' culture. Evidence gathered from a study of 40 schools nationwide indicates that students learn more effectively within a curriculum grounded at the local level rather than within a traditional educational framework (Lieberman 1998). Cajete (1994) advocates developing a culturally based education program founded upon traditional tribal values, orientations, and principles, while simultaneously using the most appropriate concepts, technologies, and content of modern education.

These changes reflect a transformation of values for Native American education in the United States, which previously only included the views of the dominant English-speaking, Western European culture. Historically, nearly all Native American groups were removed from the eastern half of the country to reservations (Forbes 1964; Nabokov 1991; Prucha 1971; Spicer 1969). In western United States, the Native American assimilation experience was varied (Spicer 1986). Although Native Americans sometimes remained on at least part of their homelands, their education reflected the assimilation views of the dominant Euro-American culture (Hoxie 2001 [1984]:54, 76–77; Quintana 2004:21–22; Simmons 2000:207–209). Secretary of the Interior Carl Schurz described education policy in his 1877 Annual Report. "Education should be compulsory, preferably in boarding schools, with English as the sole language of instruction, thereby breaking the hold of aboriginal kin and society on the minds of the young" (Schurz 2004 [1877]:9–12). Hoxie (2001 [1984]:67–70) points out that because of this policy, not only were Indian schools like mainstream modern schools of the times in philosophy and practice, they had more resources than did schools of other minorities.

The prominent philosopher and educator John Dewey summed it up in 1916:

> Countries like the United States are composed of a combination of different groups with different traditional customs. It is this situation which has...forced the demand for an educational institution which shall provide something like a homogeneous and balanced environment for the young....The intermingling in the school of youth of different

races, differing religions, and unlike customs creates for all a new and broader environment. Common subject matter accustoms all to a unity of outlook upon a broader horizon than is visible to the members of any group while it is isolated. The assimilative force of the American public school is eloquent testimony to the efficacy of the common and balanced appeal. (Dewey 1916)

A major issue in a discussion about native heritage values and curriculum is how and who develops the curriculum about values. Can the issues that are examined be truly authentic if they are written and presented by someone other than a Native American? If there is no Native American involvement in the development of curriculum, is it not another account of the victorious group's version of history? Can curriculum be created to build bridges between the groups? What is the role of archaeologists in this arena?

Heath argues that archaeologists have an ethical imperative to encourage the public to preserve and protect our heritage resources (Heath 1997:72). Implicit in this idea is the idea that the public must understand and appreciate the heritage values of those resources. Logically, this leads to another ethical imperative: to educate the public about the heritage values of the descendents. If this is true, it still leaves open the questions of determining what values are taught and appropriate ways to include the descendents in the process.

There are several ways in which Native Americans and archaeologists have been involved in efforts to create heritage values curriculum and build bridges. The authors will consider four examples with which they have personal experience. The settings represent a private institution, a federal agency, an international professional organization, and an academic institution respectively: Crow Canyon Archaeological Center, the U.S. Bureau of Land Management, the Society for American Archaeology Public Education Committee, and Northern Arizona University.

Crow Canyon Archaeological Center

The Crow Canyon Archaeological Center is located in southwestern Colorado near Cortez and the Ute Mountain Ute Reservation. Not far away are the Southern Ute and Navajo Reservations. Puebloan groups in New Mexico and Arizona are within a half-day's drive from the Center. Crow Canyon's educational program is an example of the evolving efforts of an archaeological research institution to include indigenous people in its archaeological research and educational curriculum development.

UNIVERSITY OF WINCHESTER
LIBRARY

Crow Canyon actively recruits teachers to bring students from all parts of the country to its campus for its experiential curriculum to investigate past and present cultures of the American Southwest (Davis and Connolly 2000:xv). Early efforts to incorporate Native American heritage values relied upon ethnographic information. For example, in 1988 the staff received a grant from the Colorado Council for the Social Studies to incorporate Native American games into the curriculum using ethnographic sources (Heath 1992). A similar effort was made to include Native American stories using some of the many published stories. No effort was made to gather material directly from nearby groups.

A turning point came when some of the teachers and chaperones from nearby schools pointed out that some students, particularly Navajos, were very reticent about touching artifacts; some parents did not allow their children to come to the programs. Traditional Navajos believe that when an individual dies, the best of that person goes away, leaving the malevolent part behind. This malevolency extends to objects and places.

Around 1989 teachers from Chinle, Arizona wanted to bring their sixth grade students to Crow Canyon as a part of their study of ancient civilizations. The teachers wanted their students to understand that an ancient civilization had existed right in their homeland. In the 1980s, Chinle was fairly isolated. In order to convince the school's very traditional parents that a trip to Crow Canyon would not harm their students, the teachers invited Crow Canyon staff to attend a parent meeting in Chinle. After a long conversation in their native language, the parents agreed to a trial program, provided that Crow Canyon could guarantee the students would touch no artifacts.

This agreement meant that the education staff had from November to March to manufacture a wide variety of new "artifacts" that could be used with the students from Chinle. When the first group of teachers, students, and parent chaperones arrived in March, the campus and curriculum were ready. Evaluations were positive enough that the next year more classes from the Chinle school district came for the two-day experience.

The staff learned a great deal about Navajo views and attitudes by conferring with Native American parents. Upon learning that animal stories should not be told during the summer, lest the animal hear it and become angry, the staff began further research. They found that though this belief was widespread in the Southwest, the exact dates after which stories could no longer be told varied from tribe to tribe. To resolve the dilemma, they consulted the nearby Ute Mountain Ute Tribe. Norman Lopez, one of the tribe's cultural keepers, said he believed animal stories could be told until the snow disappeared off the nearby Sleeping Ute Mountain, a place sacred to the tribe. Crow Canyon decided to stop telling animal stories after the snow disappeared off the Sleeping Ute. It was a significant step as new, different stories had to be learned or different programs offered. Thus, the Crow Canyon staff went from writing curriculum *about* Native Americans, to consulting *with* them, to *accepting* their heritage values, and *transforming* the curriculum to meet those values.

Crow Canyon began to include Native Americans more meaningfully as program instructors. It had long included Native Americans by taking its southwest tours to Native American villages to visit artists. In the late 1980s, Crow Canyon added Native Americans as guest instructors for workshops that bridged archaeology with modern artistic practices: pottery making, weaving, jewelry making, flute making, and even cooking. The instructors worked closely with the staff to create the curriculum for the workshops. In the late 1990s, a member of the Ute Mountain Ute Tribe joined the education department as a full-time member. This represented another step in the process of involving Native Americans in presenting heritage values to the public.

According to Marjorie Connolly, Director of American Indian Activities, the most significant institutional event occurred in 1995 when Crow Canyon established a Native American Advisory Board and added a Native American member to its Board of Trustees. This event signaled a long-term investment in establishing trust and respect between Crow Canyon and American Indians (Marjorie Connolly, personal communication, October 10, 2007). The Advisory Board's web page lists numerous accomplishments including members who have authored chapters in Crow Canyon research reports, collaborated in the development of the curriculum, and served as scholars for programs (Crow Canyon Archaeological Center 2007). Connolly believes the establishment in 2007 of a curriculum project with several Pueblo groups represents another leap forward (Marjorie Connolly, personal communication, 2007). According to the Crow Canyon web site, all the Pueblo educators are actively involved in developing native language and traditional knowledge programs in their respective communities, an effort which the Center is pleased to support by providing meeting facilities and a forum for the exchange of ideas. Crow Canyon actively raises funds to support its American Indian Initiative and add to its tuition assistance fund for Native American scholars, elders, and students (Crow Canyon Archaeological Center 2007).

BLM Heritage Education and Project Archaeology

The Bureau of Land Management (BLM), an agency of the Department of the Interior, manages approximately one-eighth of the land in the

United States, or 256 million surface acres. BLM established a heritage education program in 1992 as a result of two major forces. First, the agency was looking for a unique program to meet then-President George H.W. Bush's education goals. The second was a growing awareness of the need to combat vandalism.

"In May 1989, the SAA and other project sponsors held a working conference [in Taos, NM] on looting and vandalism of archaeological sites.... The conference brought together over 70 national experts... and citizens concerned with problem of archaeological looting and vandalism." A summary of their findings listed seven action items; the first two were informing the public and education. (Judge and Bruen 1990:9)

"At about the same time an Interagency Task Force on Cultural Resources formed in Utah to combat rampant vandalism and looting in San Juan County. The BLM, National Park Service, US Forest Service, and the State of Utah decided that educating the children of local citizens would be the most effective tool to combat the looting. The result was the publication of *Intrigue of the Past: Investigating Archaeology (Utah Intrigue)* in 1992. (Smith et al. 1992) *Intrigue* was a classroom-tested set of lessons for the 90s, designed to teach children about archaeology. The authors crafted it so that teachers could use readily available materials for the lessons. The agency and its partners distributed it through workshops led by teams of teachers and archaeologists." (Heath 2007) In order to expose teachers to Native American views, BLM encouraged facilitators to include Native American speakers in the workshops.

Smith and her coauthors submitted the draft lessons to representatives from all of the tribes in Utah and the Hopi of Arizona for review before publishing the book. They received responses from several and used these to revise the book (Jeanne Moe personal communication, October 10, 2007). While the authors did not work directly with Native Americans, they did make use of ethnographic sources. Several lessons include references *about* Native Americans but only one, Lesson 18, "Rock Art One: An Introduction," gives direct Native American views. Four Native American interpretations of a rock art panel are part of the lesson (Smith et al. 1992: 95–98). The book was revised for use in other states as *Intrigue of the Past: A Teacher's Activity guide for Fourth through Seventh Grades (Intrigue)* (Smith et al. 1996).

The Bureau of Land Management wanted all of its western states to have state-specific materials on prehistory available to supplement *Intrigue*. The result was the creation of a new series, *Intrigue of the*

Past: Discovering Archaeology in [state name]. Most, but not all, of the manuscripts were sent to interested tribes for review before publication. Archaeologists wrote a majority of the manuscripts, with a few exceptions. In *Discovering Archaeology in Colorado,* chapter three, "Povi of the Ancient Pueblo People" was written by Tito Naranjo of Santa Clara Pueblo (Heath 1999). The final chapter of *Discovering Archaeology in Alabama* was co-written by Darla Graves, a member of the MOWA band of Choctaw Indians and then Director of the Alabama Indian Affairs Commission, with Linda Derry, an archaeologist. "Modern Indians of Alabama," brings the story of Indians in Alabama up to the present (Driskell et al. 1999).

In 2001, the BLM and its Project Archaeology partner, Montana State University, began the process of updating its Heritage Education program. Project Archaeology is a comprehensive archaeology and heritage education program that includes publications and professional development. *Intrigue* was now nearly ten years old; education and archaeology had undergone transformative changes in the intervening years. Standards and testing had become required for all states under the No Child Left Behind Act (U.S. Department of Education 2002). American archaeology was transformed by the passage of the Native American Graves Protection and Repatriation Act of 1990 (Mihesuah 2000).

In March of 2003, educators and archaeologists from around the United States drafted an outline for a new inquiry-based curriculum on the archaeology of shelter for teachers and their students in grades 3–5. In October of the same year, Project Archaeology staff invited 10 Native American educators from 6 tribes to review the draft curriculum unit and to provide guidance for further development. At that time, the shelter unit consisted of lessons on the basic concepts of archaeology and principles of stewardship along with an archaeological investigation of a Pawnee earthlodge using authentic data from a site in Kansas. The Native American educators at the 2003 workshop suggested that a descendant be included in the curriculum to introduce his or her own culture and to provide an oral history of the shelter type and its contemporary cultural significance. Some of the workshop participants assisted with the curriculum development by reviewing draft versions of the new guide, *Project Archaeology: Investigating Shelter* (2009). They helped contact members of their communities to serve as the Native "voice" to guide students through their investigation. Drafts of the guide were professionally evaluated in 10 classrooms with significant numbers of Native American students. Native American members of descendant communities assisted with the development of four additional pre-Contact shelter investigations, which are currently available via the Project Archaeology website (www.projectarchaeology.org) (Jeanne Moe personal communication, January 6, 2009). This direct inclusion of native voices in the educational materials represents a significant leap from using ethnographic resources in *Intrigue* to using primary sources to present Native American Heritage values. By orienting students in the present, it helps them move backward in time to the archaeological past. Oral histories and accurate archaeological data allow students to draw their own conclusions about the meaning of the archaeological record, the heritage values it represents, and its significance in contemporary life.

Society for American Archaeology Public Education Committee

In 1995, the Society for American Archaeology Public Education Committee (SAA/PEC) established a Native American Education Task Group whose charge was to build collaborative relationships with Native American communities through educator workshops. The intent was to "build bridges" between archaeology (and archaeologists) and Native Americans through classroom instruction. In order to do this, the group needed to demonstrate to Native educators how they could use archaeology education materials such as *Intrigue* to develop and enhance their school curricula. In response, a total of three workshops were offered, two at Haskell Indian Nations University in Lawrence, Kansas, and one as Western Carolina University in Cullowhee, North Carolina. The Task Group also hosted two retreat sessions for planning, professional development, and reflections for workshop instructors and past workshop participants.

The first workshop was held in August 1997 at Haskell Indian Nations University. Twenty-five educators from around the United States attended this four-day workshop. According to the evaluations from this session, teachers increased their knowledge about, and interest in, archaeology. They requested more learning opportunities in archaeology. An unanticipated outcome was the enhanced cultural learning among the mixed group of Native participants. They enjoyed learning about the heritage of other Native peoples across the country and about their tribal efforts to promote their own culture, language, and history.

One Hopi teacher, Bernita Duwahoyeoma (Mrs. D) admitted that she never thought about teaching her students Hopi language and culture using archaeology as one of her methods until she attended this workshop. After participating in the workshop, she says that she discovered professionals were approaching archaeology with a new attitude that included not only studying archaeology using scientific methods, but also using a descendant culture's stories and beliefs. Now, her interest in teaching archaeology is built on a need and desire to maintain the language and culture of the Hopi people. She believes that archaeology can offer explanations for things that have been previously a mystery and that the information from archaeological work helps to support a traditional way of life. Mrs. D says,

> "Our Hopi life is changing and there is a very strong personal desire for our Hopi young people to hear about and understand what makes us who we are. Our ancestors set down a life plan for us, which is very rich and complicated and includes values and rules that were meant to help us survive. It would be detrimental to forget ourselves." She further adds, "Like the Hopi, no one knows for sure everything about why we live the way we do or do the things we do. Archaeology helps to provide scientific information and explanations for us. It gives us a reason to hold onto what remains of ourselves and to pass it on." (Clark and Duwahoyeoma 1999)

Building on the experiences learned from the first workshop, the SAA/PEC held a second workshop in Cullowhee, North Carolina in 1998. Co-hosted by Western Carolina University and the Museum of the Eastern Band of Cherokee, this workshop drew 16 educators to the hills and forests of western North Carolina. A third workshop in 1999, held again at Haskell Indian Nations University, included 14 educators and 2 Native educators from previous workshops who co-taught with 2 archaeologists (Clark 2001).

An intensive 2-day planning session involving native educators and archaeologists preceded the third 1999 workshop. A Hopi educator helping to lead the session suggested that the professional development follow the archetypical Hero's Journey in which "a hero ventures forth from the world of common day into a region of supernatural wonder: fabulous forces are encountered and a decisive victory is won: the hero comes back from this mysterious adventure with the power to bestow boons on his fellow man" (Campbell 1973). The Hero's Journey usually takes the form of a cycle: separation from the ordinary world, initiation through great trials, and finally a return with new knowledge and powers. The instructors guided participants through the hero's cycle throughout the workshop and employed the metaphor to negotiate the sometimes sensitive issues that occasionally arise when dealing with archaeology and Native American heritage. The participating teachers were heroes in a way, leaving their communities to attend this professional development. In the process they explored scientific and cultural ways of interpreting the past and communicating that with native youth.

This multi-method approach to teaching with archaeology often raised negative feelings about the dominant culture and exploitation of native peoples. By working through these trials, the teachers developed new knowledge and ideas for incorporating archaeology in their curriculum upon their return.

This Hero's Journey workshop transformed how the SAA/PEC would make future educational collaborations with indigenous communities. A poem written by one of workshop participants eloquently outlines the journey, upon which we still are traveling.

A Hero's Journey

We came together from far and wide,
To gather under the Kansas sky.
We've travel life's trails far apart,
But share a common denominator of the heart.

To challenge young minds to wonder and ask,
What is the significance of this thing called the past?
Can Indians and archaeologists teach on common ground,
With a place for all, while honoring cultural bounds?

We've struggled with tradition and method and theory,
Until smiles became strained and soul's grew weary,
But still we heard the call of a distant dream,
And now must ask if this journey has been all that it seemed.

Did we really listen and not just hear?
Was that respect, chasing anger and fear?
Do we hold one truth among us all?
That the past that defines us can make our young stand tall.

Did we find a hero inside of each one,
With the courage to continue a quest just begun?
Only time can answer the questions here pressed.
Our actions will be the score on this test.
    Jackie Rice July 1999

As 1999 moved into 2000, and after five years of planning, fund raising, meetings, and three workshops, the SAA/PEC determined it was time to assess how their efforts at "building bridges" with Native Americans through archaeology were working. To this end, it held a series of two- to three-day retreats involving native participants and archaeologists from previous workshops to reflect and plan next steps. The group acknowledged that while the three national workshops were successful, building bridges with Native American communities was going to be a long process requiring more than just workshops. A bridge is a two-way structure, and the workshops really only addressed a one-way effort to teach Native educators how to use archaeology education materials. The workshops were general and not tied to specific, local contexts. As a result, teaching archaeology in native communities was often a solitary effort of individual heroic teachers and as such has not been sustained or expanded.

Further, the group concluded that cultural relevancy, language, and community were integral to the success of any native heritage education efforts. National workshops may not be the right technique to accomplish the desire of archaeologists to collaborate with native communities. The group decided that a two-way bridge should be developed in collaboration with native educators and archaeologists: archaeologists can learn about specific cultural heritage values and issues and native educators can learn how archaeologists study the past and how their research complements (or not) traditional values (Clark 2001).

Hopi Footprints Project: Hopi Tribe and Northern Arizona University's Center for Science Teaching and Learning and Department of Anthropology

In 2003, the SAA/PEC decided to provide seed money to develop a pilot curriculum project to incorporate archaeological and cultural ideas into classroom lessons for Hopi youth. The project was proposed by the Hopi Tribe and Northern Arizona University's (NAU) Center for Science Teaching and Learning, and the Department of Anthropology. This partnership was possible due to several prior years of reciprocal efforts between Hopi communities and NAU faculty and students working side by side to address issues critical to Native communities (Vasquez and Jenkins 1994). The *Hopi Footprints* project is a curriculum and professional development project that involved the creation of culturally relevant lessons and supplemental technology resources for Hopi teachers and students of grades K-6.

The Hopi people live in a remote, high desert area in northern Arizona. They are corn farmers who have lived and adapted to a harsh environment on the Colorado Plateau for thousands of years. Their oral histories and stories of clan migrations are tangible in the many archaeological sites from which their ancestors came. These places are their *footprints* and connect them to their past and their future (Kuwaniwisima 2002). Traditional Hopi values and life ways are carried on from the teachings of the ancestors. Typically, passing on these teachings take place in village kivas where the older generations instruct the younger in Hopi ways. Although kivas are the best place for teaching this knowledge, many elders have come to believe that language and culture can also be taught in schools. Sadly, many Hopi youth are not learning the Hopi language, which is key to understanding and sustaining cultural knowledge, values, and traditions.

Using archaeology and elder oral history as a foundation, the project cultivates an understanding of past cultural traditions that are linked to today's Hopi people and to future Hopi cultural preservation. By exploring these footprints together, elders, archaeologists, teachers, curriculum specialists, and youth created a context in which cultural knowledge and continuity are shared in relevant and meaningful ways. The final results of this collaboration are 12 culture lessons with an accompanying CD-ROM containing additional videos and images to supplement student learning (Gumerman et al. 2005).

The process of developing this curriculum was iterative and included multiple opportunities for substantive interactions among archaeologists, multimedia developers, educational specialists, and Hopi elders, teachers, and tribal specialists. Field trips provided opportunities to visit Hopi heritage sites where elder oral histories were recorded as well as archaeologists' interpretations and interactive group conversations. The collaborators had lengthy dialogues about how to incorporate these ideas into appropriate lessons for Hopi youth. After many hours of dialogue in Hopi and English, the group agreed that the overarching goal of the Hopi Footprints culture curriculum is to help students understand what it means to be Hopi by learning about Hopi culture, language, and history while addressing educational standards. The lessons address four cultural themes: Hopi culture, Hopi foods, Hopi communities, and Hopi environment (Gumerman et al. 2005). These themes were selected because they represent aspects of Hopi life critical for students to understand. The curriculum includes a complementary CD-ROM that incorporates a variety of primary and secondary source information such as images, maps, and video clips of elders and archeologists. The CD-ROM is organized according to the four themes and is searchable so that the media can be viewed and downloaded by students or teachers. For instance, if a teacher is working on a clan lesson, she can find video clips, audio of clan pronunciations, and images of clan symbols. Students can also use the resources for their assignments. If they do not have someone they can interview for their village history assignment, they can watch the video of an elder talking about the history of a particular village (Gumerman et al. 2005).

Upon reflection of the overall project, participating teachers indicated that they learned most from the collaborative aspect of the project, learning from each other on the fieldtrips, and from using the *Understanding By Design* (Wiggins and McTighe 1998, 2005) curriculum development process. One teacher further commented about the benefits of collaborative work: "The bridging of cultural knowledge and teaching culture is so essential with Hopi lessons. We need to know what could be taught or what couldn't be taught with the help of elders" (Clark and Gumerman 2006). The *Hopi Footprints* project expanded in 2007 to working directly with Hopi high school aged youth. The *Footprints of the Ancestors* project now involves Hopi youth, teachers, professionals, and elders along with archaeologists, educators, and multimedia specialists visiting Hopi heritage sites, participating in community projects, and developing digital Hopi youth guides about these places.

The Changing Times

If we operate on the premise that as a global society we value what matters and that we value our heritage, then we must act upon those values. Native American heritage values have previously not been included in significant ways in heritage education. The dominant Western culture in the United States valued its own history above that of its indigenous populations. Recent efforts by programs such as the ones described in this chapter are making strides in formal and informal education curriculum to change heritage education. This shift in the paradigm of how we as archaeology educators and indigenous community educators design and implement heritage curriculum has moved us from simply writing about Native Americans using ethnographic references to including native voices in teaching about archaeology and finally, to including archaeology as part of broader-based culturally relevant ways to teach about culture and history. Native Americans become equal givers of knowledge and creators of curricula through these cultural knowledge exchanges. In essence it has transformed how archaeology educators work and are involved with indigenous communities.

References

Cajete, Gregory
1994 *Look To The Mountain: An Ecology Of Indigenous Education*. Durango, Colorado: Kivakí Press.

Campbell, Joseph
1973 *The Hero with a Thousand Faces.* Princeton, New Jersey: Princeton University Press.

Clark, Joëlle
2001 Development of Archaeology Education Programs in Collaboration with Native Americans: Accomplishments and Visions of the PEC. *The SAA Archaeology Record* 1(4):9.

Clark, Joëlle, and Bernita Duwahoyeoma
1999 A Tale of Two Strategies: Teaching Hopi Culture and Archaeology. Paper presented at 64th Annual Meeting of the Society for American Archaeology, Chicago, March 26.

Clark, Joëlle, and George Gumerman
2006 Final Report: Teaching With Archaeology: New Perspectives on Science and Culture for Native American Educators. Manuscript on file, Arizona Board of Regents, Phoenix.

Clark, Kate, ed.
2006 Capturing the Public Value of Heritage: The Proceedings of the London Conference 25–26: January 2006. Swindon, United Kingdom: English Heritage.

Cleary, Linda Miller, and Thomas D. Peacock
1998 *Collected Wisdom: American Indian Education.* Boston: Allyn and Bacon.

Crow Canyon Archaeological Center
2007 About Crow Canyon, Crow Canyon Education. Electronic document, www.crowcanyon.org, accessed October 9, 2007.

Davis, M. Elaine, and Marjorie R. Connolly, eds.
2000 *Windows into the Past: Crow Canyon Archaeological Center's Guide for Teachers.* Dubuque, Iowa: Kendall/Hunt.

Dewey, John
1916 The Democracy of Education, 1916. Chapter Two: Education as a Social Function. Electronic document, http://www.ilt.columbia.edu/publica-tions/Projects/digitexts/dewey/d_e/chapter02.html, accessed September 14, 2007.

Driskell, Boyce, Susan White Driskell, Linda Derry, Darla Graves, and Karen J. Laubenstein
1999 *Intrigue of the Past: Discovering Archaeology in Alabama.* Washington D.C.: Alabama Historical Commission and the U.S. Department of the Interior Bureau of Land Management.

Forbes, Jack D., ed.
1964 *The Indian in America's Past.* Englewood Cliffs, New Jersey: Prentice-Hall.

Gilliland, Hap
1988   *Teaching the Native American.* 2nd edition. Dubuque, Iowa: Kendall/Hunt.

Gumerman, George, Joëlle Clark, and Doris Honanie
2005   Hopi Footprints: A Cultural Curriculum for Hopi Schools. Paper presented at the 70th Annual Meeting of the Society for American Archaeology, Salt Lake City, March 31.

Heath, Margaret A.
1992   Crow Canyon 1986–1992: Archaeology Curriculum for All Ages. Manuscript on file, BLM Heritage Education Program files, Dolores, Colorado.
1997   Successfully Integrating the Public into Research: Crow Canyon Archaeological Center. In *Presenting Archaeology to the Public: Digging for Truths.* John H. Jameson, Jr., ed. Pp. 65–72. Walnut Creek, California: AltaMira Press.
2007   Getting People to Stop, Look, and Listen in America's Backyard: The Changing Face of the BLM Heritage Education Program. Paper presented at the 72nd Annual Meeting of the Society for American Archaeology, Austin, Texas, April 27.

Heath, Margaret A., ed.
1999   *Intrigue of the Past: Discovering Archaeology in Colorado.* U.S. Washington D.C: Department of the Interior Bureau of Land Management.

Hoxie, Frederick E.
2001 [1984]   *A Final Promise: The Campaign to Assimilate the Indians, 1880–1920,* Bison Books, University of Nebraska Press, Lincoln, Nebraska.

Judge, James, and Bliss Bruen (compilers)
1990   Save the Past for the Future: Actions for the '90s: Final Report, Taos Working Conference on Preventing Archaeological Looting and Vandalism. Washington, D.C.: Society for American Archaeology.

Kawagley, Angayuqaq Oscar, and Ray Barnhardt
1999   *Education Indigenous to Place: Western Science Meets Native Reality.* New York: State University of New York Press.

Kuwaniwisima, Leigh
2002   Hopit Navotiat, Hopi Knowledge of History: Hopi Presence on Black Mesa. In *Prehistoric Culture Change on the Colorado Plateau.* Shirley Powell and Francis E. Smiley, eds. Pp. 161–163. Tucson: University of Arizona Press.

Lieberman, Gerald A.
1998   *Closing the Achievement Gap: Using the Environment as an Integrating Context for Learning.* Poway, California: Science Wizards.

Mihesuah, Devon A., ed.
2000   *Repatriation Reader: Who Owns American Indian Remains?* Lincoln, Nebraska: University of Nebraska Press.

Nabokov, Peter, ed.
1991   *Native American Testimony: A Chronicle of Indian-White Relations From Prophecy to the Present, 1492–1992.* New York: Penguin Books.

Nelson-Barber, Sharon, and Elise Trumbull Estrin
1995   *Culturally Responsive Mathematics and Science Education for Native Students.* San Francisco, California: The Native Education Initiative of the Regional Educational Laboratory Network, WestEd.

Prucha, Francis Paul
1971 [1962]   *American Indian Policy in the Formative Years: The Indian Trade and Intercourse Acts, 1790–1834.* University of Nebraska Press, Lincoln.

Quintana, Frances Leon
2004   *Ordeal of Change: The Southern Utes and Their Neighbors.* Walnut Creek, California: AltaMira Press.

Rhodes, Robert W.
1994   *Nurturing Learning in Native American Students.* Hotevilla, Arizona: Sonwai Books.

Schurz, Carl
2004 [1877]   Report of the Secretary of the Interior. Washington, D.C.: Government Printing Office, pp. 9–12. Quoted in Frances Leon Quintana 2004. *Ordeal of Change: The Southern Utes and Their Neighbors.* Pp. 1–2. Walnut Creek, California: AltaMira Press.

Simmons, Virginia McConnell
2000   *The Ute Indians of Utah, Colorado, and New Mexico.* Boulder: University Press of Colorado.

Smith, Shelley J, Kelly A. Letts, Jeanne M. Moe, and Danielle Paterson
1992   Intrigue of the Past: Investigating Archaeology. Salt Lake City, Utah: Utah Interagency Task Force on Cultural Resources. Bureau of Land Management.
1996   *Intrigue of the Past: A Teacher's Activity Guide for Fourth Through Seventh Grades,* 2nd printing. Delores, CO.: U.S. Bureau of Land Management, Anasazi Heritage Center.

Spicer, Edward H.
1969   *A Short History of the Indians of the United States.* New York: Van Nostrand Reinhold Company.
1986   *Cycles of Conquest.* 8th edition. Tucson: University of Arizona Press.

U.S. Department of Education
2002   No Child Left Behind Act of 2001. Public Law 107–110. 107th Congress. January 8, 2002.

Vasquez, Miguel and Leigh Jenkins
1994   Reciprocity and Sustainability: Terrace Restoration on Third Mesa. *Practicing Anthropology* 16(2):14–17.

Wiggins, Grant, and Jay McTighe
1998   *Understanding by Design.* Alexandria, Virginia: Association for Supervision and Curriculum Development.
2005   *Understanding by Design.* Expanded 2nd edition. Alexandria, Virginia: Association for Supervision and Curriculum Development.

12

THE PAST IN THE PRESENT: ISSUES, PERSPECTIVES,
AND CHALLENGES IN TEACHING AND LEARNING
ARCHAEOLOGY

Karina Croucher

Introduction

In this chapter I hope to begin to address heritage values and their role
in teaching archaeology in Higher Education (HE) at universities in the
United Kingdom (see the chapters by Chilton; and Clark and Heath
in this volume). This paper is written from a UK perspective, resulting
from work with the Higher Education Academy's (HEA) Subject Centre
for History, Classics and Archaeology (HCA).[1] Through addressing
ideological, practical, and educational factors, I will outline changes
that are taking place in the United Kingdom, embedding them in their
motivational and historical backgrounds. I will begin with a brief outline of the history of the discipline and the question of "whose past it
is anyway?" before discussing implications for teaching, learning, and
practice, outlining some of the current initiatives and research taking
place, as well as some of the remaining challenges.

Ideology: The Background to Archaeology
in Education Today

Two key factors arise from the historical background of archaeology.
One relates to concepts of ownership of the past, and the other, to
previous notions of social evolution. The discipline's roots lie in anti-
quarianism, originating from the leisurely pursuits of the wealthy and
their "excavations" of barrows and other monuments for the treasures
they yielded. Key proponents, such as John Aubrey (1626–1697) and

William Stukeley (1687–1765), began to investigate and map sites in Britain, including the Avebury Complex and Stonehenge (Stukeley 1790 [1740], 1743). The processes of mapping and collecting influenced, and were influenced by, the construction of museums, such as the Ashmolean in Oxford, completed in 1683. The quests for the collection of items from the past, and from afar, were furthered by the following periods of colonialism, with "Grand Tours" bringing treasures to Britain and Europe from distant and exotic shores. During the late 18th century and onwards, museums including the British Museum in London, the Louvre in France, and New York's Metropolitan Museum were filled with artifacts from across the globe, involving the shipping of ancient monuments across continents in huge logistical feats. The acquisition of artifacts such as the Rosetta Stone, Sargon II's Palace Sculptures, and Ninevah Palace Treasures (to name but a few) undeniably portray an understanding of ownership of the past (and of the world's heritage) by the West (Croucher and Romer 2007). There has been a longing in Western culture for material from distant places resulting in our lavish (although undoubtedly educational) museum collections, and in many respects, these principles and desires of ownership still remain today for some. Walker commented in 1997 that, "if we could show the emotional link between the collector and the museum as an object, I suspect its label would read 'Envy, Western object based on collecting and control'" (Walker 1997; see Carman 2005; Curtis 2006; Lord and Jarron 2006; Merriman 1991, 2004; Messenger 1999; O'Neil 2006; Stone and Molyneaux 1994 for discussions on museums, concepts of value, worth and ownership, and cultural identity).

More rigorous archaeological practices of excavation and display were established by General Pitt Rivers (1827–1900). Ideals of military precision and rigor were applied to excavation, with Pitt Rivers conducting the extensive excavation of Cranbourne Chase (Pitt Rivers 1898), and the opening of the Pitt Rivers museum in 1884, ordering artifacts according to type and form. Inherent in studies of the past at this time was the underlying acceptance of social evolution (Pluciennik 2005), with peoples from the past perceived as "primitive," "savage," or even "barbaric," lower down on a social evolutionary scale which culminated in the modern, Western industrialist at the pinnacle.

While attitudes and values have undeniably changed since the early days of archaeology, it is still the case that the discipline developed in an age during which values concerning the past were considerably different from those held today. Although we now strive to reach beyond these origins, many of the structures and institutions in place still often perpetuate the ideals of the past in which they were constructed.

Practice

The way that archaeology is carried out in many regions of world still perpetuates colonial methodological and ideological practices. Many of Britain's excavation projects abroad take place under the sponsorship of British Schools and Institutions. While these organizations clearly perform a vital role—many research projects would simply not take place without their support—it is easy to see how colonial attitudes might be perpetuated, including ideas of ownership over the past. Reassuringly however, steps are being taken to ensure that the British Schools, Institutes and projects overcome such perceptions. Projects employ and work with local academics and specialists, and involve local communities, not simply in manual labour, but in gaining an understanding of the archaeological practice taking place, its relevance, and contribution to the production of archaeological knowledge. The involvement of local communities in archaeology can play a crucial role in breaking down barriers and building relationships (Parker Pearson and Ramilisonina 2004:238), as well as raising an awareness and appreciation of archaeology (Mapunda and Lane 2004; Watkins et al. 2000).

The continued work of archaeologists with local communities will hopefully go some way toward overturning perceptions of "Western" ownership over the past (arriving, excavating and removing material, with little return for local communities). Essential in all of this however, is accessibility and communication. Reassuringly, it is now common for project organizers and participants to learn the host language, with obvious implications for communication, understanding, and local involvement. However, while many site reports are written in English, clearly of value from a global perspective (without which a greater fragmentation of knowledge would result), few are translated into indigenous languages. Making material available in local languages, and making information locally accessible, including the use of visual displays (so that literacy is not a condition of access to information), allows greater access to the past and is one step in ensuring that the results of fieldwork and research projects are not retained exclusively by Western scholars. As Roger Matthews commented in 2003, "Archaeology needs to be removed from its ivory towers of the West and integrated on local terms in local languages amongst local peoples" (2003:199–201). In short, communication is vital.

Legislation is now preventing the removal of antiquities in many countries, which means that material is, at least in theory, accessible locally. However, in reality, museums can be poorly funded, and often artifacts do not make their way out of dusty cardboard boxes stored in their cellars. This is an area that remains a global challenge, that many communities do not perceive a value in archaeology—it is arguably a luxury pursuit, one that should not come before food and clothing, or indeed peace (albeit the case that heritage may have a role to play in mediation and communication). However, how do you begin to embed a "global" understanding of the value of the past and heritage values, when facing so many other issues and challenges, many of which are life-threatening? And indeed, what are the ethics behind imposing our beliefs and attitudes toward the past onto others? It is hoped that through involvement and communication, an understanding and balance can be sought between local needs and the global value of heritage, as well as contributing toward a sense of pride in local archaeology.

We are all familiar with how powerful a tool the past can be from negative contexts; the use, manipulation, and corruption of heritage is not something we are unfamiliar with. The most famous example is probably the use of Kossinna's (1911) *The Origin of the Germans* in attempts to legitimize the aims of Hitler and the Nazi Party (Arnold 1990; Arnold and Hassmann 1995; Veit 1989). Conversely, although the debates are too lengthy to be entered into here, the past often plays a powerful role in gains for marginalized and mistreated groups, such as Aboriginal or Native American struggles with presiding governments over land claims, demonstrating the importance of the past, not just in contributing toward understandings of identities, but in situating them geographically, with resulting political implications (Hamilakis and Duke 2007; Kohl and Fawcett 1995; Meskell 1998).

Alternative Narratives

An important factor in the accessibility of the past is the role of investigating alternative narratives. Rosemary Joyce (2002:2) has argued that "the creation of narratives is a practice that literally binds the discipline of archaeology together from the field through to formal and informal presentation of interpretations." Enabling alternative accounts to be voiced can be important; often these include accounts that have previously been marginalized, including those that contest the current status quo, political situation, or official narratives about the past. Research is being actively undertaken to provide alternative accounts and present research on less-mainstream themes and areas. For example, in 2007 the World Archaeology Inter-Congress saw the launch of Leslie-Gail Atkinson's (2006) *The Earliest Inhabitants: The Dynamics of the Jamaican Ta'mo*, a landmark publication produced by an Indigenous scholar working on the archaeologies of Jamaica's populations prior to slavery.

Alternative narratives can also be seen at a more local level. For example, a project in Devon (southwest England), is exploring the use of oral narratives to "augment, destabilise and even challenge existing scientific knowledge, as well as offering alterative narratives" (Riley and Harvey 2005:270). The project demonstrates the use of oral histories to both "destabilise the linear and scientifically derived narratives of landscape development," as well as "offer alternative, personally or socially embedded narratives that reflect the contingency of all processes of knowledge production—to allow a hidden community to 'speak out'" (Riley and Harvey 2005:282). Recent research has also been undertaken by Sian Jones (2004) into the Hilton of Cadboll in Scotland; an 8th century AD Pictish cross-slab. The research has investigated the role of monuments in people's understandings of and engagements with local heritage, and of peoples' senses of ownership of the past (Jones 2004, 2006). Such research demonstrates that local involvement, and investigating attitudes that are not always commensurate with policy, scientific knowledge, or other broader agendas and regimes, can elucidate relationships between local histories, monuments, landscapes, heritage, and identities. The study of alternative accounts and interpretations of the past clearly has a role to play in peoples' values of heritage.

Education

Education can be crucial in embedding an understanding of the past and a value of heritage. It can also be fundamental in overturning prejudices and misconceptions about the past. Some such misconceptions have previously been perpetuated through teaching and popular media, demonstrated for example through research undertaken in 1987 in the United Kingdom, questioning 10–12 year olds (Emmott 1987). The results demonstrated that the pupils saw people of the past, and of non-Western cultures, as less intelligent than Western people. These results were argued to be a consequence of portrayals of the past and non-Western cultures that are populated with "savages" and "barbarians," and representations that portray "a distorted, ethnocentric and sexist view of the past, which forms a lasting impression and impinges on [children's] images of the present" (Emmott 1987:139, in Pearce 1997:238). One step in changing attitudes includes addressing the language used; removing derogatory terms such as "primitive" does influence how people perceive the past and other societies (Price 1991:14), although this needs to be part of a wider effort to portray more accurate, and less ethnocentric, representations of the past and other societies.

However, it is not simply colonial attitudes and perceptions of the past that are often perpetuated; there are additionally a range of other attitudes and beliefs that are disseminated through our teaching. Many fundamental aspects of human behavior that we take for granted can be argued to be socially constructed. For instance, beliefs about families, gender roles, and sexuality are all socially constructed, yet are continually projected into the past. It has been repeatedly argued that such perpetuations of the present into the past serve to legitimize the present, making the current status quo appear "natural" and universal (Dowson 2000, 2006; Gatens 2004 [1992]; Gero 1993; Tringham 2000). In reality, we know from an abundance of ethnographic material that modern Western ways of living are far from universal and natural; there are a variety of ways that communities live and integrate, involving alternative family structures from our own, as well as different gender roles, and understandings of sexualities (e.g., Morris 1995; Strathern 1988; Yates 1993). Yet archaeologists naturally portray in their interpretations situations they are most familiar with; this is not usually a conscious decision, but rather a subconscious familiarization of the past, and a tendency to "create the past in our own image" (Shennan 1989:30).

Not only does this situation apply to gender, family roles, and sexual identities, but additionally to many of the fundamental understandings of what it is to be human, such as individuality, beliefs about the human body, and about relationships between people and animals, and people and material culture (Boyd 2004; Descola and Pálsson 1996; Fowler 2004; Ingold 1996, 2000; MacCormack and Strathern 1980; Moore 1988; Ortner 1974; Rotman 2006). Anthropological case studies have revealed a variety of alternative ways of perceiving the human body and concepts of personhood and identity, including understandings of dividual bodies, permeable bodies, and alternative understandings of animals, objects, and the surrounding world (see for example, Bird-David 1991; Busby 1997; Strathern 1988).

These factors are increasingly being taken into account in Higher Education, including recognizing alternative narratives, and alternative approaches to the past, and making them more acceptable, credible, and accessible. We are seeing an increase in modules in archaeology dealing with issues of gender, sexuality and identity, as well as encompassing different attitudes to world and regional archaeologies (Hull 2006; Romer 2005, 2006), with a growing recognition of the significance of local archaeologies.

It is valuable to encourage in students of archaeology an understanding of the variety of human experience, and recognition that the modern Western perspective is not a unique, universal one. It can be argued even, that we have a duty to open students' eyes to alternative narratives of the past, and the role of these narratives in identity constructions today. This includes an understanding of a common heritage, not one simply based on modern location, as well as recognition that the modern Western situation is not universal, and not inherent in past societies. Within this, an appreciation of both local and global scales of ownership, relevance, and context needs to be maintained.

Education: Who, What, and How

In addition to a recognition of the importance of the subject matter taught, there has been in the United Kingdom a recognition of the need to be more inclusive—to move away from elitism and "ivory towers," and make education more accessible for all. This includes measures to change *who* is being taught, as well as *how*, and *what* they are taught and learn.

Government legislation in the United Kingdom has been a driver promoting accessibility for all to Higher Education Institutions, aiming for equality in accessibility to HE for those from different social backgrounds, as well as for those with disabilities, including the implementation of the Special Education Needs and Disability Act (SENDA) (OPSI 2001), ensuring accessibility for those with disabilities. There has also been a Race Relations Amendment Act (OPSI 2000), ensuring equal opportunities based on racial background. With relation to heritage, these measures reflect Government-commissioned research by English Heritage into the need for heritage to be accessible to all (English Heritage 2000). This research highlighted the disenfranchisement felt by many communities in relation to heritage—with recommendations for the integration of historic environment teaching in schools, the need to reflect a multicultural society through education and teacher training, and the acknowledgment of the "contributions, values and needs of different social groups" in the heritage sector—encouraging educational and community involvement (English Heritage 2000:23). Such research reflects the growing climate of recognition of the importance of inclusivity and equality, and has in part led to resources being made accessible for schools, including *Archaeology for Schools* by the National Trust for Scotland (2007), and recently the *Learning Outside the Classroom* Manifesto by the Government's Department for Children, Schools and Families (2007). Research has recently been undertaken by Philips et al. (2007) addressing accessibility to archaeological fieldwork for those with disabilities, reflecting aims to ensure the discipline is more inclusive; while gender imbalances in archaeology in HE have been rectified, there remains a lack of diversity in relation to ethnicity, social backgrounds, and disabilities (Croucher et al. 2008).

The introduction of targets for 50 percent of school leavers to have studied for a Higher Education qualification by 2010 (Aim Higher 2007) has resulted in the implementation of initiatives for widening participation (see Shaw et al. 2007 and the *Learning and Teaching for Social Diversity* [Hockings and Cooke 2008] project for a more generic outlook, and Booth 2003, 2005 for widening participation and diversity in history). Events are also taking place to try to engage a broader audience in Higher Education. For example, *Diversity and the Curriculum* (HEA 2007), *Diversity and the Past* (HCA 2006, 2007; see Croucher and Tatlock 2006; Tatlock 2008), and *Curriculum Innovation for Diversity* (UK Centre for Materials Education 2006) aimed at highlighting and disseminating methods for diversification and equality, including recruitment and retention. Universities are undertaking projects to engage with local schools and communities, activities that are generally embraced by most archaeology departments (Dhanjal and Stripe 2007; Fenwick 2004; Lewis 2007; Tatlock 2007). In addition to providing master classes and taster days, universities are also using citizenship in the curriculum to foreground archaeological and historical issues prior to university attendance (Dunne and Brown 2002).

Additionally, universities are beginning to recognize the importance of making the curriculum itself more diverse (Hull 2006; Romer 2005, 2006), through addressing assessment, subject choice, and teaching methods. While many measures are usually aimed at particular defined groups (such as those from lower socio-economic groups, Black and Minority Ethnic Groups, and those with a disability), such measures ultimately benefit all students, including those with different learning styles (Croucher and Romer 2007 for more on this topic). Departments are beginning to recognize that it is not simply recruitment measures that need to be diverse, but teaching, learning, and support mechanisms to ensure the retention of students in HE.

There is also a recognition that to ensure diversity of the student body in the future, role models are needed today, encouraging diversity, demonstrating the available options, and highlighting achievements (Monk 2000; Wellens et al. 2004; Zinkiewicz and Trapp 2004 for examples from other disciplines). In archaeology, work with local communities is taking place, including research by Richard Benjamin into black peoples' engagement with heritage and the past (2006). Benjamin's research highlighted the importance of the concept of relevance in engaging black communities with archaeology and the past. Work is also currently underway at Manchester University, aimed at incorporating migrant communities into museum work, as well as the appointment of direct contacts to work within local communities. Community work continually remains a focus of archaeology in the

United Kingdom, with the Council for British Archaeology (CBA)[2] and others committed to making archaeology accessible. Recent conferences and events have been held on these issues, including *Archaeology for All* (The University of Manchester Field Archaeology Unit 2006) and *Archaeology in the Community* (UCL Institute of Archaeology 2006), as well as the establishment of the Council for British Archaeology's *Community Archaeology Forum* (2007, run by Daniel Hull), and the forthcoming employment of a community archaeology post within the CBA (Richard Lee, personal communication, June 26, 2008). The CBA has recently called for an increased involvement of academia in community and voluntary archaeology, encouraging Higher Education to take a greater role in engagement with the community and with voluntary sectors (Henson and Hull 2007).

Community archaeology also plays an important role for lifelong/adult learners. Engaging with lifelong learners is particularly important for archaeology (Speight and Henson 2004), as the subject is often taken up later in life. However, the late study of archaeology is becoming increasingly difficult as the result of recent changes to government funding policy (Department for Innovation, Universities and Skills 2009), involving the cutting of funds to universities for those studying for a second degree, as well as increasing costs for part-time courses. Consequently, the financial implications for studying archaeology part-time as an adult learner are becoming increasingly prohibitive.

The education sector faces additional problems through the marginalization of archaeology in the curriculum, including the abolition of the archaeology secondary school qualification at the General Certification of Secondary Education (GCSE) level (taken at age 15/16), the comparable threat to the Classics GCSE, and a clouded future for archaeology "A" levels (Henson 2008). The threat caused by the marginalization of these subjects not only has a direct impact on the future sustainability of the discipline, but also on the coming generations' understanding of the value of the past. Measures are being taken to attempt to redress the balance, with the continuation of archaeology, at least in some form, through a new history GCSE incorporating elements of archaeology (Henson 2008).

The initiatives and projects outlined above go a long way toward making archaeology more accessible, and broadening the appeal of the past, as well as redressing traditional concepts of ownership of the past. However, there is clearly still a long way to go and many challenges to overcome. Primarily, it is arguably through influencing policy that big impacts can be seen. However, there remains scope at a more local level to make the past more accessible to all, through research, events, and initiatives, and through changing attitudes and motivations.

Conclusion

It is well accepted that the past is re-created in the present, with the role of interpretation as prominent as scientific method (Hodder 1982, 1985, 1986; Kohl and Fawcett 1995; Trigger 1984, 1985, 1989). As Hodder (1997:18) has argued, "theory has undermined the notion of neutral practice," with a demand for interpretation and a need to "bring the past to life." It is therefore essential that archaeologists are aware of their responsibilities and positions of power in presenting the past: "We must develop a greater consciousness about our own power as archaeologists" (Parker Pearson 1997:231). The role of archaeological educators is fundamental in this, both for passing on responsible, accurate accounts of the past, and for embedding an understanding of the relevance of the past to all, and "an awareness of the self in relation to the past" (Insoll 2007:122, discussing Johnson 1999 and Hodder 1999).

In this chapter, I hope I have brought together some reflections on the role that education has to play in nurturing an understanding of the importance of the past; such values and concepts are learned, and therefore must be taught (Smith 2006:4). Education plays a fundamental role in embedding and perpetuating a value of the past and heritage. It is clear that changes are occurring, and need to continue, at a range of levels; ideological (in recognizing the role education has to play, and the associated responsibilities, including a recognition of the role of alternative narratives of the past); practical (in engaging schools and communities in archaeology); and educational (ensuring that in addition to broader recruitment, students are supported through accommodating for different learning styles, through subject content, assessment methods, and teaching). It is hoped that through approaches combining these factors, education can play an even greater role in embedding an understanding of the importance of heritage, both for today, and into the future.

Acknowledgments

I would like to thank Wendelin Romer, Janet Tatlock, and Dan Hull for their comments on this paper. Thanks are also due to the Higher Education Academy and the British Academy. Any errors are, of course, my own.

Endnotes

1. The History, Classics and Archaeology Subject Centre's website contains various resources to support teaching and learning in its discipline

areas: www.heacademy.ac.uk/hca. For more generic teaching and learning resources and information, see www.heacademy.ac.uk

2. The Council for British Archaeology (CBA) provides various resources to support access to archaeology for all (http://www.britarch.ac.uk/), including hosting the Community Archaeology Forum (http://www.britarch.ac.uk/caf/wikka.php?wakka=HomePage).

References

Aim Higher
2007   University and Higher Education. Electronic document, www.aimhigher.ac.uk/about_us/about_aimhigher.cfm, accessed November 10, 2008.

Arnold, Bettina
1990   The Past as Propaganda: Totalitarian Archaeology in Nazi Germany. *Antiquity* 64(244):464–478.

Arnold, Bettina, and Henning Hassmann
1995   Archaeology in Nazi Germany. In *Nationalism, Politics, and the Practice of Archaeology*. Phillip L. Kohl and Clare Fawcett, eds. Pp. 70–81. Cambridge: Cambridge University Press.

Atkinson, Lesley-Gail
2006   *The Earliest Inhabitants. The Dynamics of the Jamaican Ta´íno*. Kingston, Jamaica: University of the West Indies Press.

Benjamin, Richard P.
2006   Engaging the Past to Develop Black Identity and Social Inclusion. Ph.D. dissertation, School of Archaeology, Classics and Egyptology, University of Liverpool, Liverpool.

Bird-David, Nurit
1991   Animism Revisited: Personhood, Environment, and Relational Epistemology. *Current Anthropology* 40:67–91.

Booth, Alan
2003   History Survey: Supporting More Diverse Students. Electronic document, http://www.heacademy.ac.uk/hca/resources/detail/reviews/history_survey_supporting_more_diverse_students, accessed November 10, 2008.
2005   Worlds in Collision: University Tutor and Student Perspectives on the Transition to Degree Level History. Electronic document, http://www.history.ac.uk/education/sept/booth.html, accessed November 10, 2008.

Boyd, Brian
2004   Agency and Landscape: Abandoning the Nature/Culture Dichotomy in Interpretations of the Natufian and the Transition to the Neolithic. In *The Last Hunter-Gatherer Societies in the Near East*. C. Delage, ed. Pp. 119–136. BAR International Series S1320. Oxford: British Archaeological Reports.

Busby, C.
1997 Permeable and Partible Persons: A Comparative Analysis of Gender and Body in India and Melanesia. *Journal of the Royal Anthropological Institute* 3(2):261–278.

Carman, John
2005 *Against Cultural Property: Archaeology, Heritage and Ownership.* Duckworth, London: Duckworth Debates in Archaeology.

Community Archaeology Forum
2007 Electronic document, http://britarch.net/mailman/listinfo/communityarchaeology, accessed November 10, 2008.

Croucher, Karina, Hannah Cobb, and Ange Brennan
2008 *Investigating the Role of Fieldwork in Teaching and Learning Archaeology.* Liverpool: Higher Education Academy.

Croucher, Karina, and Wendelin Romer
2007 *Inclusivity in Teaching Practice and the Curriculum. Guides to Teaching and Learning in Archaeology number 6.* York, United Kingdom: Higher Education Academy.

Croucher, Karina, and Janet Tatlock
2006 Diversity and the Past Report. Electronic document, http://www.heacademy.ac.uk/hca/resources/detail/diversity_and_the_past, accessed November 10, 2008.

Curtis, Neil
2006 Museums in a Postmodern World: Collections, Exhibitions and Opinions. *Public Archaeology* 5:199–202.

Department for Children, Schools and Families
2007 Learning Outside the Classroom. Electronic document, http://www.lotc.org.uk/, accessed November 10, 2008.

Department for Innovation, Universities & Skills
2009 Advance Notice of Higher Education Funding Changes in England—Second Degree Students. Electronic document, http://www.dius.gov.uk/publications/hefunding.html, accessed February 1, 2009.

Descola, P., and G. Pálsson, eds.
1996 *Nature and Society: Anthropological Perspectives.* London: Routledge.

Dhanjal, Sarah, and Jenny Stripe
2007 Widening Participation. UCL Institute of Archaeology E-Newsletter: Issue 4. Electronic document, http://www.ucl.ac.uk/archaeology/news/2006-issue04/widening.htm, accessed November 10, 2008.

Dowson, Thomas A.
2000 Why Queer Archaeology? An Introduction. *World Archaeology* 32(2):161–165.
2006 Archaeologists, Feminists, and Queers: Sexual Politics in the Construction of the Past. In *Feminist Anthropology.* P. L. Geller and

M. K. Stockett, eds. Pp. 89–102. Philadelphia: University of Pennsylvania Press.

Dunne, David, and Peter Brown
2002   Citizen of City. Manuscript on file, Manchester Museum, Manchester, United Kingdom.

Emmott, K.
1987   A Child's Eye View of the Past. *Archaeological Review from Cambridge* 6(2):129–142.

English Heritage
2000   Power of Place: The Future of the Historic Environment. English Heritage, London.

Fenwick, Helen
2004   Residential Archaeological Training Excavation for Groups Under-represented in HE. Electronic document, http://www.heacademy. ac.uk/projects/detail/projectfinder/wp/wp2530, accessed November 10, 2008.

Fowler, Chris
2004   *The Archaeology of Personhood: An Anthropological Approach*. London: Routledge.

Gatens, M.
2004 [1992]   Power, Bodies and Difference. In *Destabilizing Theory: Contemporary Feminist Debates*. M. Barrett and A. Phillips, eds. Pp. 120–137. Cambridge: Polity Press.

Gero, Joan M.
1993   The Social World of Prehistoric Facts: Gender and Power in Palaeoindian Research. In *Women and Archaeology: A Feminist Critique*. Hilary Du Cros and Laurajane Smith, eds. Pp. 31–40. Canberra, Australia: Australian National University Press.

Hamilakis, Y., and P. Duke, eds.
2007   *Archaeology and Capitalism: From Ethics to Politics*. Walnut Creek, California: Left Coast Press.

HCA (History, Classics and Archaeology Subject Centre)
2006   Diversity in Archaeology Symposium. Electronic document, http://www. heacademy.ac.uk/hca/resources/detail/diversity_and_the_past, accessed November 10, 2008.
2007   Diversity and the Past: Progress, Challenges and the Future. Electronic document, http://www.heacademy.ac.uk/hca/events/detail/past/diversity_and_the_past_05_12_2007, accessed November 10, 2008.

HEA (The Higher Education Academy)
2007   Diversity and the Curriculum. Electronic document, http://www.heacademy.ac.uk/events/detail/developing_an_inclusive_curriculum_07_sept_07, accessed November 10, 2008.

Henson, Don
2008   History and Archaeology at 14–19. Research in Archaeological Educa-
        tion, volume 1. Electronic document, http://www.heacademy.ac.uk/hca/
        archaeology/RAEJournal, accessed November 10, 2008.

Henson, Don, and Daniel Hull
2007   Archaeology and Community. Paper presented at the European
        Association of Archaeologists Conference, Zadar, Croatia.

Hockings, Chris, and Sandra Cooke
2008   Learning and Teaching for Social Diversity and Difference. Electronic
        document, http://www.wlv.ac.uk/Default.aspx?page=14274, accessed
        January 10, 2009.

Hodder, Ian
1982   Symbolic and Structural Archaeology. Cambridge: Cambridge University
        Press.
1985   Postprocessual Archaeology. In *Advances in Archaeological Method and
        Theory 8*. M.B. Schiffer, ed. Pp. 1–26. Orlando: Academic Press.
1986   *Reading the Past: Current Approaches to Interpretation in Archaeology*.
        Cambridge: Cambridge University Press.
1997   Changing Configurations: The Relationships between Theory and Practice.
        In *Archaeological Resource Management in the UK: An Introduction*.
        John Hunter and Ian Ralston, eds. Pp. 11–18. Stroud, Gloucestershire:
        Sutton Publishing Limited/ Institute of Field Archaeologists.
1999   *The Archaeological Process: An Introduction*. Oxford: Blackwell
        Publishers.

Hull, Daniel
2006   Equality & Diversity in the Curriculum: The Development of World
        Archaeology Course, The Department of Archaeology, University of York.
        Electronic document, http://www.heacademy.ac.uk/hca/resources/detail/
        diversity/equality_diversity_in_the_curriculum, accessed November 10,
        2008.

Ingold, Timothy
1996   Growing Plants and Raising Animals: An Anthropological Perspective on
        Domestication. In *The Origins and Spread of Agriculture and Pastoralism
        in Eurasia*. D. R. Harris, ed. Pp. 12–24. London: UCL Press.
2000   *The Perception of the Environment: Essays on Livelihood, Dwelling and
        Skill*. London: Routledge.

Insoll, Timothy
2007   *Archaeology: The Conceptual Challenge*. London: Duckworth.

Johnson, Matthew
1999   *Archaeological Theory: An Introduction*. Oxford: Blackwell Publishers.

Jones, Sian
2004   *Early Medieval Sculpture and the Production of Meaning, Value and
        Place: The Case of Hilton of Cadboll*. Edinburgh: Historic Scotland.

2006 'They made it a living thing didn't they...': the growth of things an the fossilisation of Heritage. In *A Future for Archaeology: the Past in the Present*. R. Layton, S. Shennan and P. Stone, eds. Pp. 107–126. London: UCL Press.

Joyce, Rosemary
2002 *The Languages of Archaeology*. Oxford: Blackwell Publishers.

Kohl, Philip, L. and Clare Fawcett
1995 *Nationalism, Politics, and the Practice of Archaeology*. Cambridge: Cambridge University Press.

Kossinna, Gustaf
1911 *Die Herkunft der Germanen* (The origin of the Germans). Leipzig, Germany: Kabitzsch Press.

Lewis, Carenza
2007 Higher Education Field Academy. Electronic document, http://www. arch.cam.ac.uk/aca/fa/, accessed November 10, 2008.

Lord, Beth, and Matthew Jarron
2006 Thinking about Museums: Philosophical Perspectives. Special Issue, *Museum Management and Curatorship* 21(2):79–170.

MacCormack, C. P., and M. Strathern
1980 *Nature, Culture and Gender*. Cambridge: Cambridge University Press.

Mapunda, Bertram, and Paul Lane.
2004 Archaeology for Whose Interest—Archaeologists or the Locals? In *Public Archaeology*. Nick Merriman, ed. Pp. 211–222. London: Routledge.

Matthews, Roger
2003 *The Archaeology of Mesopotamia: Theories and Approaches*. London: Routledge.

Merriman, Nick
1991 *Beyond the Glass Case: The Past, the Heritage and the Public*. London: Leicester University Press.
2004 *Public Archaeology*. London: Routledge.

Meskell, Lynn
1998 *Archaeology Under Fire. Nationalism, Politics and Heritage in the Eastern Mediterranean and Middle East*. London: Routledge.

Messenger, Phyllis Mauch
1999 *The Ethics of Collecting Cultural Property: Whose Culture? Whose Property?* 2nd edition. Albuquerque: University of New Mexico Press.

Monk, J.
2000 Looking Out, Looking In: The 'Other.' *Journal of Geography in Higher Education* 24(2):163–177.

Moore, Henrietta
1988 *Feminism and Anthropology*. Cambridge: Polity Press.

Morris, R. C.
1995 All Made Up: Performance Theory and the New Anthropology of Sex and Gender. *Annual Review of Anthropology* 24:567–592.

National Trust for Scotland
2007 Archaeology for Schools. Electronic document, http://www.ntseducation.org.uk/archaeologyforschools/, accessed November 10, 2008.

O'Neil, Mark.
2006 Essentialism, Adaptation and Justice: Towards a new Epistemology of Museums. *Museum Management and Curatorship* 21(2):95–116.

OPSI (Office of Public Sector Information)
2000 Race Relations Amendment Act. Electronic document, www.opsi.gov.uk/ACTS/acts2000/20000034.htm, accessed November 10, 2008.
2001 Special Education Needs and Disability Act (SENDA). Electronic document, www.opsi.gov.uk/acts/acts2001/20010010.htm, accessed November 10, 2008.

Ortner, S.
1974 Is Female to Male as Nature is to Culture? In *Women, Culture and Society*. M. Z. Rosaldo and L. Lamphere, eds. Pp. 67–87. Palo Alto, California: Stanford University Press.

Parker Pearson, Mike
1997 Visitors Welcome. In *Archaeological Resource Management in the UK: An Introduction*. John Hunter and Ian Ralston, eds. Pp. 225–231. Stroud, United Kingdom: Sutton Publishing Limited.

Parker Pearson, Mike, and Ramilisonina
2004 Public Archaeology and Indigenous Communities. *In* Public Archaeology. Nick Merriman, ed. Pp. 224–239. London: Routledge.

Pearce, Susan
1997 Museum Archaeology. In *Archaeological Resource Management in the UK: An Introduction*. John Hunter and Ian Ralston, eds. Pp. 232–242. Stroud, United Kingdom: Sutton Publishing Limited.

Phillips, Tim, Roberta Gilchrist, Iain Hewitt, Stephanie Le Scouille, Daren Booy, and Geoff Cook
2007 Inclusive, Accessible, Archaeology: Good Practice Guidelines or Including Disabled Students and Self-Evaluation in Archaeological Fieldwork Training. Guides to Teaching and Learning in Archaeology 5, Higher Education Academy. Electronic document, http://www.heacademy.ac.uk/hca/archaeology/features_resources/guides, accessed November 10, 2008.

Pluciennik, Mark
2005 *Social Evolution*. London: Duckworth.

Pitt Rivers, Leuit-Gen
1898 *Excavations in Cranborne Chase*. Printed privately.

Price, Sally
1991 *Primitive Art in Civilized Places.* Chicago: University of Chicago.

Riley, Mark and David Harvey
2005 Landscape Archaeology, Heritage and the Community in Devon: An Oral History Approach. *International Journal of Heritage Studies* 11(4):269–288.

Romer, Wendelin
2005 Equality and Diversity in the Curriculum Report (Phase 1). Electronic document, www.york.ac.uk/admin/eo/eddevelopment/Research.htm, accessed November 10, 2008.
2006 Equality and Diversity in the Curriculum: Project Report on Development and Implementation. Electronic document, www.york.ac.uk/admin/eo/eddevelopment/Implementation.htm, accessed November 10, 2008.

Rotman, D. L.
2006 Separate Spheres? Beyond the Dichotomies of Domesticity. *Current Anthropology* 47(4):666–674.

Shaw, Jenny, Kevin Brain, Kath Bridger, Judith Foreman, and Ivan Reid
2007 Embedding Widening Participation and Promoting Student Diversity. Electronic document, http://www.heacademy.ac.uk/resources/detail/resources/publications/wp_business_case_approach_july07, accessed November 10, 2008.

Shennan, Steven
1989 *Archaeological Approaches to Cultural Identity.* One World Archaeology Series. London: Routledge.

Smith, George, S.
2006 Conference Review: Capturing the Public Value of Heritage. Electronic document, European Journal of Archaeology: News and Reviews, http://eja.e-a-a.org/2006/12/17/conference-review-capturing-the-public-value-of-heritage/, accessed November 10, 2008.

Speight, Sarah, and Don Henson
2004 Widening Participation in Archaeology and the Continuing Education Agenda, Report of a Workshop held Sept 24th 2004. Electronic document, http://www.heacademy.ac.uk/hca/resources/detail/widening_participation_in_archaeology, accessed November 10, 2008.

Stone, P. G., and B. L. Molyneaux
1994 *The Presented Past: Heritage, Museums and Education.* London: Routledge.

Strathern, Marilyn
1988 *The Gender of the Gift.* Berkeley: University of California Press.

Stukeley, William
1790 [1740] Stonehenge, a Temple Restored to the British Druids. London: Innys and Manby.

1743   *Avebury, a Temple of the British Druids.* London: Innys and Manby.

Tatlock, Janet

2007   Widening Participation. Electronic Document, http://www.humanities.manchester.ac.uk/humnet/acaserv/wideningparticipation/, accessed November 10, 2008.

2008   Diversity and the Past: Progress, Challenges and the Future, 2007. Electronic document, http://www.heacademy.ac.uk/hca/events/detail/past/diversity_and_the_past_05_12_2007, accessed November 10, 2008.

The University of Manchester Field Archaeology Centre

2006   Archaeology for All: The Theory and Practice of Community Archaeology, Conference held November 2006, Manchester Museum. Electronic document, http://www.arts.manchester.ac.uk/umfac/archaeologyforall/, accessed November 10, 2008.

Trigger, Bruce

1984   Alternative Archaeologies: Nationalist, Colonialist, Imperialist. *Man* 19:355–370.

1985   The Past as Power: Anthropology and the North American Indian. In *Who Owns the Past?*, I. McBryde, ed. Pp. 11–40. Oxford: Oxford University Press.

1989   *A History of Archaeological Thought.* Cambridge: Cambridge University Press.

Tringham, Ruth

2000   Engendered Places in Prehistory. In *Interpretive Archaeology.* Julian Thomas, ed. Pp. 329–350. London: Leicester University Press.

UCL Institute of Archaeology

2006   Archaeology in the Community Conference, June 2006, London. Electronic document, http://www.ucl.ac.uk/archaeology/events/conferences/community/index.htm, accessed November 10, 2008.

UK Centre for Materials Education

2006   Curriculum Innovation for Diversity. Electronic document, http://www.materials.ac.uk/events/diversity.asp, accessed November 10, 2008.

Veit, Ulrich

1989   Ethnic Concepts in German Prehistory: A Case Study on the Relationship Between Cultural Identity and Archaeological Objectivity. In *Archaeological Approaches to Cultural Identity.* S. Shennan, ed. Pp. 35–56. London: Routledge.

Walker, Julian

1997   Afterword: Acquisition, Envy and the Museum Visitor. In *Experiencing Material Culture in the Western World.* Susan M. Pearce, ed. Pp. 255–263. London: Leicester University Press.

Watkins, Joe, K. Anne Pyburn, and Pam Cressey
2000   Community Relations: What the Practicing Archaeologist Needs to Know to Work Effectively with Local and/or Descendant Communities. In *Teaching Archaeology in the Twenty-First Century*. Susan J. Bender and George S. Smith, eds. Pp. 73–82. Washington, D.C.: Society for American Archaeology.

Wellens, J., J. Monk, A. Bernardi, B. Chalkley, J. Vender, H. de Jong, and B. Chambers
2004   Teaching for Social Transformation. Discussion paper presented at the International Network for Learning and Teaching (INLT) Post-IGU Workshop, Glasgow, Scotland.

Yates, Timothy
1993   Frameworks for an Archaeology of the Body. In *Interpretive Archaeology*. C. Tilley, ed. Pp. 31–72. Oxford: Berg.

Zinkiewicz, L., and A. Trapp
2004   Widening and Increasing Participation: Challenges and Opportunities for Psychology Departments. LTSN Psychology Report no.5. Electronic document, http://www.psychology.heacademy.ac.uk/docs/pdf/p20040422_widen_partic.pdf, accessed November 10, 2008.

PART II

Applying Heritage Values

Section 2

Stakeholders and Heritage Values

13

Experiencing Heritage Values among the Doro Ana Pumé of Venezuela

Pei-Lin Yu

Introduction

What is it like to learn about heritage values while living within another culture? I was lucky enough to learn for myself as a young anthropologist in the early 1990s. For nearly two years I lived in a tribal Pumé community, as an assistant in Dr. Rusty Greaves's ethno-archaeological research project (Yu 1997). At that time I knew nothing of "heritage" as it is discussed in the resource management community today. But despite language barriers, constant moves, illness, the demands of data collection, and my profound ignorance of almost every aspect of foraging life, I did manage to absorb some key Pumé heritage values. I would like to share a few experiences, and then discuss how my time with the Pumé has enabled me to use my authorities and capacities as a heritage professional to acquire, document, curate, and share Indigenous heritage information in a way that is consistent with the values of its owners.

Three Stories

The Film Makers

One quiet hot afternoon, an airplane flew low over our village and the Pumé women and men leapt to their feet. They hid arrows in the roof thatch and warned the kids to stay indoors—it might be a military reconnaissance. The plane circled overhead, then buzzed away. About an hour later, we heard a Land Cruiser approaching us across the tall grasses. The vehicle pulled up and four well-dressed French film-makers climbed out. They politely asked us if it was possible to film the Pumé night ceremony, called *tohé*, for a documentary on Indian religion. But in order to film, they needed light: either to use floodlights or to stage the ceremony during the day. They were prepared to pay handsomely. We anthropologists translated their request to Francisco and Pedro Julio. The two Pumé men conferred with several other adults and then answered, "How can *tohé* be done right under strong lights? And we just can't perform the ceremony in daylight, it wouldn't be *tohé* at all. Impossible!" The French film-makers drove away, disappointed.

"Just Speak It!"

The Pumé language is mostly undocumented and was not easy to learn. I felt like a toddler again and indeed, the children teased me without mercy. I knew that my friend Pedro Julio spoke Spanish and thought I might be able to learn more easily if we used that language as a bridge of sorts. When I asked if that might be possible, Pedro Julio shook his head and answered me laughingly in Pumé. Greaves translated, "Oh no, you should not use Spanish at all. Pumé is a much better language, a beautiful language. Just speak it!"

Hungry Lighting

Summer 1992: On a stormy afternoon, some of the men hurried into camp carrying a deer they had just shot with bow and arrow. The animal was quickly butchered and chunks distributed to all the households. Dr. Greaves and I boiled ours and ate it happily in our house while the rain roared down around us and lightning flickered. We decided to clean the bones by stirring them into the hot ashes—we would put them into the trash midden after the rain let up. At once the world turned into one endless white hot moment and we knew lightning had struck, very close. When we recovered our sight and hearing, Pedro Julio and the other adults pierced their tongues with sting ray spines and stood in the pouring rain, singing and blowing sprays of blood toward the sky to chase away the storm. The lightning had struck a few feet away from our door! When the storm abated, all 60 Pumé crowded into our house to tell us that lightning is hungry all the time and its favorite meat is venison. The very last thing you should do in a storm is put deer bones into a fire and send delicious-smelling smoke skyward.

The Pumé Concept of Heritage

The Pumé have no word that approximates "heritage" although it is all around them and informs every action they take and every value they hold. Pumé children do not attend school and are taught heritage values not as history, but as the way you live your life. If they did have a word for heritage, I expect that all three stories would qualify as "Heritage Lessons for Those Anthropologists." However, as with many traditional peoples, the Pumé are experiencing accelerated rates of impact from external cultures based on global economies and raw materials. If the term "heritage" implicitly acknowledges a threat—and I believe it often does—defining heritage as distinct from everyday life may be a rearguard action. Even dominant cultures adopt the term (e.g., the Heritage Foundation) as an act of defiance against the perceived threat of alien interlopers. For this reason, the Pumé have much to tell us about the concept of heritage.

First, a little background: The Pumé, called the Yaruro by Spanish speakers, include about 6,000 individuals living in the state of Apure. They have organized themselves into two types of communities: sedentary villages along major rivers and smaller, mobile camps in the more remote savanna (OCEI 1995:24). While the river communities are partly incorporated into the national economy as agricultural laborers, traditional savanna Pumé depend on hunting, wild plant gathering, fishing, and manioc cultivation. They are among the last peoples on earth who rely heavily on wild root foods. Traditional savanna Pumé live in villages of fewer than 100 people, which vary seasonally in size and location. Savanna communities move base camps about every six months because of seasonal flooding that affects the water table, plants, animals, and human travel. In the dry season, family groups make short-term moves from the base camps to procure certain wild resources and tend small manioc gardens. The traditional community where Dr. Greaves and I lived for nearly two years is called Doro Ana, or Big Creek.

The dyad of acculturated river and traditional savanna Pumé communities makes for constant intra-cultural osmosis. People move back and forth based on age, personal preference, and life situation. Some Doro Ana teenagers became intrigued by the river lifestyle and journeyed there to stay with relatives for months at a time. Eventually they came home again, bringing home such exotic commodities as toothpaste and antiperspirant. Several adults in Doro Ana had been born in river communities and emigrated to the savanna to live traditionally. When we asked why, they told us they were afraid of local soldiers, they disliked the dirty living conditions in sedentary villages, and were disturbed by the excessive drunkenness of river Pumé. But trips to the river are essential for trade, and for visiting family. Cloth, soap, needle and thread, machetes, buckets, pots, salt, matches, hunting dogs, and other essentials are procured from Pumé trading partners or Venezuelan nationals along the river.

The Pumé do not have adequate land tenure for the areas they currently occupy. At the time of our visit, almost 90 percent of Pumé were living in Indigenous communities (OCEI 1995:163, 165, 167) and 90 percent of Pumé communities have no legally documented ownership. Of 109 Pumé communities in Apure, 8 have a provisional collective title to their land, and 3 communities have a definitive collective title (OCEI 1995:167, 179–180). For two centuries, Spanish-speaking Venezuelans have "homesteaded" in Pumé lands, filling up the landscape with small ranches and farms. Many are good neighbors, but others actively discourage Indigenous use of important resource areas and there is no legal recourse for the Pumé.

Acculturation and the Pumé

In the last decade, there has been a growing trend of savanna Pumé men joining the Venezuelan rural workforce as seasonal agricultural laborers. This puts a real strain on traditional communities, where men may leave their families for weeks or months and return with little more to show than cigarettes or a bag of rice. This disruption of traditional subsistence may lead to dependence on wage work and market foods, which could undermine self-determination in coping with cultural changes. Although Hugo Chavez has added a special chapter about Indigenous rights to the Venezuelan Constitution, Dr. Greaves has observed little governmental involvement or meaningful change in the lives of traditional or river-dwelling Pumé citizens since the 1990s (Yu and Greaves 1999: 79).

In addition to these economic and social exchanges, the Pumé have been influenced by Catholic and evangelistic missionaries established in river Pumé communities for decades. The missions have had some success; river Pumé will accept a certain level of proselytizing, but commonly visit traditional communities for a night of tohé (despite the mission efforts to discourage this practice). This is not to say that foreign elements are never incorporated; Indigenous Venezuelan tribes have been interacting with Spanish-speaking neighbors for at least two hundred years. Savanna Pumé have incorporated trade materials into traditional culture, usually in such a way that fundamental forms, properties, and uses of their technology remain: roofing nails are used instead of bone or antler for fish and bird arrows, aluminum pots are used in lieu of ceramic pots, and buckets have partly replaced gourds. Many Spanish borrow-terms (*baca*/vaca, a *chuca*/azucar, *haboni*/jabon) surface in trade conversations and India Rosa is a non-Indigenous spirit of great significance in Pumé religious life.

Traditional savanna Pumé are well aware of cultural encroachment. They differentiate between themselves and their Venezuelan neighbors in terms that are concrete, such as access to guns and boats; and value-based, such as proper parenting (no corporal punishment), family structure (men marry into their wives' home villages), and sharing all food brought into camp.

Heritage: When and How to Share?

Based upon my personal observations, Pumé heritage as we define it today is first and foremost two things: the language and the religion. Traditional Pumé guard and propagate these values, making sure that their children learn them and that outsiders understand their unique significance. As I mentioned above, traditional Pumé speak Spanish only when necessary, and do not encourage their children to learn it. They are interested in sharing their heritage values with interested outsiders, however. This may be due in part to historic disinterest in their culture by Venezuelans (although this is changing). *Niwei* are encouraged to attend tohé, and Pumé healing practices of blowing smoke on the afflicted part and then sucking out foreign objects from the sufferer's body have made their way into criollo (Spanish-speaking mixed blood) traditional medicine. As with many other tribes I have known, Pumé tribal elders in particular take trouble to educate outsiders in heritage matters. Dr. Greaves and I were considered to be worth educating, and we reciprocated with a good trading relationship and access to non-traditional medicines—this was in addition to providing daily, if inadvertent, entertainment. However, we did observe that visitors who lack respect or seem threatening will get a polite, but uncommunicative, reception.

The North American Looking Glass: Commoditization and Indigenous Protective Measures

What will the Pumé children of today say to visitors in 20 years? Events in North America may foreshadow the future of Pumé heritage stewardship. In our country, the commoditization of heritage has become a topic of serious concern for Indigenous communities. For decades, spiritual movements, advertising agencies, sports teams, the arts and crafts market, and other outside interests have freely extracted elements of Indigenous culture to provide financial enrichment, entertainment, and even identity. Scientists have built careers from the study of Indigenous heritage, in most cases giving little or nothing of value back to Indigenous communities.

The United States Congress has enacted laws and regulations that protect key tangible elements of Native North American heritage such as archaeological sites, traditional cultural places, artifacts, sacred objects, and of course human remains, from destruction and theft. But 40 years later, funding and staffing to enforce these laws and educate the public remain gravely inadequate. Further, important symbols, concepts, and narratives are not protected by intellectual property laws. For these reasons, Native American tribes with whom I have worked are taking steps to regulate the outward flow of heritage-related information. Meanwhile publicly funded heritage resource managers are required to consult with interested parties, including Native American tribes, whenever the federal government considers taking an action that could impact a heritage resource (see Section 106 of the National Historic Preservation Act 1966). Many states now follow similar processes. Therefore, the requirement of heritage resource managers to collect and retain a certain level of official documentation pertaining to this process has resulted in a potential conflict with tribal goals for protection of their own heritage values and properties.

Observations and Recommendations

At the risk of seeming facile, I would like to apply some concepts from the three stories I shared above with the goal of professional management of Indigenously owned heritage resources in a way that is consistent with cultural values.

The Film Makers

The film crew may have had good intentions, but the documentary they wished to make would have (a) created an unnatural, potentially culturally disruptive *tohé* ceremony and (b) misrepresented the Pumé people's most important religious observance, to a wide audience. The Pumé themselves would have received no benefit beyond a small cash stipend.

In order to learn about heritage values, document them, and potentially present them to outside cultures, heritage professionals need to talk directly with the owners of those values. In short, we must communicate frequently and wherever possible, face-to-face, to learn what types of heritage values may be shared and what are the culturally appropriate means to do so. This may be tougher than it sounds—it involves plenty of work, dialogue, and travel on both ends—but the pay-off is potentially tremendous and long lasting. Communication works both ways, and it is *our* responsibility to make sure that Indigenous colleagues are well-informed about the scope of resource management authorities and capabilities.

"Just Speak It!"

When Pedro Julio told me to learn his language, he was taking steps to perpetuate Pumé heritage in the face of Spanish-speaking Venezuelan culture. My Pumé family treated me like a child in my first months there, and I truly was a child, functionally! But when I began to communicate, I found that my mind worked differently; my comprehension of landscapes, plants and animals, family life, politics, and ethics became uniquely Pumé. Heritage managers dealing with Indigenous cultures frequently hear how important it is for kids to learn the language, but this experience really brought it home to me.

Stewardship of heritage values is the responsibility of its owners. I believe that professional heritage managers can help communities build their own capacity to do this important work, in a manner that is consistent with law, policy, and guidelines. Today, tribal projects are using public funds to interview Elders for oral histories about past practices and traditional stories. This information is curated and incorporated into tribal school programs (see the chapter by Clark and Heath in this volume). Public funds are helping researchers access publicly owned collections and data to investigate the scope and diversity of past lifeways. Tribal programs are also producing exciting media presentations about their heritage and agencies are helping to distribute them to the wider public, including schools, visitor centers, libraries, and museums. These media include illustrated books, DVDs, and interactive websites.

Hungry Lightning

When we learned about the behavior of lightning, we witnessed an Indigenous explanatory system at work. Needless to say, we did not toss deer bones into the fire again, even on sunny days! The scientific community also seeks to explain the way the world works; like the Pumé, we begin with generalized statements based on observations of empirical phenomena. We use those statements to derive testable hypothetical statements, to select relevant data, recognize patterns, assess the predictive capabilities of our hypotheses, and refine our explanation-atory frameworks for the next round (Popper 1960).

Many years after my lightning scare, I was in North Dakota, discussing the touchy issue of the repatriation of Kennewick Man with a young Mandan Powwow announcer. Although he deplored the legal battle, he considered science to be a system of knowledge with a unique potential to answer questions near and dear to tribal culture and well-being. "If only scientists were asking those questions!" he lamented. Indigenous domains of inquiry and explanation can indeed provide fruitful avenues for the development of scientific research questions, as the field of conservation biology, and particularly fisheries management, has demonstrated (State of Washington 2000; U.S. Department of Agriculture 2007). This approach is a major pathway for future research in the social sciences and humanities as well. We do not need to be struck by lightning to begin.

Conclusion

The future of heritage management, and the benefits we reap together, will grow from shared understanding between members of descendant communities, scientists, and heritage managers (see the chapters by Croucher; and Chilton in this volume). It is my hope that soon, growing numbers of people will be able to say, "I am all three!"

Acknowledgments

I extend my warmest regards to the Pumé of Doro Ana and all their relatives for teaching me what they could. I hope that someday these words will reach them. Dr. Rusty Greaves made it possible for me to learn these lessons and I owe him a debt I can never quantify.

The Native American tribes I work with as a federal archaeologist have been generous with their knowledge, patience, and professionalism. From the Spokane Tribe of Indians, I learned that sensitive information can be curated outside the community if the security of the data can be assured. From the Confederated Tribes of the Colville Reservation, I learned that certain traditional narratives lend themselves to sharing with the non-Native public, but others carry special significance and should be kept within the community. From the Confederated Salish and Kootenai Tribes, I learned how Elders share traditional travel routes and land use practices with the wider public. The Eastern Band of the Cherokee Indians showed me how to keep traditional practices alive in the heart of the mountains in the continuing aftermath of the Trail of

Tears. Finally, 20 years ago, Klamath Tribal Elder Reid David sat with me for several days in his tiny trailer, patiently teaching me his grandmother's knowledge about native plants and their traditional uses. He helped me learn how to listen carefully and remember.

References

OCEI
1995   Censo Indígena de Venezuela 1992. Tomo I. Republica de Venezuela, Presidencia de la Republica, Oficina Central de Estadisticas e Informatica. Taller Gráfico de la O.C.E.I., Caracas.

Popper, K. V.
1960   Truth and Approximation to Truth. In *Popper Selections*. D. Miller, ed. Pp. 181–198. Princeton: Princeton University Press.

State of Washington, Columbia Fish and Wildlife Authority
2000   FY 2001 Proposal to Monitor and Enhance the Lakes and Streams of the Spokane Indian Reservation. Electronic document, http://www.cbfwa. org/fwprogram/ResultProposal.cfm?PPID=IM2001000021020, accessed November 10, 2008.

U.S. Department of Agriculture, Natural Resources Conservation Association
2007   Conservation Showcase Homepage. Electronic document, http://www.wa. nrcs.usda.gov/news/Showcases/Showcase14.html, accessed November 10, 2008.

Yu, Pei-Lin
1997   *Hungry Lightning: Field Notes of a Woman Anthropologist.* Albuquerque: University of New Mexico Press.

Yu, Pei-Lin, and Russell D. Greaves
1999   Into the Life of the Nation: Land Use and Self-determination among Traditional Pumé Hunter-Gatherers in Venezuela. *Cultural Survival Quarterly* 23(4):78–79.

14

Articulating Culture in the Legal Sphere: Heritage Values, Native Americans, and the Law

Susan B. Bruning

Introduction

The Native American Graves Protection and Repatriation Act (Public Law 101-601, 25 U.S. Code 3001 et seq. [NAGPRA] [1990]) ushered in a new era of heritage values management. NAGPRA's legal structure is profoundly reshaping the ways in which parties with diverse interests are, through choice or through mandate, influencing the fate of objects of Native American cultural heritage (see the chapter by Soderland in this volume). Peering through the lens of the American legal sphere, stake-holders in cultural heritage seem at initial glance to be solid entities, with distinct rights, obligations, and boundaries. The federal government wields its power of "recognition" to identify Indian tribes within its regulatory reach, and various laws attempt to define and manage interests in Native American cultural heritage in specific ways to serve specific legal purposes. Museums enjoy tax-exempt status as non-profit institutions with the obligation to serve the overall "public interest," which is often accomplished through promotion of heritage values that encourage preservation, display, and promotion of research involving cultural objects. Archaeologists build knowledge by seeking information about the human past through exploration, study, preservation, and interpretation of the material record that informs on such past. Over the course of the past century, the United States has passed a variety of laws that have primarily privileged the archaeological and historic preservation communities' value systems, often with little acknowledgment of the value systems of indigenous descendant groups whose forbears created much of the heritage at issue.

As laws were implemented over time through application to real situations involving real people, both Native and non-Native, the seemingly clear boundary lines articulated in legal language began to blur, and the fluidity and dynamics of stakeholders and their various heritage values became more apparent. A more realistic and complicated picture began to emerge, one illustrating value systems of various individuals and groups that overlap at times and at other times diverge and even polarize. As indigenous groups and those aligned with their perspectives began speaking up for Native American concerns and values about cultural heritage management, North American archaeologists often found themselves at odds with indigenous communities whose perspectives on appropriate exploration, study, display, preservation, and interpretation conflicted with those embraced by the academic and scientific communities. Similarly, museums increasingly found themselves subject to criticism for failing to respect the heritage values of indigenous groups for whom objects in collections have ongoing cultural and spiritual importance. Descendant communities increasingly managed to have their voices heard above the cacophony of existing laws and organizational ethics codes framing much of the discussion.

The legal landscape, in response, has shifted significantly in the last few decades. The year 1990 turned out to be a banner year for legislation acknowledging culturally grounded and morally grounded interests. In addition to NAGPRA's passage, Congress enacted the Visual Artists Rights Act (Public Law 101-650, 17 U.S. Code 106A [1990]) to protect certain "moral rights" of artists seeking to protect their works and their reputations. The revised Indian Arts and Crafts Act (Public Law 101-644, 25 U.S. Code 305 et seq. [1990]) strengthened efforts to rid the marketplace of inauthentic "Indian-made" goods and to protect tribal names from unauthorized exploitation. These laws take steps to recognize interests previously ignored or under-acknowledged, demonstrating the possibility that innovative legal mechanisms might play a role in addressing some of the myriad interests at stake when cultural heritage—be it material objects, intangible information, or esoteric knowledge—is disclosed, interpreted, and used. However, all laws have their difficulties and flaws. Some of NAGPRA's challenges and limitations have become intensely evident as museum, scientific, and Native American communities increasingly engage each other in the process of seeking appropriate resolutions for managing cultural heritage.

The Concept of Heritage

"Heritage" has been defined as something acquired from a predecessor, or something "possessed as a result of one's natural situation or birth" (Merriam-Webster 2008; see the chapters by Altschul; Holtorf; Okamura; Russell; Silberman in this volume). The notion of inheritance suggests that a descendant individual or group has certain rights to access, control, and benefit from something created or possessed by an ancestral individual or group and, implicitly, the right to prevent others (those outside the beneficiary group) from interfering with those rights. One challenge, for those of us endeavoring to speak about rights, obligations, and interests in heritage and the values embodied therein, is to articulate the scale at which we engage the notion of heritage and its beneficiaries.

At the largest scale of inquiry, multinational coalitions engage in efforts to articulate and manage humankind's global cultural legacy. The 1954 Hague Convention speaks of the cultural heritage of "every people" as it trumpets a global call for protection of cultural sites and objects during armed conflict (Preamble, Convention for the Protection of Cultural Property in the Event of Armed Conflict, The Hague, Netherlands [1954]). The 1970 UNESCO cultural property convention declares that "cultural property constitutes one of the basic elements of civilization and national culture, and that its true value can be appreciated only in relation to the fullest possible information regarding its origin, history and traditional setting" (Convention on the Means of Prohibiting and Preventing the Illicit Import, Export and Transfer of Ownership of Cultural Property, adopted at Paris, France, by the United Nations Education, Scientific and Cultural Organization [UNESCO] [1970]). The Convention further calls for countries to be "increasingly alive to the moral obligations to respect its own cultural heritage and that of all nations" and to manage their collections according to "universally recognized moral principles." More than 100 nations have become signatories to the convention, suggesting widespread support, at least at the national political level, for the notion of a global heritage value embodied in the achievements, struggles, behaviors, and events of humanity's collective past.

While it may be tempting to look for universal values in the search for management solutions for cultural heritage dilemmas, it may be idealistic to believe that any single value system can be articulated and accepted by all stakeholders. Ethical mandates for some indigenous groups to refrain from visiting certain sacred areas, handling or viewing certain artifacts, or disclosing certain rituals, stories, or histories may directly conflict with scholarly goals of increasing knowledge about the human past through research and study of the human tangible and intangible record. Unlike the sweeping, inclusive language of UNESCO, which seeks to deal in "universal moral principles," the language of NAGPRA reflects the reality that there are competing moral and ethical principles struggling to co-exist in the realm of heritage study and management throughout the United States.

Heritage laws in the United States have evolved in ways that accommodate an increasing variety of heritage values held by constituent groups. At the same time, a review of some of these values reveals some inherent conflicts: repatriation vs. preservation; confidentiality vs. publication; ownership vs. stewardship. One century into the development of legal structures pertaining to the protection and management of Native American heritage, we continue to face daunting challenges as we strive to establish social priorities and strike balances among the diverse value systems competing for prominence.

Development of Heritage Laws in the United States

Legal protection for Native American cultural heritage in the United States has its origins in the near past. Prior to 1906, cultural sites, ancient structures, unmarked burials, and ceremonial objects accruing over millennia lay legally unprotected across the landscape, often collected, disturbed, or destroyed by natural and human forces. The legal system tolerated a "finders, keepers" approach to the discovery and possession of ancient objects. Uncontrolled excavations and removal of significant amounts of artifacts from the stunning ancient dwellings of Mesa Verde finally caught the attention of lawmakers; the Antiquities Act, the first law addressing protections for cultural sites and objects on federal lands, was enacted in 1906 (Public Law 59-209, 16 U.S. Code 431-433 [1906]). Key heritage values addressed by this Act were two-fold: preserving ancient cultural structures, and controlling excavations so that objects of antiquity would be preserved in United States museums instead of disappearing into foreign or private collections. The Antiquities Act represented an initial shift toward an organized effort to promote public preservation of cultural heritage in the United States, consistent with the developing heritage values of a young American nation (see the chapter by Soderland in this volume).

In the mid 20th century, a flurry of laws were enacted in an attempt to manage heritage values relating to built structures, historical landscapes, and the natural environment. The National Historic Preservation Act (Public Law 89-665, 16 U.S. Code 470 et seq. [1966]) and other laws created an active realm of cultural resource management, employing many archaeologists and building the knowledge base in ancient sites and artifacts. Many of these sites and objects lay in the path of development activities serving a rapid expansion of cities, highways, and related infrastructure across the country. The economic and historical values of a growing population, as well as the archaeological values of studying sites and objects from the human past, were managed by an increasingly complex legal structure. As these activities unfolded, human remains, burial objects, and other cultural material from the past rapidly filled shelves in curatorial facilities around the country, reflecting the heritage values of some stakeholders while offending the values of others.

As noted earlier, all laws have their flaws. In the 1970s, a Native American ceremonial mask placed in a cave by its creator was "discovered" a few years later and taken by a relic hunter. The relic hunter was charged under the Antiquities Act with removing an "object of antiquity," despite the recent creation date for the object (*United States v. Diaz*, 499 F.2d 133 [9th Circuit] [2002]). A challenge to that charge, which rightly raised the absurdity of presuming that an object made by a Native American must be ancient, led to a court ruling that the Act's terminology was unconstitutionally vague. Shortly thereafter, the Archaeological Resources Protection Act (Public Law 96-95, 16 U.S. Code 470aa-470mm [ARPA] [1979]) was enacted, in part to respond to the deficiencies of the Antiquities Act. ARPA established more definitive boundary lines for the management of cultural heritage objects coming under its purview. Under ARPA, an object must be at least 100 years old and "of archaeological interest" to qualify for protection. ARPA takes some limited steps to acknowledge Native American interests in the country's ancient heritage by requiring tribal as well as federal consent prior to excavations on tribal lands. Overall, however, ARPA's focus on controlled excavations, research, and institutional curation—and its definition of a protected object as an "archaeological resource"—still did not align with the heritage values of many members of the indigenous population of the United States.

In the latter part of the 20th century, Native American interests and concerns about the fate of their ancestral heritage, particularly the scores of Native American human remains in institutional collections, took shape in the form of legislation specifically seeking to protect and support indigenous values. Following negotiations over the return of several skulls of Modoc tribal members to their descendants, the Smithsonian Institution adopted its first departmental policy on repatriation. That policy authorized the Institution to return named individuals to their identifiable descendants. In the 1980s, the policy was expanded to allow for repatriation of human remains and associated funerary objects "that could be culturally linked to extant Native American groups, going well beyond descendants of named individuals" (Ortner 1994:12). Those efforts culminated in the passage of the National Museum of the American Indian Act (Public Law 101-185, 20 U.S. Code 80q et seq. [1989]).

UNIVERSITY OF WINCHESTER LIBRARY

A watershed event occurred one year later with the passage of NAGPRA, a sweeping legislation tackling important tangible aspects of Native American heritage values. NAGPRA is federal legislation applicable nationwide to Native American human remains, funerary objects, sacred objects, and objects of cultural patrimony that are held in federally funded institutions or removed from federal or tribal lands since the statute's enactment. NAGPRA embraces the notion that different groups may have different value systems for managing objects of cultural heritage and it imposes a process by which these diverse groups must seek resolution as to which group should control decision making about the ultimate disposition of the human remains and cultural objects at issue.

NAGPRA's birth was not an easy one. After years of discussion and debate—often passionate and contentious—within and among the Native American, scientific, and museum communities, Congress itself expended a good deal of effort to draft legislation that attempted to balance and articulate the diversity of values at stake. After much drafting and re-drafting, the fifth version of the House bill became law. The resulting legislation establishes a structure within which federally funded institutions, Native American groups, and the scientific community are expected to consult and collaborate to appropriately implement NAGPRA's inventory, repatriation, and disposition processes. The dual goals of respectful treatment of Native American cultural items and tribal involvement in heritage management decisions dominate NAGPRA and did so throughout its draft versions. It is also important to recognize that changes to the bill as it moved from draft to law reflect a conscious effort on the part of Congress to provide a system capable of balancing the interests of the Native American communities with recognized public interests represented by the scientific and museum communities. NAGPRA certainly dilutes control by the research community in contrast to its favored position under the Antiquities Act and ARPA. It empowers tribes and their religious leaders to consult actively with institutions curating cultural materials with which they have heritage links, and it shifts control over the disposition of certain items to those claimants who are authorized under the law. At the same time, the law does not prohibit all excavation, study, or ongoing curation of Native American cultural materials, nor does it mandate the return to tribes of all items subject to its coverage. As drafted, the law provides mechanisms within which scientific researchers, museums, and tribes are expected, and empowered, to co-exist as they pursue their interests—at times shared, at times divergent—in managing the material record of the past (Bruning 2006; see the chapter by Soderland in this volume).

Balancing heritage values under NAGPRA can quickly become contentious when certain culturally sensitive questions arise, such as how to define a "Native American." NAGPRA defines the term Native American to mean "of, or relating to, a tribe, people, or culture that is indigenous to the United States." This definition, like many others, may appear to be fairly straightforward, but when applied to specific situations it can inflame important and passionate debates. According to Vine Deloria, Jr., "The conflict between Indians and anthropologists in the last two decades has been, at its core, a dead struggle over the control of definitions. Who is to define what an Indian *really* is?" (Deloria 1997:215). Definitions, in the legal realm, serve very precise purposes as tools for use in interpreting and implementing particular laws. A term defined in one statute can be defined very differently in another, and neither legal definition may reflect larger cultural perspectives of groups who imbue terms with their own meanings. While the use of definitions is necessary and helpful in clarifying particular legal intentions, real world controversies such as the protracted litigation over the ancient skeleton known as Kennewick Man (*Bonnichsen et al. v. United States et al.*, 217 F.Supp.2d 1116 [Dist. OR] [2002]) have highlighted the complexities of attempting, within a legal framework, to define terms with strong (and varied) cultural, political, and individual interpretations.

Perspectives about the ethical and moral appropriateness of excavating, studying, curating, or handling cultural items vary widely among present-day peoples who prioritize their values in different ways. Some prioritize the value of non-disturbance of burials or sites above other values, while others prioritize the value of learning about the human past through excavation and study above the value of non-disturbance. Similarly, competing values become apparent when cultural objects are removed from sites, displayed, traded, or curated. Museums reflect their heritage values of preservation and public access as they collect, borrow, and curate objects that they identify as culturally significant. Researchers reflect their heritage values of knowledge growth as they access objects for study through controlled excavation and publish their findings. Native Americans reflect their heritage values of cultural protection and preservation as they limit access to sites, objects and information, provide their own interpretations of displayed material, and rebury their disinterred ancestors. The values of each particular constituency may seem appropriate when viewed separately, but when viewed in a shared social realm they may, in certain instances, irreconcilably clash. In such instances, laws often serve as arbiters to resolve conflicts by prioritizing interests in the manner articulated in the legal sphere.

Under NAGPRA, an Indian tribe or Native Hawaiian organization with the closest cultural affiliation to an item is entitled to control its ultimate disposition. Cultural affiliation is defined as "a relationship of shared group identity which can be reasonably traced historically or prehistorically between a present day Indian tribe or Native Hawaiian organization and an identifiable earlier group." In order to prove a claim of cultural affiliation, the statute identifies a wide range of acceptable evidence—geography, biology, archaeology, anthropology, linguistics, kinship, folklore, oral tradition, and history—as well as "other relevant information or expert opinion" (NAGPRA Section 7(a)(4)). The culturally affiliated group is empowered to determine what disposition is appropriate for the item, be it ongoing curation, limited access, repatriation to the group, or otherwise.

The concept of cultural affiliation is culturally and politically complex. It is contingent not only on how groups identify themselves and their links to ancestral peoples, but also how outsiders accept or challenge those identities and links. NAGPRA invites tribal experts to bring traditional knowledge into consultation and, if necessary, into the courtroom in order to demonstrate a present-day group's cultural relationship to an artifact from the past. A key difficulty in attempting to include certain cultural knowledge as part of legal evidence, or to include it within a "research commons" environment, stems from an inextricable link between restricted access and contemporary cultural value. Only through the control of certain knowledge elements by particular individuals or groups does some traditional knowledge maintain its vitality as an active asset of the community. A heritage value, in this context, can be identified as restricted access to powerful information. Loss of control over such information, even if ongoing access to the knowledge itself remains available, can destroy the present-day cultural value of that knowledge. Unlike the medicinal quality of a plant, for example, which is unaffected by the number of people who know of its value, the cultural quality of certain traditional knowledge dissipates upon its revelation to unauthorized individuals. The vitality of the resource fades, and the information changes its essence from living cultural asset to frozen relic of the past. Consequently, the cultural values associated with the resource lie in continued control over its disclosure and use. By requiring disclosure of the bases upon which an object meets the definition of "sacred" or "patrimony," NAGPRA arguably presses indigenous groups to violate their own heritage values by requiring them to "make their case" through disclosure of information that will allow outsiders to determine whether they will recognize their NAGPRA-based claims.

As NAGPRA matures, it finds itself suffering from inevitable adolescent awkwardness and growth pains. The drafters surely anticipated the law's applicability to many cultural items from the pre-European contact past, but it does not appear that they considered the possibility that some items, such as the Kennewick human remains, might be challenged as too old to fall within the law's definitions. NAGPRA's language also reflects a focus on the unique relationship that exists between the federal government and federally recognized Indian tribes, presenting challenges for Native Hawaiians as well as other indigenous groups that are outside the scope of current federal recognition. NAGPRA predicates its foundation on the relationships that hearken back to the U.S. Constitution itself: Article 8 speaks to Congress' right to regulate commerce with "foreign Nations, and among the several States, and with the Indian Tribes." Federal recognition (or "acknowledgement" according to the Bureau of Indian Affairs' Office of Federal Acknowledgement) requires, among other things, that a group demonstrate historically traceable group continuity and an ongoing structure of political governance and traditional religious leadership within the group (*Procedures for Establishing that an American Indian Group Exists as an Indian Tribe*, 25 Code of Federal Regulations, Part 83).

The crux of NAGPRA's allocation of control lies in an assumption that the indigenous group representatives engaging in the NAGPRA process have the authority to speak for their constituencies. Certain present-day groups may assert control over certain cultural items if the groups are able to trace their identities back in time sufficiently to demonstrate a "relationship of shared group identity" with an "identifiable earlier group" associated with the cultural items at issue. This relationship of shared group identity is the foundation for a determination of cultural affiliation, which is NAGPRA's designation for those groups authorized by the law to exercise control over the disposition of cultural items. The concept of cultural affiliation, which requires this tracing of identity, is rooted in assumptions about the historical depth of political, social, and cultural group cohesiveness, including continuity of traditional religious practices, of indigenous groups. Many federally recognized Indian tribes serve as models for this style of identity-tracing, such as the pueblos of the western United States who have occupied their landscapes for more than a millennium. The law includes Native Hawaiian groups within its folds, but the fit is much less comfortable.

Federal laws recognize the authority of tribes to establish their own governmental authorities and to determine who is a member, who is authorized to speak on behalf of the tribe, and who can decide how tribal heritage objects will be handled. The Bureau of Indian Affairs takes the position that formal federal acknowledgment of tribal status creates a relationship of government-to-government that enables the leaders of both governments to make decisions on behalf of their constituencies (25 Code of Federal Regulations, Section 83.12(a)). As discussed in the next section, Native Hawaiians find themselves in a uniquely complex position under the law: although acknowledged as qualified participants in the NAGPRA process as an indigenous group, Native Hawaiians are neither a recognized foreign sovereign nor a recognized Indian tribe. This conundrum creates challenges that the law, as it currently stands, may not be well suited to overcome. It also serves as a telling illustration of the forces beyond the law that shape efforts and outcomes in this realm.

Native Hawaiians within NAGPRA's Context

NAGPRA defines a "Native Hawaiian" to be "any individual who is a descendant of the aboriginal people who, prior to 1778, occupied and exercised sovereignty in the area that now constitutes the State of Hawaii." Archaeologists have identified pre-contact Hawaiian occupations of the landscape at levels identified as *ahupua'a* (community), representing physical groupings of interacting individuals, and *moku'āina* (district), representing political territories associated with chiefdoms (Kirch 2003). At the time of initial European contact, Kirch (2000) estimates that the Hawaiian archipelago had about thirty *moku'āina* on the islands of Hawai'i, Kaua'i, Maui, and O'ahu. Paramount chief Kamehameha of Hawai'i had effective control of the entire archipelago by the time of his death in 1819 (Kirch 2003). Prior to its annexation as a state, the United States recognized the Kingdom of Hawaii as a single foreign sovereign. Over the course of the 19th century, the two nations signed numerous treaties and engaged in commercial and other activities on a generally amicable basis. By the end of that century, however, these sovereigns experienced a dramatic shift in their relationship. On January 16, 1893, the United States naval forces actively participated in an invasion of the Hawaiian nation and assisted in the overthrow of the Hawaiian government, then headed by Queen Liliuokalani. One hundred years later, the United States acknowledged its complicity in the overthrow of the Hawaiian monarchy and issued a formal apology to Native Hawaiians (Public Law 103-150 [1993]). Apologies aside, the political transformation of Hawaii resulting from the overthrow was profound. The monarchal structure of leadership in Hawaii effectively dissolved, Hawaii eventually became a state of the United States, and the individuals that previously shared group identity as subjects of the Hawaiian kingdom entered the 21st century without a recognized indigenous governing body representing their collective interests in engagements with the United States government. Legislation seeking federal recognition for Native Hawaiians as an Indian tribe is currently pending in Congress (Native Hawaiian Government Reorganization Act, Senate Bill 344 [2004]), but it remains uncertain whether or in what form such recognition will occur.

Presently, a multitude of organizations representing various political, social, or cultural interests of Native Hawaiians participate in the NAGPRA process as the parties seeking to represent the interests of their stated constituencies. The statute allows this, through its empowerment of any Native Hawaiian organization to assert claims for control of Native Hawaiian cultural items just as an Indian tribe may do for Native American cultural items affiliated with its tribe. The law defines a Native Hawaiian organization as any organization "which (A) serves and represents the interests of Native Hawaiians, (B) has as a primary and stated purpose the provision of services to Native Hawaiians, and (C) has expertise in Native Hawaiian affairs." The first of these criteria—serving and representing the interests of Native Hawaiians—does not require clarification of which particular Native Hawaiians' interests are being represented, nor does it seek to avoid empowering multiple groups to represent the same interests.

Entities qualifying as claimants under the law are entitled to speak for the interests of their stated constituencies. This presumption certainly may be appropriate for Indian tribes that have functioned and continue to function as sovereign entities representing tribal members' interests in dealings with the federal government. However, when Native Hawaiian organizations, some of very recent creation by self-defined, rather than community-defined, representatives of Native Hawaiian interests, purport to speak on behalf of Native Hawaiians, the individuals whose interests are affected may take issue with their authority to do so. Contemporary Native Hawaiian organizations find it challenging to demonstrate contemporary group cohesiveness and a historically traceable and ongoing continuity with earlier peoples—the fodder for federal tribal recognition as well as NAGPRA claims. The historical realities of the relationship between Native Hawaiians and the United States as well as traditional anthropological and ethnographic approaches to the study of peoples indigenous to Hawaii both give rise to complications when competing groups seek control over Native Hawaiian cultural heritage under the rubric of NAGPRA's cultural affiliation standard.

The absence of a present-day pan-Native Hawaiian political authority and the resulting difficulties in determining the appropriateness of heritage claims gained widespread attention when an important group of objects at the Bishop Museum in Honolulu became the subject of NAGPRA claims. A total of 83 objects discovered in the early 20th century in the Kawaihae Caves on the Island of Hawaii ultimately entered the collections of the Bishop Museum. In 2000, the Bishop Museum transferred possession of the objects to Hui Malama Na Kupuna O Hawai'i Nei ("Hui Malama"), one of several Native Hawaiian group claimants consulting with the museum about the items. The museum reportedly had not yet made a determination about cultural affiliation for these items, but it claimed instead that the transfer of possession to Hui Malama was a temporary loan. Ultimately, at least 14 Native Hawaiian organizations formally asserted rights under NAGPRA to some or all of the objects at issue. Despite the Bishop Museum's initial characterization of the transfer as a temporary loan, Hui Malama refused to return the objects to the museum, claiming that it had reburied the objects consistent with Native Hawaiian interests. Lawsuits ensued, with groups such as Na Lei Alii Kawananakoa ("Kawananakoa") and the Royal Hawaiian Academy of Traditional Arts asking the court to demand that Hui Malama return certain objects to the Bishop Museum so that the NAGPRA consultation and cultural affiliation process could resume (*Na Lei Alii Kawananakoa and Royal Hawaiian Academy of Traditional Arts v. Hui Malama Na Kupuna O Hawai'i Nei and Bishop Museum*, Civil No. CV05-00540, filed in United States District Court, District of Hawaii, August 19, 2005).

NAGPRA requires museums to consult with all potentially culturally affiliated parties prior to making determinations about the final disposition of objects. In the case of the Kawaihae Caves collection, at least four different Native Hawaiian groups initially asserted claims to all or some of the objects at issue, and additional groups entered the fray over time. Under NAGPRA, when multiple claimants compete for control of objects, a museum is obligated to try to determine which of the claimants is most closely culturally affiliated with the objects. If it can make such a determination, it must grant control over disposition of those objects to that claimant. If it is unable to make such a determination, the museum may retain possession of the objects until the claimants' competing claims are resolved, whether by agreement or through a court ruling (NAGPRA Section 7(e)).

Hui Malama is a non-profit organization formed in 1989 to address Native Hawaiian concerns when burials were uncovered during construction of the Ritz-Carlton Kapalua hotel. It participated actively in negotiations leading to NAGPRA's enactment and is explicitly acknowledged in the statute as a Native Hawaiian organization. However, Hui Malama does not have exclusive rights to act in such capacity. One of the many claimants challenging Hui Malama's claim is Kawananakoa. According to the complaint document initiating the lawsuit against Hui Malama and the Bishop Museum, Kawananakoa was founded by Abigail Kinoiki Kekauliki Kawananakoa, great granddaughter of Queen Kapiolani and King Kalakaua, who "by Hawaiian tradition, custom, and law is the ranking member of the Alii [chiefly lineage]." Challenging Hui Malama's claim that it acted on behalf of all Native Hawaiian interests by taking the Kawaihae Caves objects and reburying them in an undisclosed location, Kawananakoa decried the removal and reburial, arguing that objects may be stolen and are "at great risk of being damaged by environmental forces or improper care." The complaint also asserts that Hui Malama "does not have a legitimate NAGPRA claim to the Items." After years of legal wrangling, protests, and incarceration of a Hui Malama leader for contempt of court due to his refusal to disclose the whereabouts of the objects, the objects were ultimately returned to the Bishop Museum and consultation with the multitude of Native Hawaiian claimants recommenced.

Is NAGPRA the best tool to determine the outcome of the Kawaihae Caves objects? By drawing on the lines of evidence articulated in the law, researchers could delve into all manner of testing and scientific analysis relating to the objects, some of which contain elements of human remains. Vigorous scholarly research may provide robust information about the nature of the objects and their linkages to past peoples, but it may not resolve fundamental disputes over which present-day Native Hawaiians should decide the fates of the objects. At a conference held during the lawsuit in an attempt to encourage settlement of the dispute, the judge summarized the case as one of "native Hawaiians versus native Hawaiians" (Transcript of status conference proceedings before the Honorable David Alan Ezra and the Honorable Kevin S.C. Chang, January 5, 2006, Civil No. CV05-00540, filed in United States District Court, District of Hawaii). The court encouraged the parties to come together using traditional Hawaiian mediation practices to attempt to work out their differences and resolve the dispute in a manner that emphasizes cultural, not legal, empowerment. NAGPRA seeks to transfer control of an object to the group with the closest historically traceable relationship of cultural group identity with an object. In the case of Native Hawaiian claimants, a significant challenge is to determine which organization has the authority to speak for which Native Hawaiians, particularly where organizations may lack a demonstrable authority to represent the interests of the individuals for whom they purport to speak.

Shared Group Identity

The wrangling over the Kawaihae Caves objects highlights the cultural complexities embedded in legal mandates to "reasonably trace" relationships between present-day peoples and past groups. The notion of heritage invokes concepts of identity anchored in the past and continuing into the present. Group identity is a cultural construct, a conceptualization shared by those within the group who, by the nature of their particular perspectives, see themselves as connected to each other in a culturally distinct manner from those outside the group. In order to operationalize a group's identity and perceived heritage when dealing in contexts such as NAGPRA's consultation and repatriation processes, stakeholders outside the group must accept that group's identity as well. Perspectives about shared group identities may connect present to past, and at the same time, they may connect multiple contemporary groups to the past through shared conceptions of ancestry. These perspectives may hinge on ancestral relationships to a place or a landscape, shared symbolic systems, paradigms of explanation about origins and migrations, and other factors.

Any effort to understand the heritage values of a particular culture group must include an effort to understand the group's perspectives of its origins and the core traditions upon which the group's cultural coherency is founded. This means delving into the historical foundations of how the group came to its present location and situation, as well as familiarizing oneself with the potentially vast array of tangible and intangible evidence that the group refers to in supporting its links to the past. It is here that the material and conceptual evidence supporting group coherence and continuity coexist, providing a nexus for the formation, reformation, and reproduction of social identities at the individual, community, tribal, regional, and national levels. In the case of Native Hawaiian groups vying for control over Native Hawaiian cultural items within NAGPRA, a significant challenge comes from the reality that many of the claimant groups have quite recent origins, often formed for the specific purpose of addressing NAGPRA issues. The law allows this, but it creates an ill-fitted context for assessing group identity and resolving claims in a manner that respects the underlying heritage and cultural values of the individual Native Hawaiians whose interests are, with or without their consent, being affected by the claims and actions of these organizations.

In light of the tensions created by attempting simultaneously to assess anthropological, indigenous, and legal perspectives of identity in the context of NAGPRA, how should parties engage in the process, particularly when multiple groups vie for control over objects of cultural heritage? All stakeholders in this realm must appreciate the complexity of any attempts to trace and contest cultural connections over long time periods with the goal of determining who should control the fate of objects of cultural heritage. Shared group identity is not a precisely constituted concept, but is rather a bundle of concepts and understandings that includes a plethora of meaningful social elements such as traditional knowledge, landscapes, specific places, histories, material objects, lineage ties, and symbolic representations. A group may utilize any number of identity elements to situate itself in the larger social landscape relative to other identified social groupings. This identity bundle includes references to time, space, history, and place, and it often hinges on relationship threads (actual or perceived) connecting particular groups in the present to the past. NAGPRA seeks traces of shared identity between contemporary claimants and earlier groups who are perceived as the origin sources of extant cultural items.

Conclusion

Heritage values are at once personal, social, and global; they arise from the multitudes of understandings about elements of heritage and their meanings in the present. Cultural heritage itself, with its tangibles and intangibles, might be described as the contents of humanity's social portfolio. It includes jewels of past human experience, embodied in story, song, dance, attire, food, drink, action, thought, object, person, and place. Heritage invokes elements of identity, history, and cultural connection, but it is not a substitute for those concepts. Heritage can embody the sacred, with struggles over differing values relating to access and control often intensified by needs for secrecy and proper engagement. It may be invoked as a sword in the fight for cultural survival, with the tensions of a post-colonial world continuing to imbue cultural values with importance grounded in contemporary struggles for recognition and priority of rights. Recognition of the varying scales and overlapping nature of heritage connections, and the diverse values jostling for position of priority in different contexts, may lead to more productive and insightful decision making and scholarship in the area of cultural heritage management both within and beyond the NAGPRA context.

NAGPRA has served as a watershed event for those interested in the cultural heritage of the indigenous peoples of the United States. It has required academic communities to engage with descendant communities at unprecedented levels, leading to increased understanding of the breadth of perspectives about cultural relationships. It has also led to some high-profile disputes, such as those involving the Kennewick human remains and the Kawaihae Caves objects, which highlight the exponential increase in tensions that occurs when the legal system becomes the venue for resolution of differences. More productive resolutions are being reached in the realms of collaborative research, where parties bringing anthropological and indigenous perspectives jointly engage in the processes of investigating connections between present and past groups and searching for greater understanding of the meanings and importance of identity and cultural heritage in multiple contexts. Laws such as NAGPRA may trigger conversations among disparate stakehold-ers through the consultation and repatriation processes, but meaningful solutions for the care, management, and fate of objects of cultural heri-tage are best developed outside the legal context, in the realm of volun-tary communication and mutual respect. Such efforts may best honor the tapestry of human experiences created by the interlaced threads of all of our ancestors, of peoples in the present, and of those yet to come.

References

Bruning, Susan B.
2006   Complex Legal Legacies: NAGPRA, Kennewick Man and Scientific Study. *American Antiquity* 71(3):501–521.

Deloria, Vine Jr.
1997   Anthros, Indians and Planetary Reality. In *Indians & Anthropologists: Vine Deloria Jr. and the Critique of Anthropology.* Thomas Biolsi and Larry Zimmerman, eds. Pp. 209–222. Tucson: University of Arizona Press.

Kirch, Patrick Vinton
2000   *On the Road of the Winds: An Archaeological History of the Pacific Islands Before European Contact.* Berkeley: University of California Press.
2003   Archaeology and Prehistory in Kahikinui, Maui, Hawaiian Islands. Electronic document, http://sscl.berkeley.edu/⊠oal/research/kahikinui/kahikinui.htm, accessed January 17, 2009.

Merriam-Webster
2008   Merriam-Webster OnLine Dictionary. Electronic document, http://www.merriam-webster.com/dictionary, accessed January 17, 2009.

Ortner, Donald J.
1994   Scientific Policy and Public Interest: Perspectives on the Larsen Bay Repatriation Case. In *Reckoning with the Dead: The Larsen Bay Repatriation and the Smithsonian Institution.* Tamara L. Bray and Thomas W. Killion, eds. Pp. 10–14. Washington, D.C.: Smithsonian Institution.

15

HERITAGE VALUES AND MEXICAN CULTURAL POLICIES: DISPOSSESSION OF THE "OTHER'S" CULTURE BY THE MEXICAN ARCHAEOLOGICAL SYSTEM

Lilia Lizama Aranda

Introduction

In his 1989 work, *México profundo: Una civilización negada,* Guillermo Bonfil argues that there are two Méxicos: "the Deep" (*México profundo*) and the "Imaginary." The "Deep México" consists of the Indigenous Indian communities that predate Spanish colonization, as well as rural mestizo communities, and the urban poor. The "Imaginary México" is formed by mainstream society, the dominant group imposed by the West, which does not acknowledge the cultural reality of the daily life of most Mexicans. Thus, those in power, who are part of the "Imaginary México," have created a model of development that does not include the communities of Bonfil's *México profundo.*

The social groups of Bonfil's "Imaginary México" form the economic, social, and ideological power that extends from the time of the European invasion until today. These groups have sustained historical projects that have not allowed space for groups that descended from Mesoamerican civilization (Bonfil 1989:102). This means that there is a dominant group that does not recognize the dominated group, the "Deep México," which is trying to survive through different strategies of cultural reproduction. The "Imaginary México" sees those of the "Deep México" as "the Other." The concepts of "Other," or "the indigenous" are invented and imposed by the dominant group. The "Other" are the various Indigenous groups that were found in the colonized territory by the colonizers—those in the "Imaginary México" (see the chapters by Altschul; Holtorf; and Russell in this volume).

Centuries after this colonization and even today, groups in power are in the quest for a Mexican identity based on symbols such as the Aztec eagle and the Castillo pyramid of Chichén Itzá, now considered one of the modern wonders of the world. It is understood that these symbols of human heritage are of Indigenous origin, yet there is still little or no space for Indigenous groups to interact with archaeology, the field that is largely responsible for interpreting these symbols for the world. The imaginary groups possess the land of sites such as Chichén Itzá, whereas the Indigenous peoples have no ownership rights and must request a special permit to perform traditional ceremonies, and are even required to pay entrance fees just like tourists.

As in Bonfil's book, we are currently experiencing in México the encounters between the two social groups. The dominant group realizes the existence of the Indigenous and asks questions: Who are these beings? Are they close to me? Are they like me? The dominant group realizes the need for answers to these questions. The communication between the two Méxicos—the Imaginary and the Deep—becomes complex in these modern times. The hegemonic group—the Imaginary—ends up imposing its brand of administrative justice, consequently building a system of cultural reproduction that compromises, but does not extinguish, the existence of the groups within the Deep México. At the same time, those who are part of the Deep México look for new strategies for cultural survival that allow the transmission and application of new cultural manifestations.

Within this complex conversation, there are also encounters between the two groups within the field of archaeology. This is especially true in México, given that before the period of colonization, some of the largest cultures and traditions in Mesoamerica were found there. Many still prevail today, forming a vast and rich tangible and intangible heritage, contributing to the symbolic identity of the country. However, for a long time, the "Other," the Indigenous, the "Deep México," were considered as something valueless, and were not recognized as part of the symbolism that constituted the country. Nor were they recognized as contributing to it. Yet today, just as in the past, Indigenous peoples are alive among us. And today, Indigenous groups such as the Maya are seeking to establish their new identity.

The Context of Mexican Public Archaeology and its Fringes

The Law of National Heritage and the Federal Law of Sites and Historical Monuments of México established that the country's historical patrimony is not transferable, inalienable (unchangeable), and unquestionable.

According to Article 27, the archaeological monuments, physical and non-physical, are property of the nation and are not transferable, and this is indisputable. These words—nontransferable, inalienable, and unquestionable—mean that when México's political constitution was written, there was no consideration of private ownership for patrimonial or cultural heritage. Rather, it belonged wholly to the state.

A negative consequence and one of the biggest problems for the type of archaeology administered by the state is that the cultural policies change every six years, each time the government changes. There are new directors, new managers, and new personnel that do not necessarily honor the agreements made by the outgoing administration. Instead, they pursue new agendas, and grant privileges and positions of power to new sectors that support their new administration. This in itself represents a status quo, whereby few initiatives for shared responsibility in cultural protection have the time needed to enter into the legislative process, gather sufficient support, and be voted on (see the chapter by Soderland in this volume).

A review of present-day archaeological practices suggests three problems related to "the Other," as defined by Bonfil:

(a) The inappropriate protection of heritage and the lack of federal legislation allowing for the creation of public and private companies to help in the protection and conservation of heritage,

(b) The ignorance of who is "the Other," and

(c) The disregard of the dominant group, "the Imaginary," toward the disadvantaged groups and the failure to acknowledge the interests of indigenous groups in cultural protection.

Federal and national behavior: the absence of connections and alliances; the disregard for "the Other" in archaeological protection and conservation

México's Constitution, formed in 1821, declares that the state possesses all the oil, gas, electricity, and water, and all the archaeological sites found within the country. The Instituto Nacional de Antropología y Historia (INAH), the government agency created in 1939 to oversee archaeology in México, has difficulty today in creating connections and alliances with civil groups to administer the tangible and intangible heritage of the nation's 62 ethnic and linguistic groups. It was not until 2001 that the federal government officially recognized the existence of Indigenous groups in the country, and created the National Commission for the Development of Indigenous Towns to help mitigate cultural projects.

In México, there are more than 39,000 archaeological sites (plus the settlements surrounding each one) located in federal, communal, and private lands, but only 173 are open to the public, and the federal government owns the land of only 6 of them: Palenque, Tulúm, Teotihuacán, Cacaxtla, Cholula, the Templo Mayor, and a part of Tlatelolco. The Castillo of Chichén Itzá is considered one of the seven new wonders of the world, but the other 38, 827 sites in México are largely ignored.

Current Protection of Cultural Patrimony: Between the Illogical and the Unreal

In México today, there are four situations related to Indigenous use of archaeological sites, in cases where sites are considered sacred by the Maya, but are restricted in their utilization:

(a) Communities that practice their religion in archaeological sites that are unknown to the state. Those places have been kept jealousy hidden by local communities to avoid tourist commercialization or takeover by the state. There are a vast number of these kinds of places documented in the south of México.

(b) Archaeological sites under the custody of INAH, where Indigenous people make agreements with the guards, usually members of the same group, so they can practice their traditions outside of tourist schedules, usually at night.

(c) Archaeological sites that used to be visited for ritual reasons, but have been discovered by the state administration, restored, and opened to the public. Access becomes forbidden for the Indigenous population, and priority is given to restoration.

(d) Places where, with the goodwill of the authorities, the projects of the Indigenous communities are supported so that they can continue performing their traditions and receiving benefits from interaction with tourists, in places such as Xochipila, Puebla, and archaeological sites in the nature reserve of Calakmul, Campeche. Unfortunately, these are exceptional cases.

In many cases, the federal government sees potential in archaeological sites on private property and takes them over without offering compensation to the landowners. The government operates under a legal system of concessions, which are made with owners who might be interested in investing in sites, and access to the site by the Indigenous community is cut off. An example of this is presented in an interview with an INAH official:

> INAH is watching the archaeological richness of Mexico, in order to do research and dissemination of knowledge, and at the same time to take care of any damages caused by other type of activities.

We get to a good agreement with the owners of those places, so they do invest in the surrounding areas with the objective to turn sites in touristic centers and in areas for economical development, so the inhabitants of the places can receive a benefit. (Sánchez Venegas 2007)

The protection of cultural heritage is carried out in many ways throughout the world. In México, one of these ways involves the acquisition of site objects by the government, with artifacts generally deposited in storerooms; often, years will go by before publication and information reaches the public. In the best cases, some of the cultural remains will be displayed in national museums and international expositions. This type of procurement and management of cultural heritage often limits the participation of the Indigenous community with its own cultural heritage.

An example of this issue developed in 2005 in the community of El Naranjal, in the state of Quintana Roo. INAH had carried out several seasons of excavations, and had recovered and "saved" artifacts and various objects, including pottery and ceramics. Inhabitants of the community confronted INAH authorities, protesting for the recovery of their cultural heritage and asking INAH to return the cultural heritage, stating that it belonged to them. After several years of these petitions, state authorities responded that in order to have the physical return of objects, the community needed to have certain facilities, including an air-conditioned room, in order to store the objects. El Naranjal is located in one of the most underdeveloped municipalities in Quintana Roo, with an infrastructure consisting of one paved street for its 140 inhabitants, mainly farmers. Many of the houses do not have basic services like electricity and tap water. In 2005, the community was devastated by Hurricane Wilma, and in 2006 a grasshopper plague ate all the crops. Nevertheless, the community worked hard to meet the conditions to recover their heritage, meeting all conditions except for providing the air conditioning unit. But the government's promise of returning objects has not been fulfilled. This example illustrates what seems to be the government's logic of taking away tangible artifacts of a community's heritage and asking in return a series of conditions that are illogical and unreal in order to exercise control, while not returning the objects.

There are dozens of cases in México where the official institution has disrupted part of the collective memory and stopped the processes of cultural reproduction, in the name of the national collective, or justified using the philosophy in the country's name. This behavior shows a particular and biased way to protect heritage, unlike the ethics of mainstream heritage protection as illustrated in other countries around the world.

In addition to the protection of archaeological sites, we should consider the protection of the communities' identities; otherwise, they may become lost by displacing the collective memory and ending the transmission of knowledge. The rapid growth of the Maya region also contributes to a loss of cultural inheritance. In a study carried out in Quintana Roo in 2005 and 2006, Lizama and Herrera interviewed 25 Indigenous persons related to an *ejido* system (lands given by the government to the Indigenous people for agricultural activities in various sizes of 20 sq. km. approximately) with a population estimated at 6,000 persons. A questionnaire sought information about many aspects of their life. For example, one question asked if the location of a specific archaeological site was known to them. Only two people responded with the correct answer. This illustrates a modern transformation in the use of archaeological sites from identity places to the current status of being "lost and buried" in touristic, urban, and commercial development (Lizama and Herrera 2005a, 2005b).

The Disregard for the Existence of "the Other" and its Heritage Divestment

México has 62 different ethnic groups and 62 linguistic groups. In 2001, México recognized the existence of "the Other" with the creation of the National Commission for the Development of Indigenous Towns (CDI, Comisión Nacional para el Desarrollo de los Pueblos Indígenas in Spanish). Interestingly, the Mexican archaeological community, as represented by INAH which was founded in 1939, also started to wonder recently who they are, in the context of including Indigenous persons and giving them their rights. At last, they seemed to be asking the questions: Where are those ethnic groups? And what am I going to do with them and their heritage? This is one of the greatest situations facing "the Imaginary" or the dominant group in archaeology today.

In 1821, the imaginary group declared that all persons in the country were Mexican; that is to say, Indigenous people at the time of the Mexican constitution were not recognized, because everybody was now considered equal. Thus, the whole country operated under one flag, one symbol, and one national song, and all features and elements of the past, or the cultural heritage, should be part of a new being titled "México." From that day on, there was no space for the existence of the other, the Indigenous. With the disappearing capacity of the Indigenous community to interact with the protection and conservation of heritage, a unique type of archaeology prevailed, dominated by the state totalitarian policy, which does not allow for competition for archaeological research in México. There has not been, nor is there, consideration for the existence of a different type of archaeology that might include an Indigenous archaeology and a private archaeology in coordination with INAH as the governing body of archaeology. Yet, today, the imaginary group is faced with realizing that at least 10.2 million Indigenous persons still exist in México, and many of them want to use their 28,000 plus sites, which are still part of their collective memory.

A reality in Mexican archaeology is that the dominant groups have the means and potential to use and exploit sites for personal and economical gains, ending up with long-term agreements with the government, whereas Indigenous groups generally lack the resources to develop and use these sites in the same capacity. A typical response by individuals when competing with the dominant group is to sell their interests or lands to developers, with no benefits for the Indigenous groups, other than the immediate cash obtained in the sale of the individual's interest or land.

It is a fact that many of the developed hotels in the Riviera Maya once contained objects of cultural heritage, ranging from structures and pyramids to artifacts and tombs. Very little heritage is rescued in any capacity prior to or during the construction of these hotels. INAH, as the government organization responsible for the protection of this heritage, can show few examples of intervention, in comparison to the overall loss of heritage over time and throughout the region.

Another example of exploitation of cultural heritage in Quintana Roo or locally within the Riviera Maya is a residential development infringing upon a site called Coxol. In this residential development plan, the site of Coxol was reduced in size to a mere 56 × 121 square meters, protecting only a residual part of the main pyramid and several associated structures. A survey and rescue was performed by INAH to determine that out of the entire site, only this small amount was worth protecting in the middle of constructing 1,200 homes. It will be interesting to see how much time will elapse between the rescue of this collected material and the publication of any of the research conducted on this material, let alone to inform the general public how the small area of 56 × 121 square meters and the cultural remains within will be protected or whether there are plans for restoration.

From the perspective of this author, change is required in order to meet and fulfill the requests made upon the cultural heritage in México. New federal legislation is needed, which would support the creation of private businesses to share in the responsibility of protection and conservation of patrimonial heritage, much like the systems found in Spain,

England, Germany, Japan, the United States, and Canada. In these countries, independent businesses participate separately and together utilize the resources of the entire nation, helping to create a higher efficiency in the archaeological recovery, prior to urban, commercial, and touristic development.

For many years in the state of Quintana Roo, specifically in the Riviera Maya, developers have been inclined to make objects of heritage found within their construction site disappear, rather than protecting the site and notifying INAH. It is widely understood that destroying cultural heritage is far less expensive than the expense of rescue or salvage. To exemplify the point, consider that the fines levied against a business for destruction of cultural material are based on increments of 100 and 1000 times the minimal daily wage of a worker, which is 50 pesos, or about US$5. Thus, the maximum fine for any one offense is about US$5000 US. Despite this, there are some positive examples where cultural heritage found within a hotel development is preserved and incorporated into the development, allowing for it to be maintained and for tourists to see and interact with it. Even in this positive example, however, the fundamental drawback is that the local Indigenous culture is not made aware of, or is not able, for economic reasons, to view their heritage. According to Gorodesky and Escalante (1996):

> A positive aspect is that the authorities of INAH, must conform to the government declaration that "...the indigenous people participate in the rescue of their heritage, not only providing hands for the reconstruction, but also providing ideas about how to do the restoration and assume responsibility in guarding the archaeological patrimony. We must remember that the restoration of sites like El Tajín, in Veracruz, was possible thanks to the cooperation and communal voluntary work provided by the community."

Gorodesky and Escalante further state that:

> In many places, the archaeological sites are protected by local guards from the indigenous communities who assume their work with responsibility, because the patrimony is a part of their past, space and identity. This proximity and permanency within the site lets them work with more responsibility and apply a coveting aspect represented in loyalty contrary to that of his government counterparts. Even in some places the constructers in charge design new and adequate ways for restoration, as well diminishing the cost of the operation using local resources (woods, cords, natural substances, etc.) instead of heavy machinery that destroys the surrounding vegetation.

Indigenous contributions and experiences make these indigenous equal in the eyes of many Mexican archaeologists, seeing them as self-taught archaeologists. The same archaeologists of INAH recognize that these restorers of the patrimonial heritage are the indigenous. Notwithstanding all of these rich and vast contributions, the indigenous rarely take part in the decisions and seldom benefit from the projects. (Gorodesky and Escalante 1996)

The concepts and principles generally associated with Indigenous archaeology, public archaeology, and private or contract archaeology in many countries are outside of the conventional representation allowed by the Mexican government. Thus, these concepts cannot be used in the protection and conservation of cultural heritage because they do not exist in México. But over 10.2 million Indigenous people do exist today in México, and professional career archaeologists are willing to assume responsibility in helping to protect their heritage. But at this time, without the modification of federal legislation, persons wishing to interact with or rescue artifacts, for example, can be prosecuted.

There is no better time to address, discuss, and analyze the possibility of including the indigenous, public, and private sectors in archaeology in México.

Current Behavior and Cultural Development in México

Lack of Dialogue and Delay of Legislation to Modernize Cultural Affairs

Since 1994, there has been discussion in México about the modernization of culture (Crespo Oviedo 2003). Currently, we find a country that is modernizing itself and trying to incorporate new policies. Yet, there are difficulties in sectors such as INAH, where there is ongoing resistance to modernizing archaeological policies, especially in relation to the communities that seek to interact with archaeology and cultural heritage.

Indigenous peoples are handicapped in the pursuit of equality because even when it is the responsibility of federal institutions to disseminate cultural heritage, they fail to reach the ears and eyes of the Indigenous. To illustrate the point, how much research performed by INAH is printed in the Maya language for the Maya? Another example is the use of Maya or other Indigenous people as a labor force in the consolidation and protection of Maya sites. This is a two-sided coin because one face presents a happy picture, whereby there is participation and employment of the Indigenous by the federal institution, but more to the reality is the fact that this labor force is temporary, by far the cheapest, and the most uneducated within the country, and thereby vulnerable to exploitation. And yet, they are still required to pay the same fee that tourists pay to enter the archaeological sites. For example, the average daily wage is 50 pesos, while the entrance fee to Tulum is 42 pesos, and to Chichén Itzá, 95 pesos.

The author believes that if the Indigenous were indeed educated to include their cultural rights, many problems related to possession, managements, protection, and conservation of heritage sites would manifest themselves immediately. The Indigenous stand to be the benefactors by logic, but they are precluded because of four factors: (1) federal legislation, (2) education, (3) the difficulty of gathering resources to petition for involvement in possession, management, conservation, and protection of sites, and (4) the need to rise above being a cheap, uneducated, and exploited labor force.

Recently, legislative proposals have been made to address these long-standing inequities, promoting deep changes in the cultural structure, especially in the field of archaeology. Initiatives for a "Law of Diffusion of Culture," which sought to promote the participation of citizenship in general, and of other federal institutions, were presented in late 2006 to the Mexican Congress. The law was stopped, not because it was good or bad, but because it was a law that was dangerous to the status quo, threatening the control and monopoly of Mexican cultural heritage, and threatening the institution of INAH.

In the legislature ending August 31, 2005, more than 30 initiatives were presented to the commission of culture of the Congress. Of these, three were approved and one rejected outright, and 26 remained to be analyzed. Of those 26 remaining initiatives, 10 are related to the creation of cultural institutions for the participation of the public and academic sectors in archaeology (Jiménez 2006)

The Mexican academic sector, however, says that the successor of the heritage and the private sector are omitted in the discussions within these more than 30 initiatives. Contained in these initiatives are discussions about the duplication of overlapping functions between the institutes and the lack of new strategies of administration (http://archivos.diputados.gob.mx). Many are also concerned about who will benefit from the creation of new alliances, with an observation that Indigenous communities could be ignored again (Hernández Navarro 2007).

All the countries in the world have problems with their heritage and México is no exception. In México, the problem is specific, with cultural groups of the "Deep México" requesting the repossession of their cultural heritage and natural resources. This pursuit is made without education, or understanding of the system they are participating in, and they face a government that is not acting in their defense, but divesting them from their culture, fields, lands, and resources in the name of creating commercial and tourist relationships.

The actual enforcement policies of the government focus on professionals related to the cultural sector and, in general, those who interact with cultural heritage. The federal government pursues the indictment of those who interfere with that process or interact with the country's heritage in particular ways. Combining this behavior with the reality that the powerful do not wish to relinquish power can lead to the corruption of a system. There is no room for the development of participation of either the Indigenous community (outside of the labor force) or the private sector in the protection and conservation of cultural heritage. The inclusion of these two communities is feared by the official government actors because there is no desire to create competitive markets against themselves, potentially jeopardizing their control of cultural heritage. On the other hand, the excluded groups perceive that their inclusion in the protection and conservation of cultural heritage would be of benefit in a new system.

The practice of archaeology has been carried out by a well-defined section of the Mexican public sector since 1939. Only a few times have improvements been made with the same rhythm of progress felt in other official institutions, linked to policy changes with each new six-year administration. Observers of behavior in México see that government policies are far from embracing dialogue as a way to solve problems. Thus dialogue, a fundamental part of politics, and relationships built by dialogues are not part of improving the politics of any science in México.

Currently, there are these questions: If we cannot have dialogue or discussion that includes the Indigenous community and the private sector, what kind of policies are being created for the practice of archaeology in México? What kind of archaeology is done if the Indigenous, "the Other," and the professionals of culture are at the mercy of those who persecute and conform to the existing policies in México? In our country, there is a wide gap in the relationships created between the Indigenous along with general participants ("the Deep") and the official governing agencies ("the Imaginary") who are in charge of creating those relationships. Instead, relationships are created by federal legislators' policy making and INAH's petitions for what they specifically recommend or directly want in the archaeological practice. While there is talk in México of modernizing and incorporating new policies, INAH still appears to be resistant to modernizing archaeological policies.

Fringe Archaeologies: from the Perspective of "the Other" in México

In México today, there is an ongoing struggle by those at the fringe of the established system to be included in the changing field of archaeology. Two key components of this clash in archaeology are the following:
   (a) Professionals in the cultural sector who do not belong to the official institution of INAH are precluded from interacting with cultural heritage by federal legislation. This demonstrates a closed door to the creation of new alliances with the private sector, and limits the creation of jobs for many unfulfilled professional archaeologists.
   (b) The practice of archaeology is diminished by a lack of dialogue with "the Other." There is limited opportunity to create alliances between official actors and Indigenous communities and other citizens who have an interest in areas of protection, conservation, and the promotion of cultural heritage. This is especially true for Indigenous peoples as heirs and rightful guardians of what was constructed by their ancestors.
Mexican archaeology limits itself and will never reach its full potential if it does not put forward projects that can involve the private sector, indigenous communities, and other citizens in the economic benefits, protection, and conservation of cultural heritage.

Final Considerations

Mexican archaeologists should be concerned with creating an archaeology that is for the public, responding to questions of who, what, where, why, and most importantly, how have cultures developed and changed over time. They need to take into consideration the interests of the Indigenous community and the public in order to design new objectives in a non-biased archaeological practice, instead of spending time and resources justifying an inadequate system.

   In industrialized countries, the parameters of archaeology are formed by and have ethical principles of the career professional, whose objectives and goals conform to systematic research and a political use of cultural heritage that is in relationship with the value and harmony of economic, cultural, and social rights. The current federal law in México does not allow the creation of space for the free expression of new actors in the cultural field. Until 2005, over 30 initiatives addressed laws of Cultural Diffusion being presented to the Congress for discussion and enactment. However, these initiatives do not include dialogue for the inclusion or the participation of the private sector and Indigenous peoples. It is difficult to modify a deficient system without free and open dialogue with professionals in the field, and the participation of Indigenous groups and the public. Two more initiatives were presented to the Congress during 2007 (see http://www3.diputados.gob.mx/camara/001_diputados/008_comisioneslx/001_ordinarias/006_cultura/004_trabajo_legislativo/001_iniciativas/002_iniciativas_turnadas_durante_la_lx_legislatura).

As a developing country, México's pace of reaching its own public and Indigenous population should be equal to the pace of creating economic relationships with other countries. The current inadequate system can do one of three things: increase or decrease relationships or die. Currently, there seems to be little connection between the values of citizenship and an honest political practice, let alone a valuing of the connection between Indigenous peoples and their cultural past. If we do not bring the value of their past back to them, they can do little to help preserve heritage for everyone.

"The Other" is a producer of memories, images, and artifacts, but is often seen as merely a producer for tourism, becoming a product and a part of the folklore of the country. In reality, Indigenous peoples— "*Mexico profundo*," "the Deep"—desire a new archaeology, more enriched, formed not only by objects and artifacts, but by the preservation of identities and community. This allows Indigenous peoples the enjoyment of proximity with their cultural past, in a nation that allows them their inclusion as a part of new cultural rights.

References

Bonfil Batalla, Guillermo
1989   *México Profundo: Una Civilización Negada*. Grijalbo, México. (Published in English as *México Profundo: Reclaiming a Civilization*, 1996, University of Texas Press).

Crespo Oviedo, Luís Felipe
2003   *Políticas Culturales: Viejas tareas, Nuevos Paradigmas. Derecho y Cultura* 2:23–42.

Gorodesky, Ari Rajsbaum y Escalante Betancourt, Yuri
1996   Los Pueblos Indígenas y el Uso del Patrimonio Arqueológico e Histórico (Indigenous towns and the use of archaeological and historical heritage). http://www.tlahui.com/arqueo1.htm, accessed January 31, 2009.

Hernández Navarro, Luís
2007   El Asalto al patrimonio cultural. Electronic document, http://www.jornada.unam.mx/2005/10/18/027alpol.php, accessed January 31, 2009.

Jiménez, Arturo
2006   Piden expertos que diputados reviertan la reforma constitucional del Senado. *La Jornada* June 14.

Lizama, Lilia, and Israel Herrera
2005a   El Beneficio Económico de la Conservación y Protección del Patrimonio Cultural a través del Diagnóstico Arqueológico e Histórico para los Municipios del Estado de Quintana Roo y del país. Presented at the National day of Consultation: "Hacia un parlamento de Cultura," Cancún, Quintana Roo, Mexico.
2005b   Derechos culturales en el área maya de Quintana Roo: La conservación y protección del patrimonio cultural frente al crecimiento turístico en la zona norte del municipio de Benito Juárez, Quintana Roo. Comisión Nacional para el Desarrollo de los Pueblos Indígenas (CDI), Programa de Promoción de Convenios en Materia de Justicia, México, D.F.

Sánchez Venegas, Adolfo
2007   El gobierno federal no es dueño de Chichén Itzá; de 173 zonas arqueológi- cas abiertas al público, sólo 6 pertenecen a la Federación. Electronic docu- ment, http://www.cronica.com.mx/nota.php?id_nota=310599, accessed January 31, 2009.

PART II

Applying Heritage Values

Section 3

Heritage Values and World Heritage

16

Global Heritage Tourism: The Value of Experiencing the Past

Ian Baxter

Introduction

This chapter aims to draw together a number of strands of thinking on heritage tourism at a global scale, in an attempt to consider the question applicable in both research and operational contexts: in tourism terms, what is the value of experiencing the past? (see the chapters by Graham; Lertcharnrit; and Shen in this volume). The underlying assertion or stance being taken is that while "heritage" is now an accepted given as a major concept in tourism development opportunity and visitor motivation, there needs to be further analysis of the relationship between the emergent trends in heritage management and understanding and tourism management and trends. While tensions are likely always to remain between the easily polarized attitudes of conservation versus development, the majority has now moved beyond this simplistic rhetoric and needs to be addressing the greater challenge of reconciling emergent subjective and objective treatments of information and data at the intersection of heritage and tourism (see the chapters by Graham; Lertcharnrit; and Shen in this volume).

Form of Answer

The chapter will not rehearse the debates and development of tourism, heritage and the cognate field of heritage tourism: such issues have much material already available on them and are typified by both generalized texts explaining the concepts of heritage tourism (Timothy and Boyd 2003; Misiura 2006), or works using specific lenses through which aspects of heritage tourism are analyzed, be they discipline-based (such as marketing), geographically based, or thematically based (Baldwin 1999; Basu 2006; Prideaux et al. 2007; Smith and Robinson 2006). The chapter thus looks again at where changing definitions and understandings of both heritage and tourism are going to affect the relationship between them (specifically around the experiential notion of a historic environment), and thus the notion of where heritage tourism will develop as a niche topic. It takes an unapologetically theoretical approach and is therefore light on facts and figures, though it does provide clear signposts as to the location of accessible data. The issue of facts and figures derived from available global tourism statistics needs to be considered in the whole, and while specific instances of heritage tourism will be illustrated, the broadly theoretical discussion will attempt to add to the debate from a perspective looking at tourism trends.

Reframing the Question

In some respects, the research question being addressed must be restated so that it is not so easily dismissed by obvious and divergent discipline-oriented responses. In asking what the value is of experiencing the past, the heritage lobby (for want of a better term) is most likely to take a socio-cultural stance. The arguments stated have tended to be centered on the role of the past as having educationally vital goals, socio-cultural aspirations around notions of society, identity and cross-cultural understanding, and intrinsic worth (Allison et al. 1996; Henson et al. 2004; papers in Clark 2006). The latter of these arguments, having been out of favor for some years, now, even in governmental circles, seems to be gaining weight once more having perhaps lost its traditional politically conservative overtones (Jowell 2004, 2005). Taken at its extreme, the value of the past as a stand-alone representation (physical or ideological) philosophically remains in certain quarters to be of greater significance than that which would place the value of the past being a handmaiden on the path to society's future. Conservation in all its forms thus gets pitted against development in all its guises, and heritage tourism then often becomes a target for both operational and academic criticism (Gordon 2007; Reynolds 2005). The tourism lobby, alternatively, tends to focus on those operational aspects and the potential limitations of heritage managers (often seen to be wielding more power and influence than they themselves feel they possess). Restrictions on development and opportunities for the varying facets of tourism development and destination management thus may be seen to suffer from a shallow relationship that stretches only as far as visual marketing of locations or configurations of management and visitor engagement at individual site specific nodes. The weightiest amount of data from this lobby comes from the economic impact of tourism, where visitors have expressed a preference for heritage as part of their tourist offering (Cuccia and Cellini 2007; Henderson 2007). These expressed preferences, as will be shown later in the chapter, are pretty much a constant at the generic level of the "heritage" label, with differentiation seen most clearly in parts of the world that have utilized heritage as a resource in a quite particular fashion. Measurements for these expressed preferences at the extreme relate not to an understanding of heritage tourists, but to the transactional value in dollars accruing on the relevant country's tourism satellite account, or via tourist flow measured in visitor numbers (Bryan et al. 2006).

A slight reframing of the research question alters the perspective on heritage tourism away from disciplinary tension toward opportunities for future co-exploration and resolving of issues. It is therefore more appropriate to ask where value can be found in the experience of the past as part of touristic activity. The emphasis has been moved to the notion of the tourist experience, as it engages with the general transformation model of heritage from concept to object in its returning cycle (i.e., from concept to object), where objects that have been labeled through processes of management as part of the authorized heritage discourse or elsewhere (Smith 2006), are reintegrated and represented with the concept of heritage through the visitor's mediated experience of that heritage object (at varying scales). This simplistic model of transformation as developed by the author elsewhere has the advantage of considering general principles at work in the management of heritage and at a generally applicable scale that does not get bogged down in such disciplinary tensions as noted above (Baxter 2004, in press).

Where the idea of the "experienced" heritage object is being transformed back into the concept of heritage for the tourist, management processes at work underneath the surface simplicity of the transformation can begin to tease out where particular values associated with heritage tourism can be located, and so in turn, an answer to the restated research question can be attempted. This is aided by the more detailed modeling specific to heritage tourism undertaken by Timothy and Boyd (2003), itself emergent from the work of others in the field (Hall and McArthur 1998; Kirk 1963; Richards 1996; Tunbridge and Ashworth 1996).

Definitions

Definitions are of course vitally important for setting the parameters of measurement and discussion: but here it is perhaps more important to recognize that the quest for agreed definitions for heritage objects and heritage tourists at a detailed level leads to a reversion into those disciplinary boundaries that we are trying to break free from. The contestation within the terms heritage and heritage tourist (as one type of consumer of heritage) is not always helpful in the broadly based values debate. It is accepted that a criticism of vagueness and woolly thinking may be leveled, but in the reframing of the problem, a generalist scale must be moved back to before the more detailed debate may continue. It is further suggested that the interplay between heritage and tourism at conceptual and operational levels, evidenced by the implication of constancy of transformation in the model already noted, by nature creates a friction that can lead to the intransigent opinion that heritage and tourism have irreconcilable aims and philosophies.

The broad groupings of definitions (and definitional value) must thus serve to illustrate the ideas proposed. The values of experiencing the past then can be found where the host and guest encounter (with additional involvement of a range of stakeholders) takes place within the location of a historic environment or culture-historic context. The encounter is usually a mediated institutional process, meaning that an organization is deliberately enabling the touristic host-guest relationship to have historic connotations by virtue of its location or presentation. The categories of experience and the defined values of the experience of the past using tourism as the method of encounter will be further explored in sections below using some of these broader definitions which more easily sit with the hard data for global heritage tourism that exists.

It is worth noting, however, that the interrelationships of the general concepts that are being dealt with here are aided by the particular refinement of the term "heritage" to "historic environment." The increased usage of this latter term sprung from one of the many persistent problems of definition that had both spilled out from the academy, and had developed from new management interventions in conservation practice. Though the term "historic environment" has existed for some time (Baxter 2004), in Western European contexts, it is only in the past decade that it has come into mainstream use in professional practice. The reason why this particular definitional example is of importance is that what looks to be a simple terminological change has achieved a number of things in terms of the tourism-heritage relationship.

As noted in Baxter (2004) considering the changing use of terminology in the United Kingdom:

> Firstly, it has clearly differentiated the academic consideration of heritage from the professional practice of managing the historic environment. Secondly, it acknowledges clearly the role of proactive

management and need for strategic direction and purpose within the sector, by recognizing that heritage assets are part of a broader physical context which must be considered as a whole environment. This second effect has also placed the sector on a par with other "environmental" disciplines with more developed management structures (and better public perception of what the sector does), i.e., natural environment and built environment. Environmental "assets" can thus be identified, compared and valued (Countryside Agency 2003). Thirdly, the tautological differences between conservation and preservation, and whether management of heritage assets is a barrier to development is removed (Kincaid 2002). Administration and application of backward looking heritage protection legislation thus becomes (in concept and perception if nothing else) modern and focused, valuing heritage assets amongst other aspects of our everyday habitat.

Most importantly…a change from heritage to historic environment, has placed the sector at the heart of tourism development and community regeneration, both as a stakeholder and strategic leader in the process, rather than simply as a provider of an asset for exploitation by tourism or other sector managers. It would be naïve to suggest that a simple re-branding of the sector from heritage to historic environment has brought about such a profound change, not least as there is no one organization which directs heritage management in the UK, but usage of the term can be measured incrementally against equivalent changes to management structures, attitudes, treatment and acceptance of the role the sector can play as its external environment has changed over the past five years. It has also potentially brought scope for clarity of thinking about the wider role of heritage within society, acknowledging the interplay of the relationships between practical and theoretical considerations of historic assets existing in the modern world. Essentially, with heritage now being valued in differing ways (De la Torre; Getty Conservation Institute 2003; Jowell 2004; National Economic Research Associates [NERA] 2003) management of the historic environment in the UK can now be compared more readily with Cultural Resource Management in the USA (King 1998) and Australia (Australian Heritage Commission, Australian Committee for IUCN 2003).

Global Heritage Tourism Data

Tourism data and its collection methodologies is a science that is fraught with difficulty (Lennon 2002). Data exists for heritage tourism at numerous different scales and configurations (from site based, through regions, nations, and international to global), dependent on the source and purpose of analysis. Reviewing the major sources of international data for heritage tourism has the advantage of analytical interest from a combination of sources. Professional market research companies, such as Mintel, Keynote, and Euromonitor International undertake investigations into tourism at a general industrial scale, and also cultural and heritage tourism as an identified niche within the global tourism market (Euromonitor 2004, 2007; Mintel International Group 2002, 2004). Intergovernmental organizations and international research organizations such as the World Tourism Organization, ATLAS, and the European Travel Commission also have relevant data allied to international standards for Tourism Satellite Accounting (TSA) reports in the context of global trade, and also via international agreements for the promotion of cultural and social goals (Bund and World Tourism Organization 2003; World Tourism Organization 1995).

The picture that emerges from the individual datasets pertaining to countries, country groupings, or types of touristic activity, as well as global overviews, identifies the key importance of heritage and culture (a conflated definition, where in general terms cultural sites may be considered to have heritage linkage through art form or location) to both transactional and experiential value chains. Indeed, heritage sites as a conglomerate group type of attraction have the highest global tourist attraction value sales after casinos and theme/amusement parks (Euromonitor 2007). Differences in the form of experience within the attractions market and the heritage attractions market must be highlighted, as it reinforces the power of the heritage tourism market: many kinds of heritage tourist attraction (such as national parks and museums) generate little in terms of revenue due to low or free admission costs, but the value share of market that these sites hold keeps them at the top of tourism sales league tables.

Market research identifying new trends in tourism additionally reports the strongest growth within the sector for industrial tourism (Euromonitor 2004, 2007), although it is still a small base level within the niche sector. Based around interests in former industrial techniques, the surge in growth has been fueled by media interest repeated across the world in cultural and technological development, and by industrial concerns themselves where a globalized economy has put manufacturing industries in greater direct contact with product consumers.

Heritage tourism and cultural activity is recognized as being less of a "high-brow" activity and more accessible to the mainstream traveler and visitor, and motivations to visit heritage sites are reported as showing steady growth across demographic groups. Of particular note are figures quoted by the World Tourism Organization, whereby 20 percent of tourist visits to Europe have cultural motivations; 60 percent of European outbound tourists have cultural motivations in their visits to other parts of the world; and 40 percent of all international trips contain heritage as a component (if not the driving force) (Mintel International Group 2004).

A globalized trend in tourism toward the short-haul/mid-distance markets of short breaks sees a niche grouping of "city breaks" coming into dominance. Tourism destination image studies as well as national tourism organization marketing strategies usually have heritage imagery as a dominant factor affecting or attempting to drive motivation (Wee et al. 1986). Such a trend brings to attention the changing definition and focus away from the individual heritage site as an attraction, to the wider historic environment, and heritage location being the attraction and motivation for the tourist to visit a destination. The most recent commercial assessment of general world tourism trends makes reference to this in saying that:

> Traditional attractions, such as historic buildings, great museums and galleries, and natural wonders have been the basis for many major tourist venues and are used as the primary marketing hook by the countries concerned. Italy, with the presence of world famous galleries and historical sites, and the presence of the Vatican, is a prime example of culture-driven tourism.

> The world's top tourism attractions include a wide range of different types of attraction. Interestingly, some of the most well-known tourist attractions, such as the Vatican in Rome, the Acropolis in Athens, the Hermitage in St Petersburg, the Tower of London, Notre Dame in Paris and many others do not feature on the list of most-visited tourist attractions, as the cities concerned have such a plethora of ancient monuments and museums that tourists tend to be dispersed. On the other hand, in a newer city like Sydney, the Opera House is usually the first port of call for tourists. (Euromonitor 2007: section 8.3)

The tourism trends with regard to heritage tourism are unmistakable: actual receipts and actual share of market have increased for the heritage tourism sector year-on-year, and are projected to continue. The reasons for this can be found within the changing form of the tourism experience and its utilization of heritage characteristics for places.

Forms of Experience and Experience Economy

The standard management tool of business environment scanning generates data to support the political, economic, sociocultural, and educational aspirations for the development of heritage tourism. This relationship implicitly and explicitly encompasses the "self-actualization" realm from Maslow's hierarchy of needs, where one considers the immersive or experiential aspects of a heritage tourism guest in any particular heritage location. The actualized value for the heritage tourism host or operator is most often derived from international and domestic tourism flows and, by consequence, political and economic stages that the cultural consumption of tourism fulfills in any particular country.

The value that an industry or supply-side approach is looking for tends to be measured through business performance indicators and a location or country (Litteljohn and Baxter 2005). The value of that performance gets defined in a number of typical methods: visitor numbers; generated admission revenue at attractions; estimated equivalent revenue or benefit derived from tourism footfall at a location; and tourism visit motivational modeling using techniques such as tourism destination image studies and projections. Variables associated with this include, obviously, the length of stay at an attraction or location; the level of immersion and additional associated revenue generation (from, for example, souvenirs or events); and the opportunity to influence present and future behaviors (through image identification, repeat visitation, and so on).

The differing and deepening of forms of access to heritage tourism additionally are reflecting broader societal developments in the realms of both culture and technology. Pine and Gilmore and, through critique, Florida's work considering globalization trends and immersive attractions within the "experience economy" are further altering the form of heritage tourism experience and also the locations where value can be found in that experience of the past (Florida 2004; Pine 1999). Visual consumption of sites and sights (as originally proposed in the seminal work of Urry [2002]); the experiential immersion or exposure to historic environments through "heritagescape" approaches to the management of historic locations (Garden 2006); and brand stretch through heritage product development all generate additional forms of heritage tourism on a global scale. The important socioeconomic and intercultural development opportunities afforded by such technological and socially motivated developments (e.g., conservation camps, archaeological excavation holidays, eco/social-tourism projects) also use heritage as a lynchpin in many parts of the developing world. The heritage niche label within the tourism industry can be hard-wired to a quest for authenticity (chapters in Rojek et al. 1997) on the part of the tourist, levering economic and social advantage out of undeveloped destinations (in terms of traditional tourism infrastructure—hotels, etc.). Mention should also of course be made of World Heritage sites due to their iconic status and driver of tourism development, particularly in developing countries

(Harrison and Hitchcock 2005; Leask and Fyall 2006; Shackley 2000). An entire canon of research relates to this particular category of heritage site, so further detailed consideration is not made here.

So, Where is the Value to be Found?

Such a question must consider both the current situation and recent history of the rise of global heritage tourism, and must not forget the future trajectory of heritage tourism as predicted (Euromonitor 2007; Mintel International Group 2004). A maturity in the understanding between the needs and desires of conservation versus development needs to take a matrix approach to the understanding of the information that can be made available. Stakeholders and consumers can be understood in greater depth through consideration of their perceived contexts for decision making and actual behaviors. Analysis of stakeholders at the World Heritage site of Stonehenge (Baxter and Chippindale 2002) considered generic groupings of the managers, the managed, the unmanaged, and the anti-managed: these generic characteristics when plotted against the behaviors associated with the tourist site of Stonehenge can be used as a useful illustration to begin to generate generic locations for those behavioral value chains—transactional, experiential, and consequential.

The typical visitor journey sequence as traditionally understood within tourism (Middleton and Clarke 2001) mirrors the building of these value chain locations. A visit to a heritage location may have a transactional value (based on admission, footfall, etc.), an experiential value (preference to visit based on tourism destination image, desire to undertake repeat visitation, other form of engagement on psychological/educational level), and a consequential value (actual repeat visit, support for heritage conservation causes, organizational ability to undertake heritage enhancement as a result of tourist engagement). It should be noted that these value labels are explicitly linked to a touristic understanding of heritage sites, and are therefore complementary to those established in other heritage value debates, notably Clark (2006).

Scenario planning as an area of increased interest to national tourism marketing organizations and policy units uses some of these generic information and data markers to take heritage tourism to the next stage of development: plotting the future (an example of this is VisitScotland's Scenario Planning Department's undertaking "crystal ball gazing" for Scotland's national tourism organization[1]). Social and economic goals which are the predominant drivers within the tourism industry are now beginning to target heritage as a particular niche for development (as seen in the industrial tourism group noted already). Combined with technological opportunity to both enhance the visitor experience, and mitigate the pressures on the conservation of the physical (and intellectual or cultural) heritage to a shared benefit, visits may become virtual, reconstructions may become more authentic, and the holy grail of commercial viability for heritage protection might be conceivable.

The teasing out of the value of the heritage tourism experience of the past can be said then to be manifold—but the manipulation of the management information about the sector (the tourism data) and the categorization and characterization of the data are of vital importance to understand. The right question therefore needs to be asked about global heritage tourism—we recognize what it is, and to some extent we can measure what it does; but we now need to strategically consider how we use our understanding of it.

Conclusions

The broad trend in global tourism toward immersion of the consumer in the experience economy has major implications for heritage sites and heritage tourism more generally. A move away from prescriptive definitions which have arisen from local operational concerns aids the comparison of guest/consumer encounter with the historic environment across different parts of the world within that overarching tourism context of global heritage tourism. The values of experiencing the past in terms of global heritage tourism can therefore be found by analyzing situations based under three broad headings: with immediacy for the host and guest, or producer, and consumer—transactional value and experiential value; and for a delayed or sequential realization of value (again for both the producer and consumer)—consequential value. The available data for heritage tourism comes from a number of contexts or stages for experience/encounter, and the forms of experience can also be assessed. The data within the field of heritage tourism is both vital and possibly misunderstood.

The remaining challenge is somewhat paradoxical—while the broader context of the touristic heritage experience is being enhanced through greater research and understanding of different value chains, processes of globalization, and intercultural exchange, the data being collected continues to be focused on particularity and individuality, making aggregation of information and misunderstanding ever more problematic. Furthermore, it has to be remembered that particularity and individuality are character traits that give heritage and the historic environment its intrinsic appeal (and dare it be said, value) in the first place. The field of understanding is not likely to be simplified as the fine-graining of data collection within tourism and heritage continues to be improved—but it does make for a rich and vital seam of opportunity for all interested stakeholders for the future of both conservation and development, indeed, heritage tourism development. Modeling and the understanding of the shared and divergent value creation mechanisms and created value chains within the broader debate on heritage values are thus vital for an industrial sector (tourism) that has global dominance.

Endnote

1. http://www.visitscotland.org/research_and_statistics/scenarios/scenarioplanning visitscotla nd.htm

References

Allison, G., S. Ball, and P. Cheshire
1996 *The Value of Conservation? A Literature Review of the Economic and Social Value of the Cultural Built Heritage.* London: English Heritage.

Australian Heritage Commission & Australian Committee for IUCN
2003 *Protecting Natural Heritage using the Australian Natural Heritage Charter.* 2nd edition. Canberra: Australian Heritage Commission in association with the Australian Committee for IUCN World Conservation Union.

Baldwin, D.
1999 *Experiencing Heritage: Making Sense of Industrial Heritage Tourism.* University of Bristol, Bristol, United Kingdom.

Basu, P.
2006 *Highland Homecomings: Genealogy and Heritage Tourism in the Scottish Diaspora.* London: Routledge.

Baxter, I.
2004 From Heritage to Historic Environment: Professionalising the Experience of the Past for Visitors. *Journal of Hospitality & Tourism* 2(2):5–25.
In press *Heritage Transformed: From Concept to Country House—the Objectification of Cultural Resources in the United Kingdom Castle Acre.* United Kingdom: Heritage Marketing & Publications.

Baxter, I., and C. Chippindale
2002 From 'National Disgrace' to Flagship Monument: Recent Attempts to Manage the Future of Stonehenge. *Conservation and Management of Archaeological Sites* 5(3):151–184.

Bryan, J., C. Jones, and M. Munday
2006 The Contribution of Tourism to the UK Economy: Satellite Account Perspectives. *The Service Industries Journal* 26(5):493.

Bund, P., and the World Tourism Organization
2003 *Co-operation and Partnerships in Tourism: A Global Perspective*. Madrid: World Tourism Organization.

Clark, K., ed.
2006 *Capturing the Public Value of Heritage—The Proceedings of the London Conference*. January 25–26, 2006. London: English Heritage.

Countryside Agency
2003 *The State of the Countryside 2003*. Cheltenham, United Kingdom: Countryside Agency.

Cuccia, T., and R. Cellini
2007 Is Cultural Heritage Really Important for Tourists? A Contingent Rating Study. *Applied Economics* 39(2):261.

De la Torre, M., and the Getty Conservation Institute
2003 *Assessing the Values of Cultural Heritage: Research Report*. Los Angeles: Getty Conservation Institute.

Euromonitor
2004 *World Market for Tourist Attractions*. London: Euromonitor International.
2007 *Travel and Tourism—World*. London: Euromonitor International.

Florida, R.L.
2004 *The Rise of the Creative Class: And How it's Transforming Work, Leisure, Community and Everyday Life*. New York: Basic Books.

Garden, M.
2006 The Heritagescape: Looking at Landscapes of the Past. *International Journal of Heritage Studies* 12(5):394.

Gordon, W.
2007 Case News: Court in the Crossfire. *Property Week*, May 11: 70–71.

Hall, C.M., and S. McArthur
1998 *Integrated Heritage Management: Principles and Practice*. London: The Stationery Office.

Harrison, D. and M. Hitchcock, eds.
2005 *The Politics of World Heritage: Negotiating Tourism and Conservation*. 1st edition. Clevedon, United Kingdom: Channel View Publications.

Henderson, J.C.
2007 Communism, Heritage and Tourism in East Asia. *International Journal of Heritage Studies* 13(3):240.

Henson, D., Stone, P., Corbishley, M.J., (eds.), and English Heritage
2004 *Education and the Historic Environment*. London: Routledge.

Jowell, T.
2004   *Government and the Value of Culture.* 1st edition. London: Department for Culture, Media & Sport.
2005   *Better Places to Live: Government, Identity and the Value of the Historic and Built Environment.* 1st edition. London: Department for Culture, Media & Sport.

Kincaid, D.
2002   *Adapting Buildings for Changing Uses: Guidelines for Change of Use Refurbishment.* London: Spon.

King, T.F.
1998   *Cultural Resource Laws and Practice: An Introductory Guide.* Walnut Creek, California: AltaMira Press.

Kirk, W.
1963   Problems of Geography. *Geography* 48:357–371.

Leask, A., and A. Fyall, eds.
2006   *Managing World Heritage Sites.* Amsterdam: Elsevier BH.

Lennon, J.J.
2002   *Tourism Statistics: International Perspectives and Current Issues.* London: Continuum.

Litteljohn, D., and I. Baxter
2005   The Structure of the Tourism Industry in the United Kingdom. In *The Business of Tourism Management.* J. Beech and S. Chadwick, eds. Pp. 21–39. London: FT Prentice Hall.

Middleton, V.T.C., and J. Clarke
2001   *Marketing in Travel and Tourism.* 3rd edition. Oxford: Butterworth-Heinemann.

Mintel International Group
2002   *Visitor Attractions in Europe: An Overview.* London: Mintel International Group.
2004   *Cultural and Heritage Tourism: International.* London: Mintel International Group.

Misiura, S.
2006   *Heritage Marketing.* Oxford: Butterworth-Heinemann.

National Economic Research Associates (NERA)
2003   *Economic Issues in the Heritage Sector (Report for the Monument Trust).* London: NERA.

Pine, B.J.
1999   *The Experience Economy: Work is Theatre & Every Business a Stage.* Boston: Harvard Business School Press.

Prideaux, B., K. Chon, and T. Dallen, eds.
2007   *Cultural and Heritage Tourism in Asia and the Pacific.* London: Taylor & Francis.

Reynolds, N.
2005   Architectural Gem Saved, but it could be the Last English Heritage Says, Government Cuts Mean no Cash for More Rescues. *The Daily Telegraph*, March 23:3.

Richards, G.
1996   Production and Consumption of European Cultural Tourism. *Annals of Tourism Research* 23(2):261–283.

Rojek, C., J. Urry, and D. MacCannell, eds.
1997   *Touring Cultures: Transformations of Travel and Theory.* London: Routledge.

Shackley, M.
2000   *Visitor Management: Case Studies from World Heritage Sites.* Oxford: Butterworth-Heinemann.

Smith, L.
2006   *Uses of Heritage.* London: Routledge.

Smith, M.K. and M. Robinson, eds.
2006   *Cultural Tourism in a Changing World: Politics, Participation and (Re)presentation.* Clevedon, United Kingdom: Channel View Publications.

Timothy, D.J., and S.W. Boyd
2003   *Heritage Tourism.* Harlow, United Kingdom: Prentice Hall.

Tunbridge, J.E., and G.J. Ashworth
1996   *Dissonant Heritage: The Management of the Past as a Resource in Conflict.* Chichester, United Kingdom: Wiley.

Urry, J.
2002   *The Tourist Gaze.* London: SAGE.

Wee, C., A. Hakam, and E. Ong
1986   Temporal and Regional Differences in Image of a Tourist Destination: Implications for Promoters of Tourism. *The Service Industries Journal* 6(1):104.

World Tourism Organization
1995   *Concepts, Definitions and Classifications for Tourism Statistics.* Madrid: World Tourism Organization.

17

Evaluating Values of World Heritage Sites and Cultural Tourism in China

Chen Shen

Introduction

In recent years, international tourists have been fervently attracted to the natural and cultural sites of China. According to the statistics reported by the Chinese National Tourism Administration (CNTA), the authoritative agency of the central government, the number of foreign tourists (excluding those from Taiwan, Hong Kong, and Macau) reached 22.2 million in 2006, a 9.65 percent increase from the previous year. Revenue from international tourism generated US$33.9 billion in 2006, adding significantly to the 622.9 billion RMB (US$85 billion) generated from domestic tourism.[1] Both governmental and private tour agencies clearly realize that the backbone of this booming tourism in China is the renowned historic sites and monuments, especially the World Heritage sites (WHS).

Cultural tourism has played a major role in marketing locations to tourists who desire to see heritage-rich countries like China, Egypt, India, and Mexico, along with many other nations usually considered "underdeveloped countries." The study of cultural tourism has only recently become an area of research (e.g., Singh 1994; Smith 2003; Mckercher and du Cros 2002; also see the chapters by Baxter; Graham; and Lertcharnrit in this volume). In China, it is a new and particularly challenging subject for heritage management professionals who are dealing with the unexpected growth in cultural tours to heritage sites, most of which have yet to be the subject of long-term preservation plans. Under such circumstances, both cultural heritage management (CHM) professionals and tourism developers in China have found a common solution, at least temporarily—applying for and promoting WHS as a measure for preservation as well as for increasing tour destinations. Since 2004, when UNESCO's 28th session of the World Heritage Committee was held in Suzhou, China has been gripped by a WHS fever that continues unabated to this day. Behind this WHS fever is a process of evaluating and re-evaluating values of cultural heritage, a situation that has led the public to wonder whether they underestimated the values of their heritages, and how they can make the most of heritage values.

This author has been asked repeatedly to accompany cultural tours to China as a resource professional, and noticed that each of these tours inevitably promotes WHS designations as the central destinations. Over the years and the course of many visits to the same sites, I have observed changes at many of China's World Heritage sites. One of these changes is that heritage values have been recognized and re-evaluated by the local government and public, and applied to local economic development through the promotion of cultural tourism.

Defined by the 1972 UNESCO World Heritage Convention, a site to be inscribed on the World Heritage List must have "outstanding uni-versal value" (UNESCO 1992). Even though today the definition of the "universal value" of World Heritage sites is still only vaguely discussed or evaluated (Pomeroy 2005), it is clear from the recently defined ten cri-teria that issues of cultural values, human traditions, and social/historic significance are most heavily considered. These criteria do not include the public value of world heritage; but in the real world, the public has an opinion of cultural values from their own perspectives (Clark 2006). In some places, the public (including tourists, owners, private and gov-ernment agencies) could evaluate the heritage with numbers in terms of investment (preservation) and revenues (tourism) (Throsby 2006). Therefore, in this chapter, I will consider how values of heritage can be evaluated and applied to events of socioeconomic development. In other words, I would like to examine how cultural value can be transformed into economic value in the event of tourism development, as well as their causes and consequences.

Cultural Value of the World Heritage Sites

The government of China ratified the 1972 UNESCO Convention in December 1985. As of 2009, 38 Chinese sites have been designated as World Heritage sites—27 cultural heritage, 7 natural heritage, and 4 mixed cultural and natural heritage—thereby ranking third in quan-tity for countries on the list (UNESCO 2009). The first 6 sites were inscribed in 1987 and included important archaeological sites, historical architecture, and monuments: These sites were the Imperial Palaces of the Ming and Qing Dynasty (the Forbidden City in Beijing), the Mausoleum of the First Qin Emperor (housing the famous terracotta statues), the Mogao Caves (also known as the Caves of the Thousand Buddhas), the Mount Taishan (the most important of the Five Sacred Mountains and an important pilgrimage site), the site of Peking Man at Zhoukoudian, and the Great Wall. The significance of the cultural values of these sites, like the Great Pyramid in Egypt and the Temple of Apollo Epicurius in Greece, does not need much clarification as they truly represent many aspects of "outstanding universal values." In the beginning, motivation for participating in the UNESCO WHS program was especially strong among the CHM professionals in China who saw it as an open channel through which they could communicate with conservation specialists in other parts of the world. Having returned to social stability after the "Cultural Revolution," China desperately needed preservation measures for cultural heritage sites that were under threat from natural erosion and human destruction. It was through international involvement that early designates, like "the Peking Man" site at Zhoukoudian near Beijing, were able to be preserved with the much-needed technology and financial investment. Moreover, through interaction with UNESCO specialists, China trained a number of conservation professionals who later worked on such heritage sites as the Mogao Caves in Dunhuang, as well as the Leshan Giant Buddha inscribed in 1996.

Before 1997, only 16 World Heritage sites in China were inscribed. Most of these sites had been well known to the world and had already been major tourist destinations in the country. The WHS title seemed to be an honor for the nation to pride. At that time, the public valued these sites highly because of their social, aesthetic, visual, spiritual, and educational significance. We have little evidence to suggest that, in those days, values of cultural or historical sites were connected in any form to revenue generation. Rather, the benefits from the UNESCO acknowledgment of their "outstanding universal value" were clearly related to conservation and preservation. Therefore, the interest in applying for WHS designations during the first 10 years of China's WHS nominating process was driven by needs of preservation and recognition of the renowned cultural value of these sites.

Economic Value of the World Cultural Sites

Since 1997, the public value of the World Heritage sites has changed dramatically, triggered by booming tourism (Xiao 2004). Heritage sites like the Ancient City of Ping Yao and Old Town of Lijiang, both inscribed in 1997, were little known to most Chinese, l   e to the rest of the world. However, once they became World He   ites, tourists, especially international tourists, descended upon t   ce small and quiet towns; local residents quickly seized the econo..... opportunities for their benefit.

Ping Yao is in the center of the Shanxi Province and in 2002 had a population of less than 500,000. In China, it is considered a typical small sized, county-administrative city. The town, which boasts 2,700 years of history and is famed for its well-preserved enclosure with an ancient layout and comprehensive traditional architectural components, was deemed to have merits of "outstanding universal value." After becoming a WHS designate, tourism increased 300 percent in the second year. Annual admission revenues of the two major museums (the Shuanglinsi Temple and the Zhenguosi Temple) increased dramatically from 180,000 RMB (US$24,000) in 1996 to 7.8 millions RMB (US$1.1 millions) in 2000. Where no public transit system had existed previously, 13 public transit routes were established. The numbers of trains stopping at Ping Yao increased to 26 daily, double from the previous 13 per day. The county of Ping Yao had an average annual revenue of only 40 million RMB (US$5 million) before the ancient town became a popular tourist destination, while in 2000 the annual revenue reached 110 million RMB (US$14 million) (Yan 2004).

In Yunnan Province, the Old Town of Lijiang, which was hardly heard about even in China, became one of the hottest destinations on international tour itineraries. After the success of Lijiang in Yunnan Province, the Old Town received over two million tours yearly. Tourist revenue reached 134 million RMB (US$17.8 million) in 2000, accounting for about a half of the county's gross domestic product (GDP). The Mount Huangshan, praised as "the loveliest mountain of China" by ancient and contemporary poets, painters, and writers, as well as modern photographers, has been an important part of the natural scenery throughout Chinese history. After Mount Huangshan was listed as a WHS designation in 1990, the number of annual visitors jumped from several million to 200 million (Yan 2004).

Without exception, all of the WHS tour destinations show an increasing economic value. These developments in China's WHS have clearly added concrete dollar figures to the idea of world heritage, effecting a transformation in the public perception of the importance of these sites away from strictly cultural values to economic values, a transformation the public clearly welcomes. Compared to the first 10 years of the WHS nominating process, which seemed to be only concerned with what the CHM professional and heritage managers of central governments would like to do, proposals for WHS nominations now are submitted in droves from local governments all over China. With the exception of 2002, China has been successful in garnering WHS designations every year since 1997. Currently there are 33 proposals that have been pre-screened by the State Administration of Cultural Heritage (SACH) and are waiting for the World Heritage Committee to review. Obviously this enthusiasm, driven by cultural tourism, comes with concerns: there are good causes and bad causes leading to different consequences that challenge CHM professionals.

Causes and Consequences

By 2006, a total of 2,351 archaeological sites and historic monuments were listed as National Major Heritage Protection Units under the SACH, the central government agency for cultural heritage management. From a view of cultural value, historical preservation, and social influences, any of these heritage sites could be a candidate for WHS nomination. In fact, all of the 38 current WHS designations are from this SACH category. In 1982, as a preservation measure to control rapid expansion and development in urban areas, the SACH designated a new category of cultural heritage: cultural city/town/village with important historic and cultural values. By 2006, the State Council verified a total of 96 such cultural heritage cities, 44 heritage towns, and 36 heritage villages. This measure for managing cultural heritage is a result of re-evaluating the cultural value of existing heritage locations to include issues of adjacent village landscape and urban size. These previously overlooked issues now require a defined management strategy if the fast urbanization of these places (a natural outcome of these establishments becoming increasingly popular cultural tourism destinations) is to be controlled.

Local politicians observed the benefits brought forth by developing heritage sites for tourist destinations, and showed their support and enthusiasm for reviving previously overlooked issues of heritage value. They have started to use the buzz word "cultural administration," indicating that local politicians are re-evaluating the cultural heritages in their administrative districts and are willing to collaborate with CHM workers to restore and preserve heritage for the benefit of local economy.

Driven by such political agendas in competition for WHS designations, many CHM workers were presented with opportunities to conduct much-needed preservation projects (Shi 2002). For example, in 1999 Chongqing Municipality, the largest and most populous city in China, restored 100,500 square meters of grassland around the Dazhu Rock Carving heritage site. In Lijiang, ironhanded administrators shut down most pollution-generating factories and invested 400 million RMB

UNIVERSITY OF ...
OF ...
LIBRARY

(US$53 million) into infrastructure reconstruction that favored the natural environment and promoted heritage preservation. In October 2001, the UNESCO Asian committee's fifth annual conference was held in Lijiang, where international representatives observed the progress and offered high praise to the CHM authorities for their efforts and outcomes (Mu 2003).

In the new wave of competition for WHS nominations, local authorities have set a relatively high priority for promoting cultural heritage. Such promotion and testimony has called for increased public awareness of the value of their cultural traditions. The youth today have many more resources than older generations for understanding the social and cultural values of heritage. Through the WHS competition, more and more people will appreciate, understand, and testify to the cultural value of Chinese heritage. Public awareness of cultural heritage value is so crucial that a National Heritage Day was established on the second Saturday of June each year. The first celebration in 2006 was a direct result of increased enthusiasm for the WHS titles.

Evaluating the heritage value for WHS competitions has had an influential impact on large infrastructure developments, like the South-to-North Water Transfer Project, currently under way in China (Shen in press; Shen and Chen in press). For example, Anyang, a modern city in central China built entirely on the ruins of a 3,300 years old Shang Dynasty Bronze Age capital (called Yin Xu), would be negatively affected by the building of transporting water channel structures. Normally, CHM managers are powerless when facing representatives from politically driven projects like the Three Gorges Dam and the South-to-North Water Transfer project (Shen in press). But this time was different, because Yin Xu was proposed by the Anyang municipality and backed by central government CHM authority, and was being reviewed by the World Heritage Committee for 2006 nomination. The local community successfully persuaded the commissioners of the South-to-North Water Transfer Project to change the Middle Route to bypass the site. Clearly, Anyang authorities made good use of the powerful political pressure inherent in the application for WHS designation to achieve this detour. As a result, Yin Xu became China's 33rd World Heritage site.

However, getting local politicians and their financial backing involved in the process of the competition has come with a price (or unfortunate consequences). Local governments clearly have their interests fixed on seeing profits generated from their investments in cultural preservation. Once a location becomes a successful WHS, heritage management issues drop substantially in terms of priority on local administrative agendas. Over the past several years, business developments at heritage sites have spiraled out of control in most places where cultural heritage departments have been pushed aside by tourism departments (Wang 2002). For example, only six years after being placed on the World Heritage List, the Wulingyuan Heritage District in Hunan Province (inscribed in 1992) boasted over 400 hotels and restaurants plus several hundred shops and service facilities. All this was within a 39 square kilometer area of the scenic valley. Pollution from human activities has badly contaminated the designated natural heritage. In 1998, UNESCO sent a review panel to inspect the site. The committee report stated:

> The Bureau invited the Provincial and Central Government authorities to augment the resources for the management of the site. Co-operation with the Chinese Academy of Sciences and other such institutions may be needed in order to assess the World Heritage values of the site's biodiversity. The Bureau drew the attention of the State Party to manage tourism development in and around the site on a sustainable basis.... The Bureau recommended that the report of the IUCN/Centre mission to China be transmitted to the relevant Chinese authorities. (UNESCO 1998)

Such local government management of cultural heritage, with a socio-economic agenda, brought a new round of destruction on the heritage environment—which is the challenge that China's CHM authorities and professionals are facing today. The best example of this is from the loss of cultural treasures in the home town of China's greatest philosopher and educator, Confucius (or Kong Zi in modern Chinese). Qu Fu, in Shandong Province, was established as a capital of the Lu State of the Eastern Zhou Dynasty (771–221 BC), when Confucius lived (551–479 BC). Today, one quarter of the city's 640,000 residents are Confucius' descendants of 73 to 78 generations. Here in the old downtown, a magnificent temple was built in 478 BC to commemorate Confucius to which many emperors throughout history came to pay their respects and to worship. The temple, mansion, and cemetery complex in Qu Fu have been well protected and preserved through the patronage of emperors for over 2,500 years, and they were designated a World Heritage site in 1994.

In 1999, the local government decided to have the site placed under the management of the Bureau of Municipal Tourism, a decision designed to benefit the city economy by expanding cultural tourism. The tourist bureau then contracted a private corporation to manage business development at the site. A series of business decisions proposed by the company was supported by the city administration despite criticism from the CHM authorities whose concerns were completely ignored. Not surprisingly, the priority given to the business decisions and disregard for the CHM concerns led to a series of incidents causing the loss of many cultural relics.

In one such incident in 2000, a car was allowed to drive into the temple courtyard, and struck a stone stele dated to the Yuan Dynasty (1270–1368). The stele, with important inscriptions detailing the affairs of the imperial court and ranked as a Grade-One treasure, was fragmented beyond repair. Next, the company used high-pressure water guns and metal scrapers on over one hundred ancient wooden structures to clean them. The result was permanent damage to large areas of lacquer-surfaced color paintings and decorations on the architecture, areas that previously had been preserved for hundreds of years.

Investigators from the SACH, on behalf of the central government, did whatever they could to correct the problems and to control the damage. The incident was widely publicized and caused a wave of national rage. The SACH used this opportunity to provide the public with a wake-up call by exposing numerous similar incidents and by criticizing bureaucratic misconduct in CHM activities.

Bureaucratic misconduct is a serious matter for policy making behind the practice concerning tourism development. There were no single acts or laws in China concerning WHS management until 2006. The Great Wall is one of the first World Heritage sites in China. However, the Acts of Great Wall Protection, released as Order #476 from the State Council, was executed on December 1, 2006, 19 years after the site's designation. This is the first regulation to control local governments' misuse of cultural and natural heritage resources like the Great Wall and provide clear procedures by which the CHM authorities can coordinate with other local government departments, including tourism, in case of mismanagement and destruction of cultural heritage. At the same time, the SACH produced another important document, Acts of World Heritage Site Protection and Management, to provide strict guidelines for managing the 38 World Heritage sites in China and two dozen more currently being considered for future applications. These guidelines and regulations may seem to have come late, but this is better than not having any regulations at all. Their creation demonstrates that Chinese heritage managers and professionals are learning from painful lessons, and are making every effort to correct deficiencies.

Evaluation of Heritage Value and Cultural Tourism

Managing World Heritage in relation to cultural tourism in developing countries has always been a challenging subject of study for many CHM professionals and tourism developers (Leask and Fyall 2006; Pomeroy

2005; Thapa 2003, in press). There are no sufficient case studies for China, a nation with 38 sites on the UNESCO World Heritage List, and with many more to come. My observations have led me to the realization that the mixed causes and consequences of desire for WHS designation, such as those discussed above, are of course a part of the progress in improving WHS management during the rapid socioeconomic transformation in China.

During such a transition, values of heritage can be measured not only by their social significance and cultural influence, but also by their capacity for generating resources for the preservation and conservation of sites. Clearly, heritage management as related to cultural tourism should be carried out by balancing both the cultural value and economic value of heritage sites in the view of the public. With the public awareness of heritage values, practices in heritage management tasks could be supported and implemented effectively. Thus, the question is how to balance the cultural values and economic values of heritage. Although answers to this question will vary in different countries and under different circumstances, obviously in cases where these values are imbalanced, managing World Heritage sites will be a difficult task.

While it is easy to blame uncontrolled local economic development, particularly in regard to cultural tourism, for interfering with the CHM process, we should also acknowledge that cultural tourism has increased public awareness for assessing heritage values in a brand new way, as well as bringing about the financial benefits needed for preservation projects. For example, in the case of Ping Yao and Lijiang, the value of this once-upon-a-time fairytale town would not have been properly evaluated and applied if it were not on the UNESCO list. Furthermore, the cultural values for Xidi and Hongcun, two villages in remote areas of southern Anhui Province that preserve ancient layouts, traditional architectures, and ritual tradition stretching back over 1,200 years (WHS inscribed in 2000), would not have been revealed to populations outside the villages. It is worth noting that of 36 nationally designated heritage villages "with important historic and cultural value" in China, only Xidi and Hongcun have WHS designation. Clearly, the cultural value of the remaining 34 heritage villages is not appreciated to the same degree by the public, or even by their own inhabitants, as that of the 2 WHS villages. The non-WHS villages could not produce the same economic value as would the 2 WHS villages. Such differences are noted by national and local governments as well as preservation specialists, who are seizing this opportunity (desire for WHS designation) to promote cultural tourism in order to plan a long-term preservation strategy, as well as to generate funding for preservation in those troubled ancient villages (Luo 2007). Therefore, cultural tourism, in its promotion of

WHS destinations using various media, has played an important role in re-evaluating the cultural value of heritage by transforming it into economic value.

However, cultural tourism is of course commercialized, even though cultural experience was the goal of the tours. Uncontrolled commercial-driven activities such as fake-antique vendors, overpriced restaurants and bars, and inferior cultural performances, are overflowing heritage sites, which certainly degrade to some degree the cultural value that heritage has attained. But the problem could be even worse if heritage management was considered a lower priority than promoting local tourism by local governments, like the case at Qufu where the cultural value of the area could be literally demolished. Large numbers of visitors also create a danger for fragile heritage sites. The millions of annual visitors to the Forbidden City in Beijing have caused serious erosion on the original ancient stepping-stones and floor tiles in the palaces. Although using the funds generated from tour admissions to carry out restoration using replicas is possible, the cultural value of this important WHS designation would be considered differently than that created by the previous assessment by the World Heritage committee.

In summary, cultural tourism provides opportunities as well as challenges for managing World Heritage sites in China, as can be seen in other parts of the world. Case studies from China during this period of fast-growing economic development should be examined, particularly in regard to how we can evaluate and re-evaluate heritage values in relation to promoting WHS and to managing cultural tourism. The foundation for examining heritage value under such circumstances is clearly built on the public evaluation and assessment for what heritage means to them, both socially and economically (see papers in Clark 2006). Such public awareness of heritage values is no doubt being promoted, to a great degree, by cultural tourism.

Endnote

1. The sources of numbers were adopted from web publication of government documents from the Chinese National Tourism Administration of People's Republic of China, accessed on October 1 2007.

References

Clark, Kate
2006 *Capturing the Public Value of Heritage*. London: English Heritage.

Leask, A., and A. Fyall
2006 *Managing World Heritage Sites*. Oxford: Butterworth-Heinemann.

Luo, Qingxi
2007 Ancient Villages in China: Troubles and Opportunities. *Chinese Cultural Heritage* 18:10–29.

Mckercher, Bob, and Hilary du Cros
2002 *Cultural Tourism: The Partnership between Tourism and Cultural Heritage Management*. New York: The Haworth Hospitality Press.

Mu, J.
2003 The "Lijiang Model" Showing a New Way of Preservation and Making Use of Cultural Heritage. *Chinese Cultural Relics News*, July 14.

Pomeroy, Melanie C.
2005 Assessing the Cultural Significance of World Heritage Sites: A Case Study from Avebury, Witshire, England. In *Heritage of Value, Archaeology of Renown*. C. Mathers, T. Darvill, and B. J. Little, eds. Pp. 301–316. Gainesville: University Press of Florida.

Shen, Chen
In press Mission Impossible: Current Archaeological Practices in the Three Gorges Reservoir, China. In *Damming the Past: Dams and Cultural Heritage Management*. S. A. Brandt and F. A. Hassan, eds. Lanham: Lexington Books.

Shen, Chen, and Hong Chen
In press Cultural Heritage Management in China: Current Practices and Problems. In *Cultural Heritage Management: A Global Perspective*. Phyllis Mauch Messenger and George S. Smith, eds. Gainesville: University Press of Florida.

Shi, J.
2002 Cooling the Thoughts During the Heat of Competition for World Heritage Sites. *Shanxi Jiji Guanli Ganbu Xueyuan Yuanbao* 10(1):105–121.

Singh, Shalini
1994 *Cultural Tourism and Heritage Management*. Jaipur: Rawat Publications.

Smith, Melanie K.
2003 *Issues in Cultural Tourism Studies*. London: Routledge.

Thapa, Brijesh
2003 Tourism in Nepal: Shangri-la's Troubled Times. *Journal of Travel & Tourism Marketing* 15(2):117–138.
In press Financial Mechanisms for World Heritage Sites in Least Developed Countries. In *Cultural Heritage Management: A Global Perspective*. Phyllis M. Messenger and George S. Smith, eds. Gainesville: University Press of Florida.

Throsby, David

2006   The Value of Cultural Heritage: What Can Economics Tell Us? In *Capturing the Public Value of Heritage*. Kate Clark, ed. Pp. 40–43. London: English Heritage.

UNESCO

1992   *Operational Guidelines for the Implementation of the World Heritage Convention*. Paris: UNESCO.

1998   State of Conservation Report: 1998. Electronic document, http://whc.unesco.org/archive/repcom98a4.htm#sc640, accessed January 13, 2009.

2009   World Heritage List. Electronic document, http://whc.unesco.org/en/list, accessed September 16, 2009.

Wang, Y.

2002   The Biggest Threats to World Heritage Natural and Cultural Sites: Out-of-Control Tourist Business Development. *Hubei Daily*, June 28.

Xiao, H.

2004   History Tells Future: Analyzing the Heated Competition for World Heritage Sites. *Urban-Village Construction* 2004(8):18–19.

Yan, Lizhong

2004   The Fate of the World Heritage Sites. *Economic Perspectives Daily*, July 10.

18

The Protection of Heritage Values while Utilizing World Heritage Sites for the Benefit of the Community

Roy Eugene Graham

> The State Party is encouraged to integrate the protection of the
> cultural and natural heritage into regional planning programs
> and adopt measures which give this heritage a function in the
> "day-to-day life of the community."
>
> (UNESCO World Heritage Centre 2000)

Introduction

UNESCO'S Convention concerning the Protection of the World Cultural and Natural Heritage adopted in 1972 has a number of goals designed principally to encourage the protection of universally important sites. Increasing tourism is not one of the goals, however, and excessive visits threaten the value and indeed the very essence of some World Heritage sites (Shieldhouse 2007; see the chapters by Baxter; Lertcharnrit; and Shen in this volume). A site's inclusion on the World Heritage List depends heavily on the authenticity and integrity of the site and the way it is protected and managed.

There is sufficient anecdotal evidence that World Heritage listing encourages tourism: "tour companies and tourist accommodation with access to World Heritage areas commonly advertise that fact in their marketing material; and tourism developers and entrepreneurs preferentially pursue opportunities in and around World Heritage areas" (Buckley 2004).

The Conservation Plan for Lunenburg and Koper/Capodistria

In the last decade, I had the opportunity to be the director of several "Community Conservation Strategies," which included a historic site in Canada and one in Slovenia. I assembled a team of experts that included planners, economists, historians, architects, archaeologists, and travel industry specialists, several of whom had been formerly on the staff of the Colonial Williamsburg Foundation.

Both the 18th century fishing town of Lunenburg, Nova Scotia and the 15th century Venetian Republic town of Koper in Slovenia were at crossroads in the early 1990s! The traditional industries connecting these historic towns with the sea that dated from more prosperous periods of fishing, international trade, and specialized maritime crafts had virtually vanished. The absence of this traditional economic base had left both towns in decline.

Thus, designation for the World Heritage List presented both communities with tremendous opportunities for new economic development through international marketing, increased tourism, new cultural industries, and rejuvenation of local business and industry. At the same time, the listing presented the sites with the considerable challenge of protecting the heritage value of the historic towns and assuring that new development and increased tourism would not diminish the communities' integrities, both as places to live and as cultural sites of international importance.

In both places, unplanned-for tourism was already beginning to change the townscape and re-direct the economy. The social fabrics were changing. The future was uncertain in both towns. These pressures, if left unchecked, would have continued to change the communities whether or not the townspeople desired change.

The communities were powerless to stop change from uncontrollable external forces. However, they both decided to influence change. To begin with, the communities needed clear visions of what they could be, and what they wanted to be. Lacking visions, the citizens of Lunenburg and Koper and their governments could not begin to manage the sites in ways so as to protect the cultural resources. The citizens did not see the benefit of the cultural resources to their communities. Without an overall strategic plan with defined goals, they had no strong commitment to motivate their involvement in change.

By engaging the professional team to produce a strategic conservation plan, they sought to make a real difference to the kind of changes that were about to occur. Instead of resisting change, the communities saw that they could direct change. Instead of fighting inevitable declines from pressures beyond their control, the communities sought to replace them with new initiatives of their own.

Although "orchestrated" by professionals, the conservation strategy that was developed actually belongs to the two communities, having been formulated through a lengthy process of consultation. Throughout the process, the primary concern was to ensure that the strategy reflected how each community understands itself and its unique visions for the future.

Preparation for the Plan

In preparation for the team of experts' involvement in the plan, various community-input meetings were held in partnership with mayoral and governmental representatives, professionals, and business leaders from the town, and cultural and educational representatives. Many problems and opportunities for improvement of the towns were identified, including the relationship between the historical centers and the surrounding infrastructure. It was clear that the sites were valuable from both a cultural and an economic point of view and that these values were intertwined.

In surveys, both communities were asked to express their ideas in a variety of ways. Regardless of "presumed" heritage value, citizens were asked to locate their "special place" in the town. This was defined as the place "that has special meaning for them and that they would like to see preserved despite whatever changes might occur" around it. The exercise was designed to get the community thinking and talking about cultural values, development, and conservation in the town. It also sought to help integrate the heritage conservation strategy into other needs of the community so that it would be supported by second nature in the "day-to-day life of the community"(UNESCO World Heritage Center 2000).

In addition to surveys, community vision workshops were held to gather ideas about the future of the towns once they became World Heritage sites and also to gain a sense of the strengths, weaknesses, opportunities, and threats that will play a part in moving toward that future.

For example, the opportunities and challenges of Lunenburg were synthesized into five visions for the future of the town as a World Heritage site. The overarching priority for these visions was an overwhelming mandate to improve the quality of life using the heritage to the community's advantage while taking every step to conserve its value. This foremost priority of conserving the heritage and improving the quality of life for future generations was also the conclusion reached by the citizens in Koper.

The five visions identified in Lunenburg were: (1) the renewal and revitalization of the marine industry; (2) the development of tourism as a sustainable industry—from heritage products and through the renewal and revitalization of traditional industries—from which all townspeople can potentially profit; (3) the enhancement of cultural and educational opportunities for the townspeople, including the establishment of a "learning institute" in partnership with local universities and schools; (4) the development of heritage products as a new industry to ensure long-term sustainability for Lunenburg; and, (5) the improvement of opportunities in the community in health care, sports, and recreation.

Common elements identified in both Lunenburg and Koper were the need to conserve the value of the heritage, culture, and architecture of the town's center, its tradition as a hub of social and business activity, and its traditional industries, records, archives, history, and town plans. Both communities desired a strong, locally based economy built on traditional strengths but augmented by newly formed partnerships concerning tourism, heritage, and cultural assets. They both wanted a sustainable economy that improved local retail and commercial activity as well as an enhanced quality of life.

Koper had once been the capital of the larger region of Istria, both during the 15th century Venetian empire and in the period of Napoleonic domination during the early 19th century. Although 21st century Venice is practically sinking because of the weight of excess tourism, Koper, with roughly the same historic architecture of even more complex historic value, was an island almost forgotten. The modern city serves as the largest port on the Adriatic, yet the town center remained devoid of tourists and townspeople alike. Storefronts were vacant and streets were deserted. Venetian palaces were vacant and rotting. Since Koper was cut off from the sea by the expanding modern port, the authenticity of the heritage resources was threatened even more than in Lunenburg which had no new industry.

In enthusiastic town meetings, the citizens of Koper were asked to analyze their town, and five distinct visions resulted there as well. The overarching priority addressed by these visions was to conserve the heritage values while using them to better the quality of life for the townspeople and for the region of Istria (which, at this time, is predominantly located in Croatia).

The first vision was to develop tourism as a sustainable business that all townspeople can potentially profit from. This is directly linked to the second vision, which was to develop heritage products as a new (old) industry. Historically, Koper was reputed as a center of craft production. The marketing potential of the site being included on the World Heritage List would provide opportunities to expand and transform craft production into a highly profitable and sustainable economic generator.

The economic stimulus expected by the first two visions would enable the remaining three visions. The third vision was to create social and entertainment activities that would benefit all generations. The promotion of cultural tourism combined with the wealth of talent, resources, and skills in Koper presented a unique opportunity for the community to become a center of culture and education in an international marketplace. The benefit of these activities would then improve the economic base, while presenting new opportunities for local citizens of all ages to be involved as students, teachers, and facilitators.

The fourth vision was to create intergenerational cultural and educational opportunities. As a consequence of the proposed cultural tourism and resultant economic stimulation, the citizens of Koper would be able to gain the requisite funding to restore and conserve their heritage resources. Thus, a new start with a strategic plan would be able to provide a better quality of life in the social realm of interchange and entertainment. The community would then become a more interesting place within which to live with an enhanced quality of life. "Quality of life" is a term used to describe the amenities a community has to offer, including clean air and water, safe streets, open space, cultural events, and recreational activities. Koper was already blessed by having many of these amenities. With the introduction of cultural tourism, however, these facilities can be better utilized by the citizens of the community, thus providing activities financed by nonlocal sources that would alleviate the burden on local taxpayers. Also relating to the quality of life in Koper, the fifth vision identified by the stakeholders was to improve opportunities for health care, sports, and recreation.

In short, the citizens of Koper wished to benefit from being inscribed on the World Heritage List, but did not wish to lose the town to a kind of tourism that diminishes the integrity and livability of the community. Instead, they aspired to utilize the potential of the listing in a careful manner that would permit revitalization of the town's economy without losing a community voice in the retention and protection of heritage and way of life—both for the people who live there now and for future generations.

Creating a Strategy

After completing the visions, the next step was to create strategies for implementation. In both towns, the final plan recommended two new "umbrella organizations" as the best vehicles to provide these means. These organizations were to be created by consolidating existing and competing groups. These new organizations were to be regulated by newly created public-private groups called Heritage Advisory Committees. These supervisory committees would work under the mayors and town councils in order to assure that standards of conservation practices and business did not affect the quality of heritage values. The recommended Heritage Advisory Committees would also serve as architectural review boards, but with expanded missions.

The first private organizations, the "Community Foundations," would manage initiatives in support of the heritage management and cultural tourism agenda. Incorporated under existing Canadian law and new enabling legislation in the Republic of Slovenia, these nonprofit organizations were designed to work with the government and private interest groups to conserve heritage, culture, and community traditions.

The second private organizations, the "Community Corporations," were to be set up as for-profit organizations that would initiate, promote, coordinate, and manage the communities' economic activities. These organizations were intended to break new ground as partners working together to market and support business enterprises to cultivate stakeholder benefits from the sites being included on the World Heritage List. These for-profit corporations would be required to submit business plans to the Heritage Advisory Boards for rulings on appropriateness and effect on heritage values.

The foundations and the corporations were conceived to work together with local government in developing and delivering the cultural tourism product, in protecting and conserving heritage resources, and in developing and sustaining the cultural, recreational, and social life of the communities. Existing organizations in the towns would be superseded or abandoned but would have a place on the board of directors of the new group. Furthermore, the directorships of the new organizations would themselves overlap in order to assure a common vision.

As not-for-profit organizations, the foundations would be tasked with directing and managing the heritage resources effort in both Lunenburg and Koper and the communities' infrastructure to support other programs. These tasks would include championing the conservation of the heritage visitor orientation, developing a memorable visitor experience and educational interpretation, publishing guides (such as architectural surveys), fundraising, devising heritage property management schemes (such as through easements), finding ways to get community involvement in heritage conservation, developing work programs and internships, providing the communities with preservation assistance, and conducting and funding research in support of preservation technology.

The Community Foundations were expected to take a major role in the management of the heritage. Some of their main goals as nonprofit organizations were to assist townspeople in restoration and other projects, to be proactive in acquiring conservation easements, to initiate revolving funds and grants, and to instigate other incentive producing methods of heritage resources management. The foundation would also develop the capacity to make professional services available at little or no cost to property owners of the towns.

The foundations were to compile a library of conservation information pamphlets and to take the lead in enhancing the beauty of the town by initiating historic building renovations, street and alley cleanups, colorful banners, landscaping, and lighting improvements. The foundations in both communities would be able to maintain special conservation-related databases for architectural restoration. By leading the effort for a managed environment and organizing the community heritage conservation effort, the foundations would ensure that the potential World Heritage site is attractive and inviting while protecting its universal value.

The respective foundations were also set up to contribute to implementing the communities' visions by staging conferences, seminars, workshops, and courses on conservation topics. In Koper, these would be taught in conjunction with the establishment of a new regional university that is to be housed in the town's historic center. In Lunenburg, this educational component would be partnered with local schools and universities in nearby Halifax. In addition, they were to establish scholarship and apprenticeship programs for the local youth to ensure that traditional building and conservation skills are available to young people.

Both historic towns are open, living communities; they are neither museums nor theme parks. In fact, from a tourism perspective, the ideal in drawing tourists and encouraging visitor spending was to provide a genuine heritage experience in a noncontrived way. At the same time, however, it was vitally important that the experience for visitors be enhanced if visitors are to stay for an extended period and/or expend more fiscally. There also was, of course, the corresponding need of having the means to generate the income to underwrite the cost of providing those enhanced experiences, such as the infrastructure improvements needed to accommodate increased visitation. To achieve this, heritage restoration in Koper and Lunenburg was determined to be a public/private partnership that fused historical interests with economic benefits.

Both Community Conservation Strategies recommended a visitor interpretation system that has proved successful elsewhere, including at many of the world's greatest heritage attractions. The uniqueness of implementing this strategy in Koper and Lunenburg was that, although the towns would be "living history museums," they would depend on the townspeople and entrepreneurship to make the experience work. Under this plan, at the arrival/welcome point, visitors would purchase a general admissions pass, which would be a badge that they would wear during their visit. Their badge would not only allow free entry to the various demonstration and interpretive buildings within the historic town centers, but also confer discounts on paid-admission attractions, special transportation, and retail and concession purchases from foundation-operated concessionaires. Existing historic craft production would go on with visitors observing unobtrusively. Visitors would, however, have to pay for the privilege of seeing the process and having it explained by a docent. The revenue generated would be used to restore and enhance the historic environment and provide quality of life improvements to the community.

On the other hand, the second organizations, the newly recommended Community Corporations, were designed to be for-profit organizations. They were envisioned to be a chamber of commerce with expanded missions and were intended to be community business organizations that work together with the Community Foundation and town governments. These for-profit organizations in both towns could then break new ground in giving the business sector of Lunenburg and Koper the ability to capitalize on their sites' inclusion on the World Heritage List.

The corporations were designed to be purpose-built business organizations that function as partnerships of the various business interests in the communities. They were to be built upon the premise that many small economic solutions provide greater long-term stability than a few large solutions. In that way, the corporations would become catalysts for the sustainable economic growth of Lunenburg and Koper.

The corporations were expected to take on responsibility for marketing the towns, their products, and their educational and recreational facilities. In this capacity, each corporation would work with the corresponding foundation in the areas of heritage tourism, special events, arts and craft products development, and heritage commercial initiatives. The corporations thus become the marketing arms for both their own initiatives as well as for those of the foundations. The corporations were also tasked with tourism program management and marketing and the economic development programs. The parameters of these tasks are wide-ranging and include managing and marketing the tourism experience, establishing and supporting commercial and industrial partnerships, facilitating the growth of existing—and the establishment of new—commercial enterprises and economic activities, finding new ways to jump-start the economies, finding financing and funding for existing and new businesses and tourism, providing business advice and support, introducing micro-enterprise programs, orchestrating special events and hospitality packages that promote the heritage product, and enhancing the range of tourism product offerings and the retail and commercial sector in the historic town centers.

Corporation marketing would also comprise licensing designs from the artist/artisan for production by a third party. A royalty on sale would go to the artisan. In this instance, the corporation would work with vacant working areas/studios to provide them to community members at affordable rates. The intention was to create a "craft village," or an area that would become a demonstration area in each town.

For businesses that manufactured their own products, the corporations typically would manage co-op marketing programs under a common branding, such as branding products with "Heritage." Alternatively, the corporations would contract with the manufacturer to handle the marketing. In addition, the corporations would manage and market packaging programs. Packages would solicit tourism through "getaways," learning products, adventures, and the like. The corporations would also work with local ground operators and tourist services in delivering products on the ground. To survive, many local producers of traditional crafts would have to diversify into other products and other markets.

With the drive and industriousness typical of the entrepreneur, many of these efforts have succeeded and today, the economy in both towns is more diversified than it has been in the past. There are now a mix of craft items and assembly-line-based businesses, manufacturers that produce different products (many of which are globally exported), and an active and growing tourism sector.

Conclusion

The recently evolving patterns of economic development in both towns can be expected to continue in the future. Craft industries will continue to be important in this development. Product and market diversification of manufacturers will continue to be a successful strategy. Bearing in mind the visions developed in community' workshops in Koper and Lunenburg, a number of initiatives were proposed, both to enhance the communities' traditional craft and maritime economies and to develop new economic opportunities in the fields of cultural tourism, education, and heritage craft production.

An enhanced craft economy based on traditional strength is presently being developed at both sites. The five interrelated initiatives for the historic sites which will be utilized to enhance the traditional, craft-based economies are: (1) to establish a craft consortium and marine consortia; (2) to enhance the heritage experience for visitors; (3) to establish incentives for traditional industries to participate in tourism; (4) to enhance the towns as Artists' Villages; and, (5) to establish telecommuting industries.

Since the strategies proposed introduce expanded parameters to the business of heritage conservation, there was a need in both instances to have a clear and fair process established by which public preservation interests and private development interests can be negotiated and balanced. The Heritage Advisory Committees (HACs) were established as watchdogs for community conservation. They were therefore conceived to be strong, professional, and proactive bodies that would report to the mayors and town councils.

The broadened mission of the HACs in Koper and Lunenburg are the preservation of sites and structures of historical, cultural, archaeological, or architectural significance and their appurtenances within the designated historic districts or as listed on the World Heritage List and control of any proposed physical development within it. Each member of the committees possesses a demonstrated special interest, specific knowledge, or professional or other training in such fields as history, architecture, architectural history, planning, archaeology, anthropology, conservation, landscape architecture, urban design, or related disciplines.

Review applications for "Certificates of Appropriateness" for projects that will have an effect on the exterior appearance of sites in the official heritage sites and in the determination of the appropriateness of any proposed development or construction project that is of such nature that could effect the authenticity and conservation of the heritage districts is the responsibility of the two Heritage Advisory Commissions. It should also be noted that the new organizations would not spend the respective town's funds, thus allowing local governments to concentrate on such projects as the harbor cleanup, expanding infrastructure, traffic control and rerouting, and other pressing matters.

While both the Community Foundations and the Community Corporations required initial new enabling legislation and hopefully, seed funding, from governmental sources, it was intended that both organizations eventually would become self-sustaining—the corporations from their profit-making ventures and the foundations from private fund-raising sources. One essential element of the relationship between both sets of organizations is that a portion of the corporation's profits is channeled into the Foundations, in support of the mutual aims in the realm of community cultural conservation.

With the drive and industriousness typical of entrepreneurs, many of these efforts have succeeded and today, the economy in both towns is more diversified than it has been in the past. There are now a mix of craft items and assembly-line-based businesses, manufacturers that produce different products (many of which are globally exported), and an active and growing tourism sector. In the end, the enterprises will pay for the conservation of these World Heritage sites while acting in the interest of the stakeholders. Economic values will be part and parcel of the protection of ethical and historical values. This will give "heritage a function in the day-to-day life of the community" (UNESCO World Heritage Centre 2000).

References

Buckley, R.
2004   The Effects of World Heritage Listing on Tourism to Australian National Parks. *Journal of Sustainable Tourism* 12(1):70–84.

Shieldhouse, R.
2007   Economic Effects of World Heritage Listing. Working Paper. College of Design, Construction and Planning, University of Florida.

UNESCO World Heritage Centre
2000   *Information Kit: The Convention.* Electronic document, http://whc.unesco.org/cid+175, accessed January 15, 2009.

19

Heritage Values and Meanings in Contemporary Thailand

Thanik Lertcharnrit

Introduction

The past is not a "foreign country" in the sense that it exists as another world. Conversely, the past is with us today and tomorrow, and has a wide variety of values and meanings for the modern and contemporary world (see e.g., Carver 1996; Darvill 1995; Holtorf 2005; Lipe 1984). The past also has been consumed (e.g., Gathercole and Lowenthal 1990; Holtorf 2007; Misiura 2006; Peleggi 2002; Rowan and Baram 2004). This paper attempts to explore the use of the past in modern Thailand using Lipe's (1984) and Darvill's (1995) models as a framework.

Informational Value

Heritage, both tangible and intangible, (see the chapters by Altschul; Baxter; Bruning; Clark; Clark and Heath; Okamura; Russell; and Silberman in this volume) has been part of an educational program in Thailand to educate people about the origin and history of the Thai people. Thai and foreign archaeologists have made significant contributions to the understanding of human and cultural evolution in Thailand in particular, as well as in Southeast Asia in general, during the past four decades. For instance, it was once mentioned by a prominent Thai elite historian that the "Thai" originated in Altai Mountain in the Russian Far East and Siberia and after that migrated southerly to China and then further south to modern day Thailand. This historiography was without any supporting evidence, but it was well received among general audiences and some well-educated people, and it became a dominant statement and theory about the origin of Thai people. However, the theory has been challenged by a corpus of archaeologists that, based on archaeological evidence, the modern-day area of Thailand has been occupied by anatomically modern people since 40,000 years ago, if not earlier. This statement is supported by a series of excavations at various prehistoric sites including the Lang Rongrien Rockshelter (Anderson 1990), Moh Khiew Cave (Pookajorn 1996), Spirit Cave (Gorman 1970), and Tham Lod Rockshelter (Shoocongdej 2006). Some scholars further point out that the roots of human evolution in Thailand may further go back to 500,000 years ago referring to fossils of possible hominid classified as *Homo erectus* found in Lampang Province (thus called "Lampang Man"), northern Thailand (Pramankij and Supawan 2007). It is now a strong consensus that modern Thai people might have descended from those first anatomically modern humans who first settled in the area since prehistoric times (see e.g., Natapintu 2007; Wongthes 1984), not from immigrants from the Altai Mountain.

Educational Value

Knowledge about the past and cultural heritage is considered as a very important portion of social and economic development plans in the country. Salvage programs must be implemented before development plans, such as dam building, road construction, and real estate development, are carried out. It is also required that archaeology or heritage in general be included in curriculums for elementary and high school students, and in college and university educational programs. In 2008, a master's program in cultural resource management was offered at Silpakorn University; it is the first graduate program in CRM in the country, and it was relatively well received (15 graduate students for the regular program and 15 graduate students for the special program).

According to a law concerning the protection of culture resources, types of cultural heritage including archaeological sites, ancient objects, and art objects, wherever they are found, belong to the nation. Those cultural heritage types are deemed important because they can provide a great deal of knowledge about history, archaeology, and art in Thailand.

Informational values and meanings of heritage are also transmitted to the public through museums, historical parks, and academic Thai and

English journals, including *Muang Boran Journal*, *Silpakorn Journal*, *Silapawatthanatham Journal*, and *Journal of the Siam Society*.

In sum, heritage and the past are a major source of information for the interpretation of the history of the nation and local history.

Symbolic Value

Heritage also yields symbolic or spiritual value for modern people in Thailand. Heritage has been exploited for creating group/community identities. There is a cohort of local people across the country using surrounding heritage to build their identity. For example, in a border province of southern Thailand, there is an ancient mosque locally known as "Kru Se," which was built during the middle Ayutthaya period (15th–16th centuries AD). The mosque is the origin of a myth told from generations to generations by people in the area of about 90 ha (see e.g., Fraser 1960; Syukri 1985 for further detail). The myth may have no relation to the abundant archaeological remains, but it is very important to local people in identifying who they are and where they come from. The myth ties villagers together and helps create a sense of identity and self-defense. More importantly, the mosque has been a center for religious ceremonies that provide village members with a great opportunity to meet each other. Sometimes people in the village refer to the myth when they need to call for meetings about fighting against possible attacks from the outside world, including Buddhists and government officials.

Heritage also appears in provincial mottos and emblems. That is, almost all provinces in Thailand have mottos, and some mottos incorporate sites, architectural monuments, buildings, historical places, and ancient cities. The following are the mottos of some provinces with accompanying explanations.

> "Prang Sam Yod, San Phra Kan, Wang Narai, Din So Pong, and Phaen Din Thong Somdet Phra Narai."
>
> (Lopburi Province)

> Prang Sam Yod is an ancient Khmer-style sanctuary, dating to the 13th century AD. San Phra Kan is ancient Khmer-style sanctuary, dating to the 12th century AD. Wang Narai is a historical royal residence built by King Narai in the 17th century AD. Din So Pong is a kind of clay lime, a natural resource that is abundant in the Lopburi Province and the local

people widely use it as powder for the face and other purposes. Phaen Din Thong Somdet Phra Narai literally means the land of King Narai who ruled the ancient city of Lopburi between 1656–1688.

"Fah Dad Song Yang, Pong Lang Lertlam, Wattanatham Phu Tai." (Kalasin Province)

> Fah Dad Song Yang is the name of an ancient town (6th–12th century AD). Pong Lang Lertlam means the great zylophone, which is a kind of indigenous musical instrument first invented in Kalasin Province. Wattanatham Phu Tai literally means "culture of Phutai." Phutai is a Lao-speaking ethnic group, which has long lived in the province and has a unique culture.

"Muang Ying Kla, Pha Mai Dee, Mee Khorat, Prasat Hin." (Nakhon Ratchasima Province)

> Muang Ying Kla literally means "the city of the brave lady." Pha Mai Dee means excellent silk. Mee Khorat refers to the Khorat-style rice noodle. Prasat Hin is an ancient stone sanctuary.

In addition to its use in mottos, heritage is symbolically used to mark provincial identities. As is often seen, monuments, objects, historic buildings, and ancient structures are used as emblems of many provinces in Thailand. For example, a Sukhothai-period Buddha image represents northern Thailand's Province of Pitsanulok; an early historic stupa or pagoda called Phra Pathom Chedi is the emblem of Nakhon Pathom Province in central Thailand; a historic Khmer-style sanctuary represents the Province of Si Sa Ket in northeastern Thailand; and an ancient cannon is used to symbolize Pattani Province in southern Thailand.

Intangible heritage, including language, traditions, and performances, is also employed to create a sense of Thainess and to build Thailand as a civilized nation. For example, in the 1930s, Luang Wichitwatakan, an upper class historian and key figure in the Thai government at the time, called for the use of Thai language and traditions to promote a public awareness of "Thainess" (Sattayanurak 2001).

Economic Value

Thai heritage has been used to stimulate the national and local economies for decades. As Thailand is rich in cultural heritage, heritage tourism is promoted to generate revenues for the country. It is now known that tourism is a major source of the country's income.

Archaeological sites and ancient cities are among the most commonly used types of heritage in Thailand that not only promote national economic growth, but also help improve the well-being of local people (Natapintu 2006). Some of the historic towns are ranked highly as important tourist attractions. For example, Ayutthaya, an ancient capital of Thailand (14th–18th century AD) and a World Heritage site, is included in the "501 must-visit destinations" among world tourist destinations (Walder et al. 2006).

There were successful campaigns promoting heritage tourism in Thailand, resulting in an increasing number of overseas tourists and visitors in the country over the past 10 years, increasing from over 7.2 million in 1997 to over 11.5 million in 2005. It should be noted that tourism in Thailand increased in the early part of the 21st century in spite of war in the Middle East, an epidemic (bird flu) and a natural disaster (tsunami) in Thailand (*Thansetthakit Newspaper* July 26, 2007).

The business of nostalgia is currently booming in Thailand. There are hundreds of shops and places across the country that sell or do the business of nostalgia ranging from traditional customs, ancient massage, old market places, and the Thai traditional way of life, to indigenous food.

Entertaining/Recreational Value

Heritage has been a perennial source of information for public entertainment in the mass media and places of entertainment like theme parks and amusement arcades. There are increasing numbers of mass media presentations dealing with heritage for public audiences, including TV series, radio programs, newspapers, magazines, and works of nonfiction, as well as representations in other media like post cards, phone cards, and stamps. There are fun parks, historic parks, and theme parks where lay people can enjoy seeing and learning about various types of heritage in Thailand. For example, at Muang Boran, literally meaning *ancient city*, which was set up in 1963, there are models and reproductions of key archaeological and historical sites, buildings, structures, and objects presenting various aspects of Thai culture and history. Moreover, there are 10 historical parks in the country (Fine Arts Department 1989) and more similar parks are being developed.

Conclusion

Thailand is rich in heritage, and the heritage is highly valued by contemporary Thais, and it means a great deal to them. Some types of cultural heritage are considered nationally significant, whereas some heritage resources are locally important. Heritage has been widely used, and will continue to be used for various reasons and meanings ranging from educational, associative, and symbolic, to those with political and economic determinations. As such, heritage is not dead and cold; on the contrary, it is with us and it is lively.

References

Anderson, D.
1990   *Lang Rongrien Rockshelter: A Pleistocene, Early Holocene Archaeological Site from Krabi, Southwestern Thailand.* University of Pennsylvania, Philadelphia: The University Museum.

Carver, Martin
1996   On Archaeological Value. *Antiquity* 70:45–56.

Darvill, T.
1995   Value Systems in Archaeology. In *Managing Archaeology.* M.A. Cooper, A. Firth, J. Carman, and D. Wheatley, eds. Pp. 40–50. London: Routledge.

Fine Arts Department
1989   *Ten Historical Parks in Thailand.* Bangkok: Fine Arts Department.

Fraser, Thomas M.
1960   *Rusembilan: A Malay Fishing Village in Southern Thailand.* Ithaca: Cornell University Press.

Gathercole, P., and D. Lowenthal, eds.
1990   *Politics of the Past.* London: Unwin Hyman.

Gorman, C.
1970   Excavations at Spirit Cave, North Thailand. *Asian Perspectives* 13:79–107.

Holtorf, Cornelius
2005   *From Stonehenge to Las Vegas: Archaeology as Popular Culture.* Walnut Creek, California: AltaMira Press.
2007   *Archaeology is a Brand! The Meaning of Archaeology in Contemporary Popular Culture.* Walnut Creek, California: Left Coast Press.

Lipe, W. D.
1984   Value and Meaning in Cultural Resources. In *Approaches to the Archaeological Heritage.* H. Cleere, ed. Pp. 1–11. Cambridge: Cambridge University Press.

Misiura, Shashi
2006   *Heritage Marketing.* Oxford: Butterworth-Heinemann.

Natapintu, Surapol
2006   Contribution of Archaeology to Quality of Life Improvement at the Village of Ban Pong Manao, Lopburi, Central Thailand. Paper presented at the Exchange Project on Cultural Heritage between Thailand and Cambodia, Bangkok, Thailand, August 3.
2007   *Roots of Thai Ancestors: History and Development of Prehistoric Cultures.* Bangkok: Matichon Press.

Peleggi, Maurizio
2002   *The Politics of Ruins and the Business of Nostalgia.* Bangkok: White Lotus.

Pookajorn, Surin
1996   Human Activities and Environmental Changes during the Late Pleistocene to Middle Holocence in Southern Thailand and Southeast Asia. In *Humans at the End of Ice Age: The Archaeology of the Pleistocene-Holocene Transition.* L. G. Straus, B. V. Erikson, J. M. Erlandson, and D. R. Yesner, eds. Pp. 201–213. New York: Plenum Press.

Pramankij, Somsak, and Wattana Supawan
2007   Fossils of the Oldest Prehistoric Humans in Thailand. In *Tracing Human Root: Physical Anthropological Research in Thailand.* Korakot Boonlop, ed. Pp. 61–68. Bangkok: Sirindhorn Anthropology Centre.

Rowan, Y., and U. Baram, eds.
2004   *Marketing Heritage: Archaeology and the Consumption of the Past.* Walnut Creek, California: AltaMira Press.

Sattayanurak, Saichon
2001   The Creation of Thai Identity by Luang Wichitwatakan. In *Luam Kot Ngao Ko Phao Phan Din (Forgetting the History is Burning the Land).* K. Laongsri, and T. Apornsuwan, eds. Pp. 265–311. Bangkok: Matichon Press.

Shoocongdej, Rasmi
2006   Late Pleistocene Activities at the Tham Lod Rockshelter in Highland Pang Mapha, Mae Hong Son Province, Norwestern Thailand. In *Uncovering Southeast Asia's Past.* E. Bacus, I Glover, and V. Pigott, eds. Pp. 22–37. Singapore: National University of Singapore Press.

Syukri, Ibrahim
1985   *History of the Malay Kingdom of Pattani.* Conner Bailey and John Miksic trans. Southeast Asia Series No. 68. Athens, Ohio: University Center for International Studies.

Walder, R., J. Brown, and D. Brown
2006   *501 Must-Visit Destinations.* London: Bounty Books.

Wongthes, Sujit
1984   *The Thai Are Not from Anywhere: The Thai Are Always Here in Southeast Asia.* Bangkok: Matichon Press.

Appendix

Heritage Values Needs and Questions

Needs

- The need to understand the full range of heritage values and be able to quantify those values so that they can be taken into consideration in local, national, and international policies, strategies, and financing as well as how to enlist the fiscal and human resources of developers, national and local governments, local communities, non-governmental agencies, professional and international organizations, funding agencies, regulators, researchers, educators, and the public to ensure that heritage values are defined broadly and applied fairly.

- The need to overcome isolation of the global cultural sector with respect to development, tourism, and international partnerships and networks in order to build reciprocal cooperative bridges.

- The need to develop and promote a cultural sector as an advocate for heritage values that could assist in integrating institutional and financial support and insuring input at the level of policy-crafting, resource allocation, and actual planning of government assistance and collaboration.

- The need to intensify the education and training at local, regional, and global levels with respect to heritage values.

Questions

- What is being done to protect our global patrimony and what needs to be done effectively to increase the understanding of heritage values?

- What resources and initiatives are currently available that pertain to defining, measuring, applying, and teaching heritage values and how can we improve efforts worldwide?

- How can we infuse heritage values into public policies and how can the cultural sector become more involved in advocating for both national and international policies?

- How can we empower the cultural sector and develop the necessary skills, knowledge, and abilities to provide effective public policy and heritage resource management? How can this be incorporated into the educational system (from the graduate and undergraduate level to secondary and primary school)? What can be done to assist nations that may not have the political, educational, or fiscal resources to protect and/or manage their cultural patrimony?

- How we can further our efforts in terms of future workshops, national and international conferences, publications, grant writing, and collaborating with professional, governmental, and private organizations? What are possible sources of funding?

- How can we define heritage values in ways that achieve greater public involvement in heritage decision making?

- How can we develop a clear understanding of how heritage values influence our daily lives and how shared heritage connects us to our past, not only as individuals but also as communities and nations so that heritage values are able to compete with other public concerns and agendas?

- How can we develop a broad and clear definition of heritage value and effective means to measure this value so that it can be applied to public policy, spending, management, and delivered services relating to a collective heritage in a manner that demonstrates public accountability?

- How can we make it clear that knowing the price of something is not necessarily the same as knowing its value?

- How do we ensure that an understanding of the past gives equal voice to our commonalities and differences?

- How can we examine and present heritage values in such a way that captures individual experiences of heritage, social or economic aspects of heritage, and the processes and techniques used to create heritage value?

- How can we balance the fact that heritage value cannot be quantified easily and differs from economic value that assesses worth relative to other things as indicated by price, while value as ascribed to heritage encompasses preferences and satisfaction associated with the moral and ethical sphere?

- How can we take into account market forces and globalization's impact on heritage values and how governments and policies deal with these issues?

- How can we find methods to track data so that in a market-dominated world, a case for reflecting heritage values in our efforts to protect and manage heritage resources can be made effectively?

- How can we present heritage values in terms of "cultural capital," that is the stored and long-lasting value, as a method of achieving a quality that stands apart from financial worth while allowing economic principles to be applied to cultural heritage that are both measurable and applicable to heritage policy and long-term sustainability?

- How can we engage the public in the discussion and decision-making process involving heritage values and their application?

- How can we acknowledge that experts provide critical information to the public about the past based on rigorous research and peer review, while enabling the public to draw their own conclusions about their relationship to the past and what value they place on it?

- How do we promote the teaching of heritage values not only in our academic institutions at all levels but also in our communities as well?

- When values collide, how do we deal with conflict?

Index

ABOUT THE EDITORS AND CONTRIBUTORS

Editors

George S. Smith is a Registered Professional Archaeologist and former Associate Director at the Southeast Archeological Center, Tallahassee, Florida, United States. He taught public archaeology at Florida State University for ten years and has served on the Society for American Archaeology (SAA) Public Education Committee as well as on the Board of Directors and co-chaired the SAA Task Force on Curriculum, which received a National Science Foundation (NSF) grant to enhance the undergraduate curriculum in archaeology. In addition to numerous journal articles and reports, he has co-edited the books *Protecting the Past* (1991); *Teaching Archaeology in the 21st Century* (2000); and *Cultural Heritage Management: A Global Perspective* (in press). He participated in the international workshop Interrogating Pedagogies: Archaeology in Higher Education and helped organize several international workshops dealing with heritage management and values. He received the 2007 SAA award for Excellence in Cultural Resource Management and is co-chair of the SAA Heritage Values Interest Group.

Phyllis Mauch Messenger has focused on cultural heritage issues since her first encounters with Maya archaeology and looters in the 1970s. She has taught courses on museums, archaeology, and culture in the United States, México, Peru and Southeast Asia. She was Founding Director of Hamline University's Wesley Center and the Center for Anthropology and Cultural Heritage Education, and has co-directed many public archaeology projects. She has edited *The Ethics of Collecting Cultural Property* (University of New Mexico Press 1999) and contributed articles for several volumes, including *Ethics in American Archaeology* (SAA 2000). She has co-edited *Cultural Heritage Management: A Global Perspective* (in press). Her doctoral research focuses on women archaeologists as change agents in the cultural heritage sector. In the Society for American Archaeology, she served as Vice Chair of the Public Education Committee for six years, served on the Task Force on Curriculum, and is co-chair of the Heritage Values Interest Group. Currently, she is a grants consultant for the Institute for Advanced Study, University of Minnesota.

Hilary A. Soderland was awarded the Gates Cambridge Trust Scholarship for her MPhil and PhD in the Department of Archaeology, University of Cambridge. Her research interests and publications cross the disciplinary boundaries of archaeology, law, history, and heritage. She has been a Visiting Scholar at the American Bar Foundation, Chicago and at the Cegla Center for Interdisciplinary Research of the Law, Buchmann Faculty of Law, Tel Aviv University. She is currently undertaking her Juris Doctorate at Boalt Hall School of Law, University of California-Berkeley. A Registered Professional Archaeologist, her teaching and research have been supported by grants and fellowships in archaeology, law, legal history, and American studies. Her museum work in the United States, the United Kingdom, and Israel has encompassed archaeology and ethnology curation, accessioning protocol, exhibition preparation, and legal compliance. She serves on the Society for American Archaeology Repatriation Committee and in collaboration with this book's editors is co-founder and co-chair of the Heritage Values Interest Group.

Contributors

Jeffrey H. Altschul: Chairman, Statistical Research, Inc., Tucson, Arizona, United States; Chairman, Nexus Heritage, Hampshire, England; and President, SRI Foundation, Albuquerque, New Mexico, United States.

Brenda Barrett: Director, Recreation and Conservation, Pennsylvania Department of Conservation and Natural Resources, Harrisburg, Pennsylvania, United States.

Ian Baxter: Senior Lecturer, Glasgow Caledonian University, Glasgow, Scotland.

Susan B. Bruning: Founding Attorney, concentrating in the areas of Fine Arts, Antiquities, Archaeology, and Cultural Heritage, Bruning Carpenter PC, Southlake, Texas, United States; Adjunct Professor,

Southern Methodist University, Dallas, Texas, United States; and Visiting Associate Professor of Law (Spring 2010), Texas Wesleyan University School of Law, Fort Worth, Texas, United States.

Elizabeth S. Chilton: Chair and Associate Professor of Anthropology, Department of Anthropology and Director, Center for Heritage and Society, University of Massachusetts-Amherst, Amherst, Massachusetts, United States.

Joëlle Clark: Professional Development Coordinator, Department of Anthropology, Northern Arizona University, Flagstaff, Arizona, United States.

Kate Clark: Director, Historic Houses Trust of New South Wales, Sydney, New South Wales, Australia.

Suzanne Copping: Project Manager for Star-Spangled Banner, National Historic Trail, National Park Service, Annapolis, Maryland, United States.

Karina Croucher: British Academy Archaeology Postdoctoral Fellow, School of Arts, Histories, and Cultures, University of Manchester, Manchester, England.

Arlene K. Fleming: Cultural Resource and Development Specialist; Advisor to development and cultural organizations including the World Bank and the United States Millennium Challenge Corporation, Great Falls, Virginia, United States.

Roy Eugene Graham: Beinecke-Reeves Distinguished Professor and Director, College Preservation Programs, College of Design, Construction, and Planning and Director, Center for World Heritage Research and Stewardship, University of Florida, Gainesville, Florida, United States.

Margaret A. Heath: Chief Heritage Education Project Manager, Bureau of Land Management, Dolores, Colorado, United States.

Cornelius Holtorf: Head of Archaeology and Director, Heritage Studies Programme, School of Cultural Sciences, Linnaeus University, Kalmar, Sweden.

Lilia Lizama Aranda: General Director, Empresa del Manejo Cultural, Puerto Morelos, Quintana Roo, México.

Thanik Lertcharnrit: Associate Professor, Department of Archaeology, Silpakorn University, Bangkok, Thailand.

David W. Morgan: Director, Southeast Archeological Center, National Park Service, Tallahassee, Florida, United States.

Nancy I. M. Morgan: Principal, Point Heritage Development Consulting, Tallahassee, Florida, United States.

Katsuyuki Okamura: Museum Project Manager, Osaka City Cultural Properties Association, Osaka, Japan.

Ian Russell: Associate Fellow, Humanities Institute of Ireland, University College Dublin, Dublin, Ireland.

Chen Shen: Bishop White Curator of Far East Archaeology, Department of World Cultures, Royal Ontario Museum, Toronto, Canada.

Neil Asher Silberman: Lecturer, Department of Anthropology and Center for Heritage and Society, University of Massachusetts-Amherst, Amherst, Massachusetts, United States.

Hilary A. Soderland: PhD Archaeology; JD Candidate 2011, Boalt Hall School of Law, University of California-Berkeley, Berkeley, California, United States.

Pei-Lin Yu: Assistant Professor, Department of Anthropology, California State University-Sacramento, Sacramento, California, United States.

UNIVERSITY OF WINCHESTER
LIBRARY